The
OPERATORS

The
OPERATORS

MIKE RYAN

Collins

Collins
a division of HarperCollins Publishers
77-85 Fulham Palace Road
London W6 8JB
www.collins.co.uk

First published in Great Britain in 2005 by HarperCollins Publishers

A catalogue record for this book is available from the British Library.

ISBN 0 00 719937 6

Edited and designed by Focus Publishing,
11a St Botolph's Road, Sevenoaks, Kent TN13 3AJ
Project manager: Guy Croton
Editors: Vanessa Townsend, Caroline Watson
Designer: David Etherington

Collins team:
Editorial direction: Fiona Hobbins, Louise Stanley, David Palmer
Design direction: Wolfgang Homola

Printed and bound in the UK by Butler and Tanner, Frome.

Frontispiece: Australian operator with night vision goggles, enabling him to work around the clock. Those who can fight at night rule the battlefield.

DEDICATION
This book is dedicated to the brave and selfless men and women of our special forces, who daily put their lives at risk in the name of freedom, justice and democracy. And long may they do so, as they are the shield that protects us from the spear of terrorism, which we see played out on our television screens virtually on a daily basis. They are the faceless and anonymous shadows who fight on our behalf against this evil presence. They are the only ones capable of such an undertaking, lest we should forget.

CONTENTS

Preface

Ever since the events at the World Trade Center in New York on 11 September 2001 – known simply as 9/11 – the phrase 'special forces' has become commonplace when discussing terrorism and modern warfare. Few members of the general public, however, have any real understanding of what the special forces actually do. Using my unique contacts, and personal experience working with special forces in the US and the UK, I will reveal the true story of today's special forces and their capabilities.

Some of the conflicts featured will be familiar, but you will find out more about what *really* happened. Throughout the book there are stories of daring missions to rescue hostages, tales of operations deep behind enemy lines, as well as explanations about what makes an operator tick.

The tough standards of the special forces operator are also explored in the Selection and Training chapter, which reveals in detail the requirements, from enlistment to passing out, placed upon an individual who dares to put him or herself forward as a potential operator. In addition, I will walk you through the history and make up of the major special forces units in the world. I will also give an insight into how special forces plan to operate in the future and how they will transport themselves.

I hope *The Operators* inspires you or, at the very least, leaves you with a healthy respect for those who have made the grade – as only the best of the best make it.

ACKNOWLEDGEMENTS

I would like to thank the following people, organisations and companies for their kind help; without them, there could be no book:

Major I, Taff, Gonz, Robbo, JR, Col S, Oz, Major M, USAF PA, SOCOM, US Navy, 160th SOAR, 75th Ranger Regiment, 16 Air Assault Brigade, 101st Airborne Division (Air Assault), UK MoD, US DoD, SASR, 4RAR, 131 CDO, Australian DoD, USMC, DVIC, NARA, DSTL, Avpro Aerospace, 'The Wild Bunch' and finally, my brother, John Ryan – who served in Iraq under Operation Telic.

All photographs, unless otherwise stated, are courtesy of the UK MoD, US DoD, Australian DoD, DIVC, US Navy, US Army, US Marines, USAF and Avpro Aerospace.

Finally, a special thanks to my wife Fiona, my daughters, Isabella and Angelina, and last, but by no means least, my son, Jamie.

AUTHOR'S NOTE

Due to ongoing military operations in Iraq and Afghanistan, certain technical, tactical and procedural details have had to be either changed or omitted to comply with both UK and US operational security (OPSEC) requirements. I make no apology for this, as the safety of both our military personnel, and those of our allies, is paramount.

Introduction

Special Forces Roles

For many governments, special forces are now seen as the key tool in future conflicts, against both the terrorist threat, as well as conventional forces.

Their proven ability to deploy unseen and unheard gives their governments a powerful weapon that is both efficient and effective – their enemies do not know when or where they will strike. Special forces are also a great tool for governments who want an official footprint on the ground, without risking conventional forces who could be highly vulnerable to attack.

A good example of this tactic can be found as recently as 2001, when British and US special forces personnel entered Afghanistan just days after the collapse of the Twin Towers. Their mission was to kick-start a war against terrorism by means of a proxy force – in this instance, the Northern Alliance. It was a clever strategy, because it gave the Bush Government a discreet military presence in Afghanistan, without the political complications of getting approval from Congress for a full-scale military operation.

There is also the question of casualty sensitivity to consider as, by definition, a small force of special forces can only sustain small-scale losses. And because no members of the media ever witness special forces activities, no detailed reports can be made of any losses. For politicians, it's a win/win situation. They can always leak details of a successful special forces operation to the media, should they want an increase in the opinion polls. The failures can simply get buried in the depths of the national archives for decades to come.

A mean and moody US Navy SEAL, pictured during a counter-terrorist exercise.

Behind the Scenes

There are many different aspects to modern-day warfare, ranging from large conventional forces operating on post-conflict, peacekeeping missions, through to ultra stealthy aircraft that can bomb targets deep behind enemy lines without being detected.

Another aspect of modern warfare is the anonymity of the special forces soldier – anonymous because that is what helps keep them alive. To be successful in today's battle space you have to be fit both mentally and physically; you have to be intelligent, skilful and resourceful, because only two types remain after a modern battle – the quick and the dead.

The special forces world is completely different to that of the conventional soldier, because operators have to wage war against forces who often outnumber them; and they can only do this through superior firepower or tactics.

Unlike the warriors of old, who often fought unlawfully, today's special forces must fight within internationally recognised codes of conduct. Indeed, they must have personal standards of the highest order. Their aim, at all times, must be to aspire to perfection, and to take and hold the moral high ground, regardless of the enemy's methods of fighting war. In addition, each operator must become the most useful, deployable and feared person on the battlefield.

In Afghanistan, the role of the special forces soldier came under scrutiny like never before. Here was a place that may as well have been on the dark side of the moon as far as most people were concerned. And yet within its mountain and desert regions, British and US special forces were fighting a war using B-52 bombers as close support aircraft – something that would have seemed ridiculous to a Vietnam veteran. But that wasn't the most bizarre sight: there were even photos released showing US special forces riding horses into battle, as if they were back in the good old days of the Wild West (*see page 55*). Why would they do such things? Well, the answer is really quite simple – it seemed the right method at the time, and it worked, end of story.

Such tactics were only made possible by men who were willing to take chances and to push the envelope until it broke. They would operate in the very midst of the enemy until they were destroyed by calling in deadly air strikes from high above. In effect, *they* were the precision weapons, rather than the aircraft's bombs. Even in Iraq there were acts of bravado, when British special forces used old Iraqi petrol tankers to smuggle in key personnel before the official commencement of hostilities – with some even having the bare-faced cheek to tip the border guards.

Special forces operators are men, and in some cases women, who have been trained and equipped to carry out special missions. Their deployment in a crisis is always considered first because they give politicians a chance to resolve a problem quietly, before having to take the open military approach and send inconventional troops.

The role of special forces is increasing. They are seen as being capable of carrying out seemingly impossible tasks. This was ably demonstrated during the first Gulf War in 1991, when British SAS and US Delta Force operators located and destroyed Iraqi mobile

The mighty B-52 is still in use today, but as a close support aircraft as opposed to a strategic bomber. In many cases it is older than the operators it supports.

Scud missile launchers that had been causing severe problems for the Allied Coalition.

So great was the admiration for special forces at that time that tremendous pressure arose within the military to increase their numbers; in theory this may work, but in reality it is far different.

One only has to look back at the American example in Vietnam to see what happens when standards are dropped in an effort to increase the number of operators in the field. In their wisdom, the Americans decided that more special forces equalled more victories and therefore a quick end to the war. However, this was not to be the case.

Indeed, the standards were lowered so much that many special forces units were withdrawn prematurely from Vietnam, because there was simply no confidence in them. In short, there is no way to mass produce special forces because their qualities are rarely found, even within the ranks of conventional forces. To be a member of any elite force is no easy matter – only the best candidates are selected.

Training is usually divided into three phases.

Phase One: candidates are tested for physical fitness. This usually takes the form of punishing exercises designed to reveal psychological determination and character.

Phase Two: candidates are instructed in the key skills of the unit. This will involve weapons' handling, tactical reconnaissance and covert operations.

Phase Three: candidates receive specialist instruction in subjects such as communication, sniping, demolition and counter-revolutionary warfare (CRW) operations.

Candidates can be rejected at any stage of the process, and with courses lasting for almost a year, this creates enormous mental pressure.

The rejection rate for special forces is around 80 per cent, and the upshot of such rigorous selection is that only the most determined and intelligent make it. Soldiers serving in special forces units are generally multi-skilled because they need to be self-sufficient. In addition to their combat skills, they also learn languages, engineering, defensive training and combat medicine.

In today's unpredictable and unstable world, units have to be able to deploy at short notice; in some cases this can mean hours. Special forces can be sent anywhere in the world, so it is imperative for them to train in varied and diverse environments, from hot deserts to steamy, snake-infested jungles.

Deploying from one part of the world to another is no easy task as it often takes soldiers days, and in some cases weeks, to fully acclimatise. For instance, a special forces soldier deploying from a lowland area in Europe to a mountainous region in Afghanistan will suffer a 50 per cent reduction in combat performance without adequate acclimatisation time. Operating in a jungle environment is also very difficult due to the constant dangers of heat exhaustion, poisonous snakes and infection. There is little point in fighting the heat and humidity of the jungle environment. The best solution is to live *with* the jungle, not against it. Wars against indigenous forces can be fought and won in the jungle, just as the British proved after the Second World War in Malaya and Borneo. No matter how sophisticated the special forces operator becomes with new weapons and equipment, he will still have to train to fight guerrillas on their home territory, in the hostile, jungle environment –

> They move around the battlefield unseen, unheard and unsung. No-one knows when they leave or when they come back or even how many started out. They are the best that their countries have to offer. They are the face of future warfare.

Conventional forces operating in Iraq are always glad to have SF support – even if it is covert, as in this post-ambush image taken shortly after an insurgent attack.

should the need arise. There is more likely in the future to be a new desire to penetrate and dominate the world's jungles that offer sanctuary to those who oppose freedom and democracy.

Special forces generally receive more funding and resources than conventional forces because their requirements are often higher. The US 75th Ranger Regiment, for example, (one of many US special forces, *see pages 184–205*), is only three battalions strong, yet receives more money than an entire division. That might not make financial sense, but if you were an ordinary GI, trapped behind enemy lines and awaiting reinforcements, you would be glad to have the Rangers come to your rescue, as you would know that they will never quit until the job is done.

Since 9/11, there has been a dramatic increase in spending on special forces, mainly due to their success in Afghanistan and Iraq, and there will be more to come as further danger lies ahead from other countries, such as Iran and North Korea, particularly as the North Koreans have now declared a nuclear

weapons capability. This is in stark contrast to the Gulf War in 1991, where special forces and their capabilities – before the conflict – were not really appreciated. This was especially true in the US, where air power was viewed as the ultimate weapon of choice.

In fact, before the launch of Operation Desert Storm, General Norman Schwarzkopf, Commander of the US Central Command, felt that air power alone would be enough to soften up the Iraqi forces before the ground invasion phase. His justification for this stance was that the US and its allies in the Coalition Force had overwhelming air, sea and land assets at their disposal, so special forces were deemed superfluous to military requirements. However, Gen Sir Peter de la Billiere, the joint British Commander-in-Chief in the Gulf, was a veteran of the SAS and knew the value of such forces. He persuaded Gen Schwarzkopf to relent on his original decision and as a result permission was given to deploy two SAS squadrons on 20 January 1991. The rest, as they say, is history. Both the SAS and the US Delta Force played a key role in this conflict, especially regarding the Scud missile threat.

It is important to understand that the hesitancy to use special forces mainly stemmed from the Vietnam War (*see page 11*). The failure of Operation Eagle Claw in 1980, which was mounted following the seizure of American hostages in Iraq, didn't help this negative attitude towards special forces. Although meticulously planned, Eagle Claw failed following a series of unforeseen events;

> **It is not the critic who counts, not the man who points out how the strong man stumbled or where the doer of deeds could have done better. The credit belongs to the man who is actually in the arena; whose face is marred by the dust and sweat and blood; who strives valiantly.**
>
> *Theodore Roosevelt (Sorbonne, Paris, 1910)*

Train hard, fight easy – it's that simple...

A US **Navy** SEAL team intercepts a suspect dhow at the height of Operation Iraqi Freedom.

namely, the worst sand storm in living memory and a collision between a transport helicopter and a refuelling aircraft at Desert One, the mission's rendezvous (RV) point in the Iranian Desert.

After Desert Storm, the attitude of the military towards special forces changed, both in the United States and elsewhere. They were now seen as essential forces.

Special Operations

According to the US Special Operations Posture Statement 2000, the meaning of the term 'Special Operations' is as follows:

'These are actions which are conducted by specially organised, trained and equipped military or paramilitary forces in order to achieve military, political, economic or psychological objectives by unconventional means in hostile, denied or politically sensitive areas. They may be conducted in peacetime, in periods of conflict or during all-out war, independently or in co-ordination with conventional forces. The military and political situation frequently dictates such special operations, and such operations usually differ from conventional operations in their degree of risk, the operational techniques involved, their modus operandi, independence from friendly support and dependence upon essential operational intelligence, and the knowledge of the indigenous assets available.'

(Taken from: US Special Operations Posture Statement 2000)

I have mentioned that special forces are generally far better armed and equipped than conventional forces; and they need to be, as their operational requirements are much more demanding.

Just to illustrate this point, in the case of both the US Delta Force and the British SAS, a typical eight-man patrol will carry more firepower than 100 conventionally-armed soldiers.

Typical weapons include the M249 squad assault weapon (SAW), the Colt M4 assault rifle fitted with 40mm M203 grenade launchers, at least one heavy machine gun per section, plus copious amounts of ammunition, grenades and explosives. In addition to this, a section will usually carry a light armour weapon (LAW), such as a LAW 80 or AT-4. US forces will also carry anti-personnel mines, as the US government has not signed the UN protocol banning their use.

Personal kit usually consists of a side-arm, knife and a compass, just in case. Each team has at least one of the following items: a global positioning satellite (GPS), a secure radio with burst transmission capability, a Sat-phone and a tactical location beacon (TACBE).

If all this isn't enough, they can also call upon air support, naval artillery (NAVART) and, of course, conventional artillery, be it guns or rocket systems.

Special Forces

Selection and Training

According to the British SAS, 'Death is God's way of telling you that you have failed selection.' Sounds dramatic, but how true is such a statement? Well, by the end of this chapter, you will know exactly what is required of those who receive the calling – so you can make up your own mind.

Ask anyone to describe their perceived visual image of a special forces operator and you will probably get a description of someone who is a cross between Sylvestor Stallone in *Rambo* and Arnold Schwarzenegger in *Predator*. The truth is that over the years the film industry has been working in overdrive producing a plethora of action films that portray special forces operators as muscle bound meatheads with little intelligence, bristling with weaponry, who never seem to run out of ammunition and, it would appear, never miss their target.

The truth of the matter is that they are far removed from their screen image in terms of physical and mental stature, and far from being loud-mouthed and arrogant, they are generally very quiet and unassuming men. As you read through this book and look at each country's special forces and their entry criteria, you will see that the incredibly high standard needed for joining is a common thread. Countries simply want the best and can afford to be extremely selective about those whom they recruit because at some point, these men – and in some cases, women – may one day be required to serve their country.

Over the years I have worked with operators from many countries around the world and have always been impressed that, regardless of their nationality, they were decent and honourable people who were clearly highly trained and extremely professional in their work. Apart from looking fit and healthy, there was nothing distinguishing about them that would lead you to believe that they were special forces personnel. Indeed, many of them could easily walk into a bar or shopping mall without anyone looking at them twice, which is the ultimate test for those who want to be grey men (a person who blends into their surroundings without attracting attention to themselves).

The following chapter tells you everything required of a potential special forces recruit in three different world famous units. Many of the training methods used by these forces form a basis for the selection process for other countries around the world.

Better to have and not need rather than need and not have – especially when dealing with communications.

United States – Delta Force

Unlike the us Navy SEALs, who are open and frank about their selection and training process for potential operators, Delta Force is completely the opposite and discusses little about its requirements. However, what is known about Delta, from former members, is that, twice a year, representatives from the unit make a trip to the Army's main personnel centre in St Louis, Missouri, to examine soldiers' military records. Their mission is to find outstanding captains and sergeants among the Green Berets and Rangers, those who have skills that would be of use to Delta.

They then send these soldiers a letter, which states that Delta is interested in them. If the feeling is mutual there is a telephone number for them to call. However, if the answer is negative, they are instructed to destroy the letter. For those that make the call, an interview follows which quickly weeds out unsuitable candidates. Potential candidates are then subjected to a tough physical training (PT) test that is more demanding than the usual Army test. Those who pass who are not already parachute qualified must undertake a course at an airborne school before they can progress.

Before commencing selection, each soldier is put through an intensive week of PT that involves running, swimming and forced marches with heavy packs. The idea behind this is that it gives candidates a chance to improve their physical fitness and also highlights any injuries or medical issues that need to be addressed before selection proper.

Once through these initial hurdles the candidates go to Camp Dawson, an Army National Guard post in West Virginia's Appalachian Mountains for a one month selection and assessment phase – the first two weeks are seen as pre-selection, where soldiers are pushed to their physical and mental limits. This part of the course is very similar to that of the British SAS because Delta's founder, Colonel Charles Beckwith, felt SAS selection was the best in the world. Like SAS selection, only a small percentage of each intake passes; in most cases this number rarely gets into double figures.

Testing the candidates

During selection itself, candidates are again subjected to long marches with heavy packs over areas that are both mentally and physically demanding. They are never given timings or any information regarding their progress and they literally live from day to day, not knowing whether they are in or out.

Although Delta's original selection course was modelled on the British SAS one, over the years it has been slightly changed to better reflect us requirements in relation to course health and safety issues.

One of the toughest aspects of selection for candidates is the isolation factor, as they have little contact with anyone, apart from the instructors. For many this a difficult concept to deal with, because they are used to working as part of a team and the idea of being a loner goes against the grain. This is the purpose of the exercise, because Delta wants operators who can react quickly to change: part of a team one day, acting independently the next.

One of the most interesting and

Look sharp, stay sharp – that's how you survive in a modern battlefield.

controversial aspects of Delta's selection process is the psychological examination that each candidate must undergo before being considered as a potential operator or 'D man'. During the this phase, candidates are subjected to a barrage of questions from a number of different doctors such as: What is your relationship like with your family? Do you like foreigners? Do you do drugs? Are you running away from something? How do you feel about gays in the Army? and so on.

The questioning is relentless as the doctors want to build up a detailed psychological profile on each candidate; they don't want anyone with violent personality disorders entering Delta's ranks.

The ideal candidate is a stable individual who has an emotional anchor in his or her life, such as a family or religion, as they tend to be the most reliable soldiers. The other key area of a candidate's profile that greatly concerns Delta relates to their ability to handle extreme stress situations while carrying a gun. What Delta is looking for is someone who is willing to pull a trigger in the right circumstances. After completion of the psychological evaluation each candidate is asked to write a short autobiography that must be frank and honest.

> These are guys that are putting their lives on the line, taking on some very serious bad guys. The less anyone knows about the unit, the better.
>
> *Former Delta Force soldier quoted in* Stars and Stripes

Hanging tough with a US Ranger. If he does well, he may one day become a 'D man'.

During the second week of the pre-selection phase, candidates are physically worn down by seemingly endless forced marches that eventually end with a tough 30km (18 mile) march at night through dense woodland. The idea behind this phase is to exhaust candidates before they begin the next 18 days of formal selection.

As the candidates begin the formal part of selection they are given a number and a colour. The number identifies the individual and the colour designates their squad. They are not allowed to talk to other candidates and the Delta instructors say little to them as individuals. When addressing the candidates the instructors are very matter of fact and do not engage with them in conversation or give them any clue as to how they are doing.

The instructors never shout at the candidates, but never praise them either. They don't frown and don't smile, which often unnerves the candidate as they have no idea of their progress at any given time. A typical day begins with a self wake-up at 6am, as there is no reveille. Within each barrack room is a blackboard with the day's instructions written on it. For example, 'Red 3 report to vehicle 6 at 07.00hrs with full kit and a 40lb [18kg] pack.'

Every day the reporting times differ as do the weights, with no two days the same. Even during the day the weights can be changed, sometimes in the candidate's favour, but mostly not. Any candidates found with underweight packs are punished on the spot by instructors who give them a heavy rock to carry. Generally, candidates receive two hot meals a day, one in the morning and one at night, but at some point they will get nothing as the instructors want to see which candidates have prepared for such an event.

A typical candidate's march will start with a truck picking him up shortly after breakfast and dropping him off on a back road somewhere in the forest as part of a small four-man group.

He will then be given a point on a map and told to make it there as quickly as possible. As he heads towards the checkpoint, he has no idea of what the expected reporting time is and this will play on his mind throughout the journey.

Once he arrives at the checkpoint he will be tired, blistered and anxious, as he will not

Carrying heavy packs over long distances really puts candidates to the test.

know if he has passed or failed this particular exercise. The impassive instructors give nothing away as they mark their notebooks and only speak to advise the candidate of his next checkpoint: 'Red 7, these are your next co-ordinates, the standard is best effort.'

The candidate has to keep going until he reaches the next checkpoint, where he will hopefully get some food and rest. Before bedding down he will be given a time for meeting up with the rest of the cadre (unit) next morning. However, if he oversleeps there will be nobody to wake him up; should this happen, he will miss the truck and fail selection.

Throughout the next few days the routine varies from eight hours of marching with three Meals Ready to Eat (MRE) packets, to 36 hours of marching with only one MRE. To help in disorientating the candidate, his number and colours are changed on a frequent basis so he never really feels safe or secure. At any point he can be stopped by an instructor and ordered to strip and reassemble a foreign weapon, while being asked difficult mathematical questions. On occasions he will be approached by doctors who briefly observe and scribble notes without saying a word. Little does the candidate know that at some point or other he will photographed by Delta instructors who want to make sure that he is ploughing his way through the woodland and not cheating by using the paths.

If caught once by the intructors on a path or road he will receive an official warning, caught twice and he is out. For many of the

candidates the stress is just too much for them and they quit, while others have already failed but just don't know it yet. To help confuse the cadre, instructors often place failed candidates within their ranks so they have no way of gauging the general standards.

Every candidate is allowed a number of 'lives', but they are never told how many of them they have left – or indeed how many they had when they started out. If a soldier drops out or is failed during selection, he receives a pep talk from the Delta instructors who praise his efforts and point out his good points, as well as his bad ones. They try to let the failed candidates down as softly as possible as they don't want to damage his confidence or future career.

In addition to the talk, Delta also makes a point of writing to the candidate's parent unit and thanking them for providing a good soldier who is a credit to his unit. This process may seem a little over the top, but it is done for the very good reason that one day Delta may need the support of this soldier during an operation and they want no ill feelings that could cause possible friction.

When a candidate is failed during selection, there is no scene or melodrama as they are simply whisked away without the other candidates ever being told why. For most candidates each day that goes by is a victory for them as many of their fellow cadre members will have been either failed or dismissed by now, leaving only about 20 per cent of the original intake for the final phase.

The final phase

The last phase of selection involves a march of 65km (40 miles) in two days, with little or no sleep, along the open and winding Appalachian Trail with full kit. It is a difficult march that breaks many of the candidates, but for those who pass this gruelling event, a hot meal and a warm shower await them back at base camp.

Once back at the barracks the remaining candidates are given a number of intellectually challenging books to read. They then have just 18 hours in which to write a detailed report on the contents of each book. The instructors set this exercise as a means of evaluating how alert the candidates are after two days without sleep. After handing in their reports, the candidates are subjected to a further series of interviews in which they have to answer questions on their

Calling in an air strike is great fun during an exercise but is critical during a firefight.

childhood, family, military career and the selection course itself. Those who survive this interview move on to the final hurdle, the commander's board.

During this interview the candidate sits in a chair surrounded by Delta's commander and his five squadron leaders. The board reads through the candidate's psychiatric reports and starts asking difficult questions, such as: Would you give your child's life up for your country? You are on a mission and a young shepherd stumbles across your hide; are you prepared to kill him? You have been ordered by the President to kill one of his political rivals – are you willing to carry out this order? etc. The idea behind this questioning is to see how a candidate reacts to pressure from a higher authority. For example, does he get flustered easily? Does he panic while under pressure? Can he be trusted with secret information?

On some occasions during a board, a candidate will be asked if he cheated at any point on the course by using roads or paths. If he did so and admits to it, he may be kept on; however, if he lies about cheating, photographic proof will be shown to him, which will result in his instant dismissal.

After the candidate's interview is over, the senior Delta officers meet up to discuss him. All aspects of his performance throughout selection are evaluated and if there are still any lingering doubts about anyone at this stage, they are rejected.

Technically, Delta's commander can overrule any rejection decision; however, he rarely does. The decision to accept a candidate is made by majority vote only. Once a candidate is accepted into Delta, his selection and assessment reports are sealed for good, and nobody, including the candidate, is allowed to see the scores or know what the pass mark was on this selection course.

After passing selection the candidate is sent on the Operator's Training Course (OTC), which consists of six months of instruction in covert operations, commando assaults, close quarters battle (CQB) and sniping.

The pace of the OTC is relaxed compared to that of selection, but there is still a formal air to the course because all new students are on probation for the first year. A typical training course sees students spending over 1,000 hours in the Delta shooting house where they will learn about every aspect of combat shooting until it becomes second nature.

In addition to the practical exercises, students attend numerous lectures on subjects such as psychology, combat theory, world politics and terrorism. However, it is not all studying, as the students also learn how to ride motorbikes as part of vehicle familiarisation training, as well as detailed instruction on clandestine operations and image projection, for example, how to dress while working undercover. After this phase is over the students spend six weeks' studying

Officer assignment opportunities in Delta Force

The US Army's 1st Special Forces Operational Detachment-Delta (1st SFOD-D) plans and conducts a broad range of special operations across the operational continuum. Delta is organised for the conduct of missions requiring rapid response with surgical applications of a wide variety of unique skills, while maintaining the lowest possible profile of US involvement.

Assignment to 1st SFOD-D involves an extensive pre-screening process, successful completion of a three to four week mental and physical Assessment and Selection Course, and a six month operator training course. Upon successful completion of these courses, officers are assigned to an operational position within the unit.

As an officer in 1st SFOD-D, there will be opportunities to command at the Captain, Major and Lt Col levels. There is also scope to serve as an Operations Officer.

After service with 1st SFOD-D there are many staff positions available at the DoD, Joint Chiefs of Staff (JCS), US Army Special Operations Command (USASOC), US Special Operations Command (USSOCOM) and Joint Headquarters due to the training and experience in 1st SFOD-D. In addition, there are inter-agency positions available.

Prerequisites for an officer are:

- Male
- Volunteer
- US citizen
- Pass a modified Class II Flight Physical
- Airborne qualified or volunteer for airborne training
- Pass a background security investigation and have at least a security clearance of 'Secret'
- Pass the Army Physical Fitness Test (APFT), FM 21-20, 75 points each event in the 22–26 age group (55 press-ups in two minutes, 62 sit-ups in two minutes and a 2 mile run in 15:06 or less wearing your unit PT uniform)
- Minimum of two years' active service remaining upon selection into the unit
- Captain or major (branch immaterial)

- Advance course graduate
- College graduate (BA or BS)
- Minimum of 12 months' successful command (as a captain)

1st SFOD-D conducts worldwide recruiting twice a year to process potential candidates for the Assessment and Selection Course. Processing for the September course is from October through January. Processing for the September course takes place from April through July.

Assignments with 1st SFOD-D provide realistic training and experiences that are both personally and professionally rewarding.

(Taken from: US Army PERSCOM Online)

communications, combat medicine and advanced infantry skills. This is followed by nine weeks of assault and rescue operation training that includes two- and four-man assaults, how to enter buildings, rope work and helicopter insertion. The students then work with the CIA on real tasks such as VIP protection and intelligence gathering operations, which is usually carried out against low level criminals.

Once they have finished this training they are now 'operators'. Even though the formal aspect of training is over, there will always be other courses in subjects such as Explosives Ordnance Disposal (EOD), Scuba and High Altitude Low Opening/High Altitude High Opening (HALO/HAHO) parachute infiltration.

In addition to their training in the US, Delta operators frequently cross-train with other counter-terrorist units around the world, including the German GSG-9, the French GIGN, the Australian SASR and, of course, the British SAS, with whom they work very closely.

Delta Force officer requirements

Joining a special forces unit as an ordinary soldier is hard enough but becoming an officer is something else, as very few possess the exceptional qualities needed to lead such troops. In the box (*top left*) are the opportunities available if you became an officer in the US Army's 1st Special Forces Operational Detachment-Delta (1st SFOD-D), as well as the basic prerequisites for becoming an officer (*bottom left*).

Bugs, snakes and flies wreak havoc during jungle training, but at least it's the same for your enemy.

UK – SAS (Special Air Service)

The British SAS have one of the most demanding selection courses in the world. It is designed to challenge a candidate, both physically and mentally, to the point of absolute exhaustion, as this is the only way to judge if a candidate has the right aptitude for SAS training. The regular SAS Regiment only considers applicants that are already serving in the British Army and have completed at least three years of service. However, the Territorial Army Reserve Force (TA) SAS accepts potential candidates from both serving members of the reserve forces and outside civilian volunteers. They are looking for men who have physical and mental strength, initiative, self-reliance and the intelligence to work through highly complex issues while tired and exhausted and under extreme stress.

The selection process is designed to weed out the unsuitable as soon as possible because there are always those who apply for SAS service without realising what is actually required of them. Typical candidates are generally in their mid-20s, although older applicants do apply for selection.

Selection courses are run twice a year, once in summer and once in winter and candidates have no choice as to which one they attend. There are many schools of thought on which one is the easier to pass,

The Pen-y-Fan in the Brecon Beacons, Wales – known by the SAS simply as 'The Fan'. This landscape scene looks idyllic and pretty, but it is tortuous going at SAS marching pace.

as both have their good and bad points, however, the ratio of success on both courses is more or less the same.

Selection and Training programme
It is assumed that if a man feels confident enough to apply for the SAS, then he must also appreciate the physical and mental tasks that lie ahead of him and therefore must prepare for them as best he can. The Selection and Training programme lasts for one month and is run by the Training Wing of 22 SAS at Credenhill, Hereford. It was originally designed in 1953 and has changed very little over the years as it has been proved to work.

It begins with a build-up period of two weeks for officers and three weeks for all other ranks. The reason why the officers' work-up period is shorter than other ranks is because SAS officers are expected to outperform their men in every aspect of military knowledge and skill, otherwise they have no business being officers in the Regiment.

To attend Selection all candidates must undergo a medical at their parent unit and

Map reading is a prized skill. If you cannot move around, then you cannot fight or evade capture.

be certified fit by their Regimental medical officer. Before the candidates commence Selection they are given a chance to work up their strength because some of them may have been on operational tours where they will have had little time to prepare. Therefore, during the first week of Selection candidates start the course with a series of training runs that get progressively longer each day. Each candidate must be capable of passing the standard Battle Fitness Test (BFT) in the same time as an average infantryman; anything longer and he will fail Selection.

As the Selection programme continues, the candidates are sent on a series of long, hard, forced marches over the Brecon Beacons and Black Mountains of South Wales. The marches are designed to test their navigation and map reading skills, as well as their physical strength.

The marches place relentless demands on the candidates as they are given ever more complex and daunting problems to solve by day and night in all weathers, carrying a pack that starts off weighing 11kg (24lb) and by the end of the week will increase to 25kg (55lb). During the winter months these mountains are often covered in mist and snow, making navigation extremely difficult for the candidates as they cannot see visual reference points. The winds blowing over the mountains can frequently reach gale force, making it very difficult for a man to stand upright let alone walk. Another problem will be the ground itself, particularly if it has been raining hard, as it becomes extremely marshy and tough going. Although Selection is designed to test candidates to their physical limits, there are frequent checkpoints throughout the route that candidates must pass through. These checkpoints serve three purposes: they prevent cheating, they provide information about the candidate's next route and they ensure the candidate's safety – there have been numerous fatalities over the years on the Brecon Beacons, mainly from hypothermia and severe falls (at one stage the SAS even trialled satellite tracking devices as an additional safety measure).

Throughout Selection the emphasis is on the individual candidate and not the entire cadre, which generally numbers 120 men. Each candidate must rely on himself for motivation; the instructors are not there to help or indeed hinder them, they are there for providing information and safety cover only. At no time will they give a candidate any indication of how they are doing or how much time they have left to complete a task. Throughout Selection, candidates voluntarily drop out or are told that they have failed. Indeed, for many it is only when they report for the next march and see their name on the instructors' list that they know they are still in Selection. For those who are not on the list, a short journey back to the base camp awaits them where they will be thanked for attempting Selection and given a travel warrant back to their respective unit. Some of the candidates will be given a second chance to attempt Selection, but for most this will be the end of the line. The SAS makes a point of talking to those that have failed to reassure them that they are still good soldiers and possess many good qualities, but not the ones they are seeking.

Pushing hard

As the remaining candidates ponder their fate each morning, they take some comfort from the fact that they are still in the programme and a day closer to passing Selection. As each day begins they are given a new route and a series of RV points that they must make in

Going uphill is always hard work, especially if you have the weight of the world on your back.

The jungle phase is always the hardest part of Continuation.

order to gain further information. They are not allowed to write anything down and are forbidden from marking their maps in any way, as this could give away valuable information. Since they are on their own at all times and have no idea of timings from checkpoint to checkpoint, they just have to push as hard and as fast as they can until they are told to stop by the instructors. On occasions the instructors will order a candidate to stop and strip his weapon down, and then reassemble it again. They usually pick a time when the candidate is clearly cold and exhausted, and therefore vulnerable as his co-ordination will be slower than normal.

One favourite trick of the instructors is to place a map and a magnetic compass on a metal hood of a vehicle so that it distorts its reading. They then brief the candidates around the vehicle and issue them with a new bearing to march on. However, once the compass is lifted from the hood the bearing will change quite significantly and if the candidates fail to pick up on this point, they are likely to get lost.

During one exercise on the final week of Selection, the instructors take away the maps from the candidates and provide them instead with poorly drawn sketch maps that

have little on them apart from a few marked points. The candidates then have to use all their navigational skills to find the checkpoints that will provide the missing data. On another exercise known as the 'Fan Dance', the candidates have to negotiate an extremely difficult geographical feature known as Pen-y-Fan (or 'The Fan' as the SAS often call it) three times in four hours from three different points. However, at no point are they told about the number of times they will be required to climb the 880m (2,900ft) peak or how much time has been allocated for the task. All of the climbs are extremely tough, especially when carrying a heavy pack and a rifle, and it comes as no surprise that this exercise is the most demanding.

As the Selection phase reaches its climax, the candidates are marching all day and even through most of the night, ending on the final day with an 80km (50 mile) march across the Brecon Beacons. This march includes 'The Fan' and other local geographical nasties. Bearing in mind that an average person walks at a pace of 2–3mph on flat ground, these men have to walk over very high and treacherous terrain carrying a 25kg (55lb) pack and a rifle while exhausted, in less than 20 hours. It is a daunting task to say the least. Needless to say, the failure rate during the Selection phase is high, with on average only seven to 15 per cent of each cadre completing it successfully.

Continuation

For those few who pass the Selection phase the worst is yet to come, as they now go into a six-month training period known simply as Continuation. The first phase of Continuation lasts for 14 weeks and is designed to teach new recruits basic SAS skills such as movement behind enemy lines, contact drills, signalling and the operational roles of the standard SAS four-man team.

All recruits have to reach basic signaller standard, regardless of their rank and future specialisation, as communications plays such a key role in special forces operations. In addition, all recruits learn basic field medicine, sniping, ground control of air, mortar and artillery fire, survival skills, sabotage and demolition skills, and foreign weapons handling.

After completing the skills phase of Continuation, the recruit moves on to the

Driving foreign vehicles and firing strange weaponry is all in a day's work in the SF world.

combat and survival element of Continuation which teaches new SAS members how to fight and survive behind enemy lines with little or no support. The recruits are taught how to find and build shelters, locate food and water, and how to escape and evade enemy capture. Once this training is completed the recruits embark on a five-day escape and evasion exercise in the Brecon Beacons in which they have to evade capture from an enemy force. The enemy part is usually played by a local infantry battalion or on occasions a NATO battalion if any happen to be in the UK on exercise at the time. No matter how good the recruits are throughout the exercise, the instructors ensure that they are caught at some time or other because they cannot move forward without completing the 'Resistance to interrogation' (RTI) phase of Continuation.

Resistance to interrogation

The RTI phase lasts for around 24 hours and is one of the harshest elements of Continuation

– and it has to be. The SAS must be sure of its men at all times as much of their work is behind enemy lines. The Regiment has to be confident that they will not crack while working under pressure and betray their fellow operators. RTI is probably the best means of finding out if the SAS has a potential weak link. Much of the RTI phase is classified. However, some aspects of it are public knowledge – and it is clearly no secret that it is both physically and mentally challenging. Although no physical torture takes place, there is no shortage of mind games that border on severe mental torture, as the instructors and expert interrogators do their utmost to unhinge the recruit.

They have methods of breaking a man down without so much as touching him. This can be done in many ways, including subjecting the recruit to constant deafening white noise that can sheer metal if the decibel level is high enough; blindfolding recruits and then handcuffing them to active railway lines;

and pouring petrol over them and leaving them near an open fire. Again, it must be stressed that no physical harm comes to recruits from these methods. Many people may well ask why the SAS subjects its men to such barbaric treatment in this day and age. There is a very simple answer: it works.

After the SAS phase is over, recruits are sent on a jungle survival course that lasts up to six weeks. The SAS has fought many of its most spectacular campaigns in the jungles of Malaya and Borneo, for instance, and places great emphasis on its jungle warfare training. Those who pass the jungle phase move to RAF Brize Norton in Oxfordshire to undergo parachute training with No 1 Parachute Training School. As many of the Regiment's new recruits are ex-Paras, they are excused this course. The others undergo four weeks of static-line training, followed by eight jumps, which includes one at night.

After passing parachute training the recruits are awarded their 'Sabre' wings and on return to Hereford they are presented with their sand-coloured beret complete with winged dagger cap badge. They are now members of the Special Air Service Regiment and regardless of their previous rank they revert to the lowest rank in the SAS, which is that of trooper. They do, however, continue to be paid according to their former rank. Even though they have been accepted into the SAS, they are on probation for their first year and can still be dismissed at any point during this time. The new soldiers are assigned to one of 22 SAS Regiment Squadrons and have a choice between joining Boat, Air, Mountain or Mobility Troop.

Those selecting Boat Troop learn about maritime operations and how to handle small boats such as rigid raiders, kayaks and

Balance is key during HALO jumps, as shown here. HAHO jumps involve opening the parachute at a high altitude and gliding long distances.

submersibles. Troopers also undergo Scuba and specialist diving training, which includes underwater demolition and maritime counter-terrorist operations.

Troopers joining Air Troop undergo specialist training in HALO/HAHO techniques both in the UK and overseas. In addition, they learn about all aspects of airborne insertion, conventional and unconventional, including the use of heavily modified long-range helicopters.

Those who join Mountain Troop learn about mountain and arctic warfare, including survival training, climbing techniques and the use of equipment such as skis, sledges and skidoos.

Troopers joining Mobility Troop train in vehicle operation both in conventional and unconventional roles such as deep reconnaissance and hit and run type missions, for which the SAS is renowned. Troopers learn how to drive defensively and offensively in different types of terrain ranging from woodland to desert, and practise ambush and counter-ambush techniques until they are second nature.

At some point each trooper will rotate through counter-terrorist training, as the SAS is the UK's primary counter-terrorist unit. Training includes CQB, sniping, fast-roping, insertion techniques, tubular work and unarmed combat.

Since the SAS is the world's most feared and respected special forces unit, there are many opportunities for troopers to cross-train with other units around the world, such as the US Delta Force, German GSG-9 and KSK, and both the Australian and New Zealand SAS.

Troopers in Mountain Troop need to be adept in all aspects of arctic warfare.

South Africa – Special Forces Brigade

Both the selection procedure and the actual training for South Africa's special forces – known as the 'Recces' – is extremely tough. The unit is keen to avoid macho 'body-builder' types, as they rarely fit in and in fact seldom pass the initial selection phase. Although physical fitness plays a major part in the Recces Selection and Training phase, it is not quite the be all and end all part of the course.

Equally as important is a candidate's personality, which comes under a great deal of scrutiny as well. What the instructors are looking for in the Selection phase is a candidate who is fit, intelligent, patient, determined, flexible and tenacious. During the Training phase, there are just two key requirements that potential recruits need: initiative and plenty of guts. In a typical year, over 700 potential Recce recruits will undergo Selection; however, less than 50 of the candidates will make the grade.

The Special Forces Brigade holds two Selection courses each year, prior to which potential recruits visit a number of units to find out more about their training and operational roles. The recruiting team then shows potential candidates film footage of the actual Selection and Training course, so that they are under no illusions of what is required

'Recces' are expert in bush warfare – they have to be because they are always outgunned.

of them. If this film fails to frighten them away, they move on to the next phase, the PT test, which they must pass. The PT test requires the candidate to complete a 30km (19 mile) course in six hours with normal kit and rifle, carrying a 30kg (65lb) sand bag; an 8km (5 mile) run wearing boots and carrying a rifle in under 45 minutes; 40 press-ups, eight chin pulls and 68 sit-ups in a set time; 40 shuttle runs of 7m (23ft) each in under 90 seconds; and a freestyle 45 minute swim. If they pass this test, they are then considered as serious candidates and undergo a thorough medical and psychological examination in which they are questioned about their reasons for joining the Special Forces Brigade, and more importantly what they have to offer the Recces.

Passing the first hurdle

For those who pass the initial PT test and medical examinations, a three-week pre-selection course awaits them. This phase starts with two weeks of tough PT sessions that last for eight hours a day and are designed to prepare candidates for the full Selection programme.

Even at this early stage, some 20 per cent of the candidates drop out, mainly because of the harshness of the physical training. For those who are still left on the course there is no let up in the punishing schedule. Candidates are sent to Zululand for a week's water orientation course which tests their watermanship skills and instructs them in the use of two-seater canoes, kayaks and small motor boats.

Following this phase of boat training, candidates carry out navigation exercises in swampy terrain and then have to take part in an 8km (5 mile) race, which requires them to team up in pairs and carry a pole between them without dropping it. However, the catch in this exercise is that each pole is extremely heavy and normally requires a four-man lift. The candidates are watched throughout this

Sunset or sunrise after a hard day's work –
sometimes it is impossible to tell the
difference during the Selection phase.

exercise by their eagle-eyed instructors, who
are looking for teamwork and initiative, and
for those who show leadership skills. By the
end of the week, candidates will have noticed
a reduction in their rations and will have
been assessed for adaptability, co-ordination,
fitness, claustrophobia, resistance to cold,
and their ability to work in difficult and
demanding circumstances. For some,
however, this week will have proven too
much and they will have quit.

Survival phase

Those who are still left on the course get no
rest and are quickly flown to an operational
area for the final part of the Selection
programme. The first week of this final phase
involves bush orientation and survival
training, as many of the candidates will have
little or no experience in this area. One of the
first tasks for the instructors is to search each
person for tobacco, sweets, food and toiletries,
as these items are strictly forbidden. The only

Special Forces Brigade

The South African Special
Forces Selection course is one
of the toughest in the world and
has been described as the
'Ultimate Challenge' by those
who have undertaken it. Before
a soldier attends Selection, he
must first meet the following
requirements.

• Must be a South African
  Citizen (however, exceptions
  are often made for British
  subjects)

• Must have graduated high
  school
• Must have at least one year's
  service in any of the
  following forces: Active,
  Reserve, Voluntary or Police
• Must speak at least two
  languages
• No serious criminal offence
• Must be between 18 and 28
  before Selection
• Ranks: NCO; Private to Staff
  Sergeant
• Officers: Candidate Officer to
  Captain

item of personal kit allowed is a first-aid kit. During the survival phase, candidates are taught about plants, obtaining water, starting fires and techniques for dealing with animals such as elephants and lions. Once they have received their survival lesson, they are on their own and have to build a shelter using only their groundsheet and brushwood. The shelters are then judged for their practicality, neatness and camouflage. At this stage their rations are reduced again and each man is restricted to 5 litres of water per day.

In addition to the survival lectures, candidates are still subjected to at least an hour of PT each morning before they are allowed breakfast. At this stage of Selection, breakfast consists of little more than a biscuit and a small amount of water. Once through the survival element of the course, the candidates move on to the observation test, which is a set route that contains ten hidden items that they have to find and correctly identify. Once they finish this task an assault course awaits them that has to be completed three times – twice without kit and once with a 35kg (77lb) cement-filled, mortar-bomb container. After completing this task the candidates go for a 5km (3 mile) run along a gully that is strewn with loose rocks. At the end of the run they have to pick up a tree trunk and carry it back to camp without dropping it.

Those who successfully complete this phase of Selection are evaluated for their performance during the previous week and

A Recce candidate is given the worst that the Selection course can throw at him, even down to automatic gunfire and an assault of incendiary devices.

Contact drills have to be efficient and effective in the special forces world or you simply won't survive.

are assessed on their water discipline, ability to cope with heights, navigation, observation skills, ability to take in information, weapons handling, leadership skills and ability to work with others while under stress.

Final challenge

As the candidates ponder their fate during the final phases of Selection, they come under real automatic gunfire, which tests both their reflexes and reactions. For those who survive this test, the final challenge awaits them. The remaining candidates are gathered together and given a magnetic bearing and an RV point which is some 38km (25 miles) away. They must arrive at the RV point at a set time if they want to eat, but are not told that the ration biscuits that are there for them are contaminated with petrol. As they make their way towards the RV they pass a checkpoint where they receive some water, while their instructors drink ice-cold cans of soft drinks in front of them. At the RV point there is plenty of good food, but only for the instructors and those who want to quit the course.

As the candidates reach the RV point they are briefed on their final exercise: five days in the bush with just a tin of condensed milk, half a 24-hour ration pack and 12 biscuits, of which eight are contaminated with petrol. Throughout the five days the candidates are subjected to numerous problems, such as dealing with wild animals, brush fires and insects, to name just a few. As they reach their final RV, they are told that there has been a mistake and that they have to continue

Another day, another jump. But each day could be the last, so SF operators can never switch off.

walking for a further 30km (20 miles). At this point some candidates will lose their tempers and quit, while for those who continue, they usually find the instructors waiting nearby for them with copious amounts of fresh food and cold drinks. In general, only 17 per cent of each recruitment cadre make it through Selection.

Once a candidate has passed Selection he must attend and pass a parachute course before being accepted into the Recces. Further training lasts for some 42 weeks and includes survival, tracking, explosives, weapons handling, unarmed combat, navigation, first-aid, unconventional warfare, bushcraft, guerrilla tactics and signalling. In addition to learning about western weapons, the candidates are also taught how to handle enemy equipment, which is usually Russian or

Chinese. Even though the candidates have passed Selection, they are still subjected to regular PT and are expected to better their physical standards. The final test for the candidates is a night out in lion country with only a rifle, ammunition and a box of matches.

Once qualified, the new Recce joins an existing team and specialises in whatever subject they were best at during selection. After a period of time the Recce can further refine his skills by joining a dedicated specialist unit such as the combat divers or maritime assault unit.

Whatever element of the Recces a candidate joins, he knows that he is serving in one of the world's most respected units and that a lot will be expected of him throughout his career.

Politically Correct Warfare

The Balkans

The Swedish military works alongside US Marines as a part of Multinational Brigade South in Kosovo during Operation Dynamic Response.

Following on from selection and initial specialist training, the key thing any budding operator wants to do is to put it all into practice. For the special forces operator, his or her return is to serve their country – and serve it well by achieving any mission task put before them.

As the British SAS say: 'You have to beat the clock'; and if you do, that means you are alive. The time spent passing gruelling and arduous selection courses are for nothing if you cannot pit your skills and talents against an adversary – even if it might be only once. After the first time, you never need to prove yourself again – you are a fully-fledged operator.

The only way to really understand what it means to be an operator is to look at them in action. The action that I have

chosen to open with features the Balkan conflict. It is a theatre of war where special forces were considered to have had a dramatic influence. If ever there was a war that highlighted the diverse skills an operator needs to have in order to perform a mission, then surely this must be it.

This is the true story of SAS patrol, Alpha Two-One.

A brace of RAF Chinooks insert a spearhead force on day one of the Kosovo invasion.

Ethnic Tensions

For the British, the conflict in the Balkans began as a humanitarian operation, but eventually led to immense frustration as the British Army became embroiled in a war that knew little compassion, with ethnic hatred fuelling some of the world's worst war criminals in an orgy of unprecedented violence.

The background to this outbreak of violence can be traced back to the summer of 1992 when the former Yugoslav republic of Bosnia-Herzegovina found itself embroiled in a civil war that involved Serbs, Croats and Muslims. Fearing that a domino effect could develop from the Balkans, the UN authorised a UN Protection Force (UNPROFOR) to carry out escorts for the aid convoys and their workers who were being attacked and murdered as they attempted to help those who were in need of their support.

The first British troops to arrive were members of the Cheshire Regiment who set up bases in Vitez, Gornji Vakuf and Tuzla. Attached to the Cheshires were members of the SAS who acted as liaison officers and interpreters for the difficult and frustrating task of negotiating with the various warring parties for permission to move aid through their territory. At this time the situation was highly volatile and there were genuine fears in the UK that British soldiers might be taken hostage by the warlords. Should this happen the SAS were ready to go into Bosnia and perform rescue missions at a moment's notice. To that end they had a troop based in Split, Croatia that was assigned to both hostage rescue tasks (HRTs) and general forces support duties.

Around this time former SAS commander Lt Gen Sir Michael Rose was appointed commander of UN forces, Bosnia. Gen Rose belonged to a new generation of British Army officers, and was well liked and respected by his men. Although he was reluctant to say anything in public about his fellow UN colleagues, Gen Rose was frustrated by the sheer lack of knowledge and purpose that seemed to dog this well-intentioned, yet (some would argue) rather naïve UN mission. To enable him to operate with more confidence in Bosnia, Gen Rose wanted eyes and ears on the ground that he could trust to gather well-informed and reliable intelligence; the only people qualified to fulfil his expectations were the SAS.

The first task he set the SAS was to monitor the newly formed Bosnian-Croatian alliance and its leader. In addition they were to ensure that everything ran smoothly and that any difficulties between the two sides were quickly ironed out. To soften their true purpose in Bosnia they were called Joint Commission Observers (JCOs) and were given permission to drive around the various warring factions in their highly conspicuous white Landrovers.

In March 1994 the SAS had their first major success when they negotiated the withdrawal of Croatian forces from the Muslim town of Maglai. Gen Rose was pleased with the results and decided to send them to the Muslim town of Gorazde, which was surrounded by the Serbs. When the SAS arrived in Gorazde they were shocked by what they saw. The town had been decimated by constant shelling from nearby Serbian artillery located in the

USAF MH-53s arrive in Bosnia at the outset of the Balkans conflict.

A cold and miserable Sarajevo airport before USAF Special Operations Group (SOG) operations – the most famous being the stealth pilot rescue.

The Balkans, the Balkans, never ever get involved in the Balkans.

Otto von Bismark, 19th Century German Chancellor

surrounding hills. As if this wasn't enough, the Muslim civilians were also regularly sniped at as they they went about their business, making life very difficult for them.

On their way into Gorazde, the SAS team had sensed hostility from the Serbs as they passed through their checkpoints. At the time the Serbs were unaware of the fact that they had just let in a British special forces team as they believed them to be casual UK liaison officers and nothing more. To help with their cover the seven-man team was only armed with standard British Army SA-80 assault rifles and wore normal issue combats. Once settled into Gorazde, the SAS set up an observation post (OP) on top of the wrecked Hotel Gradina as it offered a good view of the surrounding hills and local roads. Their HQ was an old bank as it seemed the most secure building in the town and its strength would later prove to be something of a lifesaver for them.

As standard operational procedure (SOP), the SAS commenced local patrols around the Serb positions in a bid to monitor their build-up and to report back to Gen Rose on any significant activity. The Serbs didn't take kindly to the British snooping around their lines and

opened fire on them on several occasions. In response, the SAS called in airstrikes and a confrontational mentality started to develop between them. The situation finally came to a head when, on 15 April 1994, an SAS patrol came under effective enemy fire and two SAS troopers were seriously wounded.

The SAS negotiated a cease-fire with the Serbs to allow a Casualty Evacuation (CASEVAC) helicopter to come in and extract the wounded soldiers. Not wanting to appear difficult, the Serbs agreed to a short pause in their shelling and one of the soldiers, Cpl Fergus Rennie, was evacuated but sadly later died of his injuries. The other wounded soldier refused to be evacuated and insisted on staying with his colleagues. The SAS then called in further air strikes against Serbian tanks and artillery, but on this occasion the air attack backfired with disastrous consequences for both the pilot and the SAS. In modern air warfare there is a rule that if you don't hit a target on the first pass you leave it as it's very likely that you will become a target yourself. Easy words to say but hard to follow when you have an SAS Forward Air Controller (FAC) calling for your support as he and his fellow troopers are being shelled from all sides.

The unlucky pilot was Lt Nick Richardson of the Royal Navy who was flying a Sea Harrier on a practice air-support mission when he received a request for air support from the SAS in Gorazde. As he lined up for an attack on some Serbian tanks positioned on a hillside, his head-up display (HUD) failed to lock-on when he tried to release his bombs and he was forced to break away from the attack and try again. As he lined up for the second time, his HUD failed again and he was forced to abort the attack run. The FAC was now getting frustrated with the whole situation and asked the pilot to go around again.

Lt Richardson was between a rock and a hard place; he knew that if he went around again he would really be pushing his luck, but at the same time he could not let down his fellow countrymen. As he rolled in for a third attempt, disaster struck. A Serbian surface to air missile (SAM) hit him and he was forced to eject from his stricken aircraft. Fortunately he landed near some friendly Muslim forces, who took him to the SAS in Gorazde.

On arrival he was greeted by an SAS officer

All around the valley the distant sound of artillery could be heard as the Serbs shelled Gorazde, and burning fires could be seen ahead of the SAS team.

who explained that he had just jumped out of the frying pan and into the fire. Lt Richardson at first wasn't sure what he meant by this comment, but soon found out. It transpired that the SAS themselves were now in serious trouble as the local Muslims had turned against them because of NATO's failure to protect them from the Serbs. As the SAS officer appraised the situation, a lynch mob gathered at the front of the bank and began smashing down the front door. The situation was now clearly untenable and the SAS officer contacted his superiors and asked for permission to withdraw as he didn't want his men to get into a firefight with the very people they were supposed to be helping. The permission to withdraw was refused and the SAS were told to tough it out for the next four days until a relief convoy could get through to Gorazde. They would have been lucky to survive four hours let alone four days. With this in mind the SAS officer went direct to Gen Rose and again asked for permission to withdraw and this time it was granted. It was impossible for a helicopter to land in Gorazde as the risks were just too

great, so they would have to make their way to an extraction site that had been located for them in a valley some distance away.

The main problem now was getting the team out of Gorazde with an injured trooper, a downed pilot and a local guide called Ahmed, without being spotted by either the Muslims or the Serbs. It was decided that the best time to leave would be just after dark, as the SAS had good night vision sights and the Muslims had none. With typical SAS stealth the team and their guests slowly made their way out of the town without anyone seeing them. They went through a forest and were making good time when they suddenly faced a climb up a hill that was practically vertical in places. For the SAS this climb was tough enough, but they had a pilot and an injured trooper to think about as well. For Ahmed the climb wasn't a problem, but he was having difficulty getting his bearings and at one stage he got the patrol lost. As they were on a tight schedule there was no choice but to climb the hill. Despite having lost a lot of blood from his injured arm, the injured trooper bravely carried on, even though he was in agony.

Time was now running out for SAS patrol Alpha Two-One and they knew it. As they struggled to make up time there was a further setback ahead of them. All around the valley the distant sound of artillery could be heard as the Serbs shelled Gorazde and burning fires could be seen ahead of the SAS team. This could mean only one thing: the area was crawling with Serb soldiers and there was no way that a helicopter would be coming in. As they pondered their fate, a Serb patrol passed close to their position. In a firefight the SAS could easily beat them, but once the shooting started other Serbs would reinforce the patrol and they would, in effect, be cut off from escaping. After a few tense minutes the Serbs moved on, much to the relief of the SAS.

With this delay there was no way that they could reach the original RV point, so they tried to radio the pilots, but there was no response. They were roughly on the perceived flight-path so even if they did not make radio contact they could place landing markers down that the helicopter would see. As they waited, it suddenly dawned on them that there was not going to be a helicopter as nobody in Sarajevo believed they would make it this far. Infuriated by this thought the team set up their SATNET

Above: SAS patrol Alpha Two-One as seen through the FLIR (Forward Looking Infa-Red) camera of the French Puma that extracted them.

Top right: Kosovo, a Para looks on while his fellow countrymen search for booby traps on a bridge. A time-consuming but vital job.

Bottom right: Chinooks drop in a spearhead unit in order to secure a vital bridge on day one of the Kosovo invasion.

communications system and called Gen Rose in person. There were now only 30 minutes until dawn, and they knew that no rescue crew would fly in broad daylight over enemy territory, but fortunately their luck was in and Gen Rose personally arranged for a French helicopter to come in and rescue them.

With only minutes to go until first light, they heard the welcome sound of a Puma helicopter as it made its way up the valley towards their position. Within minutes they were safely on board and speeding back towards Sarajevo. After landing, the SAS team walked to the front of the helicopter to thank the crew for their bravery in risking their lives for them. They commented about it being an uneventful flight back until the pilot showed them the bullet holes in his Puma. It turned out that they had been laughing and joking so much on the way back that they hadn't heard the bullets hitting the airframe.

Thankfully, for the rest of the Bosnia tour, nothing like this happened again. Eventually 400 British UN troops moved into Gorazde and restored some semblance of normality for the Muslim population.

On another occasion, however, a JCO team in the Bihac area found itself under threat of attack from Serbian forces. Fortunately they backed off after being threatened with NATO air strikes as Gen Rose favoured an aggressive line against the Serbs, although the UN preferred a softly, softly approach.

In May 1995 the UN paid heavily for its inconsistent policy in Bosnia; the Serbs seized hundreds of UN soldiers, including 40 British troops. To counter this situation the UN Rapid Reaction Force was formed. The force included two SAS squadrons who were tasked with breaking through Serb lines and relieving the UN garrison in Sarajevo.

Despite their best efforts the UN failed to prevent the massacre of Muslim prisoners at Srebrenica, where over 8,000 local citizens were murdered by the Serbs in cold blood after Dutch troops surrendered to them. Prior to this massacre a JCO team had been with the Dutch forces and was involved in directing air strikes in support of the people of Srebrenica but, sadly, the attacks failed to stop the Serbian advance.

In August 1995 the UN retaliated against the Serbs by launching constant air attacks against Serbian positions throughout Bosnia, which caused considerable damage to their war effort. These attacks were supported with artillery barrages from both the British and French on Mount Igman, who acted in response to SAS teams who were identifying targets for them. In addition the SAS infiltrated deep behind Serbian lines to act as FACs in support of NATO air strikes. Their primary task was to find and designate targets for the attacking aircraft and to act as a rescue force should a pilot be downed.

Eventually the Serbs gave in to NATO and began to withdraw from Sarajevo under the supervision of the SAS, who fully understood

Paras always lead the way – at least the overt way, that is.

SF operators often use regular military vehicles for intelligence gathering as they rarely arouse attention in a conflict situation.

how devious the Serbs could be. Building on this success they helped the new NATO Peace Implementation Force (IFOR) by providing detailed information on the known troop lines and their levels of equipment. They played a key role in keeping the various factions under observation until conventional forces were deployed to police the peace.

On one occasion an SAS team attached to US forces helped to diffuse a potentially dangerous situation after Muslim refugees attempted to reoccupy their village which was in Serb territory. Thanks to the tact and diplomacy of the SAS a potential crisis was averted.

With the ink barely dry on the Dayton Accord (the peace agreement that ended the war in Bosnia), it was only a matter of time before trouble flared up again in the Balkans. In March 1999, the storm clouds of war were gathering over Kosovo, a country barely the size of Wales which borders Albania, Macedonia, Montenegro and Serbia. Under the orders of Serbian president Slobodan Milosevic, Kosovo was invaded by both Serbian military and paramilitary police forces.

In appalling acts of almost medieval barbarity, the Serbs began to ethnically cleanse Kosovo in an evil and systematic way. As a huge refugee crisis developed in Kosovo, NATO warned Serbia that it faced military action if it failed to reign in its military forces, who were carrying out human rights abuses on an unprecedented scale. A deadline was set for Serbian compliance in halting their actions but this was ignored by Milosevic. As a result NATO had no choice but to embark on an intensive bombing campaign against both Serbia and its fielded forces in Kosovo.

As the air operations gathered pace, an unexpected factor began to hinder the safety and accuracy of the air strikes – the weather.

NATO was now facing severe operational problems due to adverse conditions, with many sorties either cancelled before take-off or aborted over their intended targets as there was too much risk of collateral damage.

This situation could not be allowed to continue and so it was decided that special forces should be sent in to identify targets using laser designators. Since the SAS had performed so well in Bosnia it was felt that they were best placed to carry out this mission.

In response to the NATO request for SAS support, a number of squadrons were deployed to Kosovo for immediate action. Their key role was target designation for air strikes and a number of four-man teams were sent in to Serbia and Kosovo to find and identify targets of value and destroy them.

In addition to this role, NATO was desperate for reliable and accurate information on Serbian troop movements within Kosovo, as air-based intelligence gathering was failing them. The problem for NATO was that, far from not having any information on the Serbs, they actually had far too much. Their analysts were getting so much information from aircraft, unmanned air vehicles (UAVs), satellites and ground sensors, that they were simply unable to cope with it. In some cases it was taking three days to evaluate the information, which meant that by the time strike aircraft were tasked with acting on the intelligence it was often too late as the intended target had moved.

The SAS were also tasked with training and supporting the Kosovo Liberation Army (KLA) in its operations against the Serbian field forces in Kosovo. At first the KLA struggled to make any headway against the Serbs, but with SAS direction and guidance they became a potent and highly effective force. The SAS would often use the KLA as intelligence gatherers, as they had

great knowledge of their own country and its geography. One invaluable piece of intelligence that the SAS discovered for NATO concerned the bridges in Kosovo. It was found that very few of them could take the weight of modern tanks and that if a land invasion was launched this would become a serious issue. As a result NATO decided to invade Kosovo by mounting a helicopter assault using British Paras from the 5th Airborne Brigade. Following SAS recce missions near to the border with Macedonia, a number of invasion routes were identified as being suitable for both troops and vehicles. Small teams were also deployed to ridges overlooking the roads to ensure that the Serbs were not able to carry out ambushes against NATO ground forces as they entered Kosovo on 12 June 1999. The invasion went very smoothly and no resistance was encountered until British forces entered the city of Pristina, and even then it was very light. There was, however, one incident that caused immense concern to NATO: the Russians and Pristina airfield. Due to NATO dithering over the role of Russia in Kosovo's future, the Russians decided their own fate by occupying Pristina airfield and taking responsibility for it. This led to a temporary stand-off between the Russians and NATO which caused serious concerns for everyone. The Americans, under Gen Wesley Clark, had asked the British to block the airfield's runways and use force if necessary to prevent their occupation. However, the British, under Gen Mike Jackson, refused to comply with this command and as a result diplomatic efforts were used to resolve the crisis. It's fortunate that the situation was resolved peacefully as the SAS could have found themselves in the thick of a potentially very serious confrontation.

Eventually the Serbs agreed to leave Kosovo, and were supervised by the SAS to ensure that they complied with the withdrawal procedures as laid down by NATO. After the conflict ended the SAS were involved in tracking down and apprehending known Serbian war criminals and their associates. On one occasion as they went to arrest a known suspect, a firefight broke out between the SAS and the Serbs in which a war criminal was killed and one SAS soldier was slightly injured.

For the troopers in the SAS, they can look back on a difficult job done well – in tough circumstances.

A British KFOR soldier secures the perimeter of a church following a sweep and clear mission involving SF personnel from several countries.

Special Forces Tactics

Techniques and Procedures

Many people ask how special forces personnel plan and execute missions. It's a fair question as few books ever discuss the planning of a mission – merely the execution and outcome. It would seem from some military accounts of operations that they just happened, although this is clearly not the case.

For most soldiers recalling a tale of their endeavours, the general assumption is that the planning phase of a mission is boring and of no interest to anyone – except for those participating in the action. It's an arguable point, but actually the planning phase is critical to its success: failure to plan equals plan to fail – according to the British SAS, that is.

It is not always possible to hear from all sides involved in the planning and execution of a mission as Operational Security (OPSEC) has to be observed, even many years after a military operation has taken place. This is due to many considerations such as ingress and egress routes which may still be viable in a current conflict – such as in Afghanistan or Iraq – or it may be that a tactic worked so well in one action, it's worth keeping it quiet for another occasion, where its tactical effects and viability may still be valid for the next generation of operators.

Planning and preparation prevent poor performance.

Sierra Leone

On 6 May 2000, Britain launched Operation Palliser in response to the advance of rebel forces on Freetown, the capital of Sierra Leone, as they were endangering the lives of British, Commonwealth and European citizens. For the British Armed Forces this was their largest solo operation since the Falklands War of 1982, involving just over 4,500 military personnel from all three services.

Their potential enemy was the Revolutionary United Front (RUF), a bunch of cold-blooded murderers who took great pleasure in raping women and butchering young children by hacking their limbs off. Although the RUF was large in number there were also other maverick militias for the British to contend with, the most renowned being the West Side Boys (WSB), a bizarre group who paraded around in odd clothing and frequenty wore women's wigs during public parades. They were a motley crew, made up of ex-RUF members and deserters from the Sierra Leone Army (SLA), who were more often than not drunk or high on drugs. Although at first treated as something of a joke, the WSB were good fighters and totally unpredictable.

Within Sierra Leone there was a UN presence but it was virtually ineffective. The troops rarely ventured out of the main urban areas for fear of being attacked and, as a result, the rebels were having a field day as there was nobody to challenge them. With the arrival of the British it would be a different story though, and the rebels knew it. The first official British forces to arrive in Sierra Leone were members of the elite Pathfinders and two companies from the 1st Battalion of the Parachute Regiment who flew into Lungi airport on 7 May. Within hours of their arrival they had secured the airport and were mounting patrols in the local area to reassure the citizens of Freetown that they were safe from rebel attack.

Prior to the arrival of 1 Para, Sierra Leone had other visitors who were not 'officially' there. They were members of the SAS and their job was to gather intelligence on the rebel forces and to recce good defensive positions for 1 Para. For mobility the SAS used a number of locally commandeered Toyota pickup trucks for liaison and utility duties. Once their role became more overt they drove around in heavily armed Land Rover 110 Desert Patrol Vehicles (DPVs), which were armed with a mixture of 7.62 general purpose machine guns (GPMGs) and .50 calibre heavy machine guns or, occasionally, a 40mm grenade launcher.

In a highly unusual procedure for the SAS, they patrolled during daylight hours making no attempt to disguise who they were or what their intentions were. In a way their tactics were designed to intimidate the rebels and provoke them into making a move against them, a plan that eventually paid off.

The locals despised the rebels and openly welcomed the British forces, and SAS intelligence gathering amongst the local population revealed that the WSB were bragging about launching an attack on British forces but their exact target was never made clear. In a bid to set a trap for the WSB the SAS started to patrol aggressively near to their favourite haunts, especially around the area of Masiaka where they had set up road blocks for the purpose of looting trucks and cars that happened to be passing. In some cases their victims were able to pay them off with money

Timing was critical during the rescue mission because civilian lives were at stake. Too soon, and all the assets would not be in place; too late, and it would be disastrous for all concerned.

Elements of the Royal Marines SBS played a key role in acting as cut-off groups for the paras and SAS, as every contingency had to be covered.

or alcohol, but on many occasions they were robbed and then murdered.

To further increase the pressure on the rebels, both the Paras and the Pathfinders mounted extra patrols in set areas, but quite deliberately ignored others, the idea being that the WSB would enter a designated trap area that had been set up for them. One particular area had been cleared of brush and vegetation so that its road checkpoint could be easily seen from a distance, giving the impression to the rebels that it was a soft target. However, hidden out of sight were a

number of machine gun nests and mortar pits that were manned by 1 Para.

The plan was aimed at the WSB, but it was the RUF who took the bait and launched an attack against a patrol of Pathfinders at Lungi Lo, 16km (10 miles) east of Freetown airport. A fierce firefight developed and many rebels were killed in the first stage of the attack, but there was more to come. As the Pathfinders sprung their trap, reinforcements were flown in by Chinook helicopters and they engaged the rebels with both machine guns and mortars. The overwhelming firepower halted

The Scenario

Flash one:

Location	–	Sierra Leone
Time	–	16.25 local
Details	–	as follows

'A small group of British soldiers, while out on a UN peacekeeping patrol in the West African bush, have been kidnapped and are being held hostage by a local militia group, known as the WSB (West Side Boys). More details to follow.'

Upon hearing this news, all relevant members of the military and Government would be notified and an IAP (Immediate Action Plan) would be activated – pending the planning and approval of a more detailed OPLAN (Operational Plan).

An IAP focuses on a basic outline plan that can be executed rapidly, should the need arise, prior to a fully detailed OPLAN being developed.

To focus on the needs of a mission, the tactical mission planners involved in formulating the OPLAN work to the following acronym:

P Preparation and proportionality
L Lethality and legality
A Achievability and accessability
N Need and necessity

Taking each point seperately:
- Preparation: this involves reviewing every aspect of a plan including all forces available, both in theatre and readily deployable; intelligence – strategic and tactical; local issues, ie. will mounting a rescue cause further problems to friendly forces; location – how do we infiltrate target; is comprehensive medical cover available; and finally, actions on contact?
- Proportionality: what size of force is required, compared to known threat?
- Lethality: what level of combat power is required and available to neutralise threat?
- Legality: is mounting a hostage rescue mission in an overseas country justified under the circumstances?
- Achievability: does the tactical planner believe that his force can overcome the enemy, without heavy loss of Blue forces, compared to that inflicted by hostage takers?
- Accessibility: can SF forces easily infiltrate and extract from target location – if not, how far is

it to a drop-off point and RV point and is this viable?
- Need: is this a life-threatening situation and, if so, what is the estimated time line before crisis point is reached and direct action is needed?
- Necessity: is it absolutely necessary to use military force, and have all peaceful and diplomatic alternatives been pursued and exhausted?

The threat
Is this threat deemed plausible, bearing in mind that threat is defined as both means and motive to carry out a threatened action?

If the answer is an overall 'Yes' to the relevant PLAN matrix, then an OPLAN can be formed.

Usually an OPLAN involves holding an informal Chinese Parliament, where all options are discussed ranging from the sublime to the ridiculous.

Once these options have been narrowed down, the OPLAN goes to the next phase, Evaluate, Decide, Execute (EDE).

This phase is basically the final one and involves dismissing all the implausible options, until only the plausible ones are left. Once these have been narrowed down then it is decision time.

Murder board
After making your decision you then allow a group of tactical planners and senior soldiers to critique your OPLAN. Those personnel chosen for this phase will generally be members of your unit, who are aware of the tactical situation but have had no part to play in the planning phase, thereby remaining impartial.

If they have too many negative points about the OPLAN, then it is not a good one. However, if there is little to say, then it's a runner.

Once the OPLAN is sanctioned by the powers that be then it's showtime. The execution of this particular OPLAN – for the rescue mission – was named Operation Barras.

the rebels' attack and they fled into the bush to escape, but the British had more surprises in store for them. Above the fleeing rebels were a number of heavily armed Chinooks that opened fire on them with both their mini-guns and machine guns. The effect was devastating for the RUF and their attack force was totally decimated. To add further insult to injury the RUF leader, Foday Sankoh, was

The overwhelming firepower broke the rebels attack and they fled into the bush to escape, but the British had more surprises in store for them.

Members of the elite Pathfinders also served during operations in Sierra Leone, their principal role being that of intelligence gathering.

The mighty Chinook, workhorse of British special forces during Operation Barras. At one stage the crews used them as bullet magnets to divert heavy enemy fire away from vulnerable Paras who were struggling through chest-deep water.

captured in Freetown by the SAS and taken into protective custody. As the news spread of the British victory, it was tempered by the tragic loss of one Nigerian soldier serving with the UN and six members of the SLA, who were killed by the RUF in an unrelated attack.

For a time everything settled down in Sierra Leone with only the odd rebel attack being mounted against the UN peacekeepers and these were generally ineffective. After a couple of weeks the Paras were withdrawn and replaced by Royal Marines who kept up the good work and enjoyed a relatively quiet deployment. For the SAS, however, it was business as usual and they continued to patrol the coastal areas in an effort to force

the rebels back further into the bush where they would be of little threat to the locals.

Just as everything seemed to be going well for the British, disaster struck on 25 August 2000. An 11-man patrol from the Royal Irish Regiment (RIR), along with a Sierra Leonean colleague, strayed into an area that was crawling with members of the WSB and they were taken prisoner. This was a nightmare scenario for the British and 22 SAS were rapidly tasked with locating the rebels' base and mounting an OP. The British Government decided to play the patience card first to see what transpired, whilst at the same time formulating a rescue plan.

Once contact had been established with the WSB a dialogue was slowly developed that took on a non-confrontational tone; the British knew how temperamental the rebels could be and they did not want to antagonise them. At first the rebels' demands were quite modest in that they wanted food and drink for both them and the hostages, but once they got what they wanted their demands grew. The British decided to be compliant and gave in to them, asking only that their soldiers be treated decently and humanely. As a relationship started to develop between the WSB and the British negotiators, the British asked for the release of some of their soldiers as an act of goodwill. Much to their surprise on 30 August 2000, five members of the RIR were released unharmed and in good health, considering what they had been through.

As negotiations continued with the rebels,

Operation Barras section battle drills

Battle preparation
To be carried out by Section Commander:

P Protection: sentries, cover, camouflage, NBC (nuclear, biological, chemical), alarms, innoculations
A Ammunition: supply, reserves
W Weapons: scales, distribution, checking and preparation
P Personal: camouflage, hygiene, food and water
E Equipment: scales required, distribution
R Radio: communications, rehearsals
S Specialist equipment for tasks: cutting, assaulting, climbing, etc.
O Orders: 'O' Group timings

Battle preparation
Section Commander's orders:
• Ground: ref points
• Situation: enemy and friendly forces – platoon formation and tasking
• Attachments and detachments
• Mission: the section's mission
• Execution: Fire team group (if altered), route, section formation
• LSW and LAW (light weapons) tasking
• Service support: information from platoon Commander's orders

Reference points and anticipatory orders
In the 'advance to contact' the Section Commander will look out for:
• Positions giving cover, anticipating enemy fire
• Reference points for fire control orders

Reaction to enemy fire
The drill to be adopted is: on the order of the Section Commander, 'Take cover, dash – down – crawl – observe – sights – fire.' Get off effective fire zone, move to nearest cover as indicated. Take cover, crawl into chosen position to observe. Return fire – use tracer to indicate enemy position.

Location of the enemy
Location of the enemy will be difficult, which means casualties and loss of initiative. Actions on effective enemy fire are:
• Observation – look in area of thump, then use SUSAT (sight unit) or Binos. Look for smoke, etc.
• Fire – fire orders to riflemen, grenadiers or LSW gunners is to fire on possible enemy locations if no obvious target
• Movement – Section Commander will order rifleman to move while rest of section observe

Winning the firefight
Once Section Commander knows the enemy's position, a fire order will be given to neutralise or pin down, depending on tactical advantage.
• Where possible ammunition expenditure levels must be closely monitored
• Aimed single shots for long range
• Bursts for short close quarter engagements only
• High volume usage may jeopardise mission

The attack battle orders
On reaching the forward enemy position, Section Commander will look for other defended positions. If part of the objective, he will issue snap orders.
   Assault phase will be as follows:
• The approach
• The fight through
• The attack, which will be the following:
   One stage attack
   1. Fire and movement to close with enemy, L or R flanking
   2. Assault fire team prepare to move, fire support team fires
   3. Assault fire team moves
• All movement by either fire team to be covered
• Use 1,600mm distance between fire teams
• Support fire should fire across objective, prior to final assault, then switch to enemy in-depth positions making sure all flanks are covered
• Section Commander to battle appreciate throughout this phase

Reorganisation
Once objective is cleared of enemy and hostages are rescued Section Commander is to prepare for possible counter-attack. Section Commander is to:
• Allot fire tasks to each member of section
• Post sentries
• Check on casualties
• Check ammunition, arrange redistribution of ammunition
• Supervise re-digging of shell scrapes
• Send captured prisoners, kit and documentation to rear RV point
• Report to Platoon Commander for further orders

Patrolling guerrilla-held areas is key to defeating the enemy. This action puts the guerillas on the run and gains the trust of the indigenous population.

attempt as soon as possible.

As the British Government deliberated over what action to take, the decision was made for them in the light of a serious new development. It transpired that a UN helicopter had strayed over the WSB's base by accident and, believing that they were about to be attacked, the WSB dragged the prisoners out into the open as if to shoot them, but then thought better of it. Fortunately for the hostages, the British negotiator managed to convince them that it had been a genuine mistake and the WSB accepted this explanation. The British Government realised that something like this could easily happen again and that next time they might not be so lucky. With this in mind they sanctioned a rescue mission, which was codenamed Operation Barras.

Time was now of the essence as the media in the UK was openly speculating about an imminent rescue attempt, which was further reinforced by the announcement that 1 Para was to return to Sierra Leone immediately. The planners of Operation Barras were well aware of the fact that the WSB regularly listened to the BBC World Service, and that if they suspected something was in the air they would just go ahead and execute the hostages. As a result the decision was taken that a tri-service operation would be mounted on 10 September 2000.

At 06.16hrs local time, elements of the SAS boat troop and members of the Royal Marines Special Boat Squadron (SBS) sealed off the river that led to Rokel Creek. At the same time members of the Jordanian UN battalion secured the main Massiaka highway to prevent the WSB from escaping during the rescue.

Once all the security elements were in place, the main thrust of the operation commenced with an assault on Magbeni and Geri Bana by three troop carrying Chinook helicopters, supported by two smaller Lynx helicopters providing fire support. The timing of the operation was crucial as there had to be just enough light for the helicopters to see their target, but not enough for them to be seen easily by the rebels. The speed of the operation was also essential as the hostages were in one place, which meant that their captives could execute them very quickly. However, from the rescuers point of view, this also made them easier to find.

As the helicopters swooped in at low level

the SAS moved more troopers into the vicinity of the rebels' base which was located in the hamlet of Geri Bana. As they continued to observe the rebels, they discovered that they also had another camp located about 300m (330yd) away from where the hostages were being held. This camp was located in another hamlet called Magbeni which was just south of Geri Bana and was well placed to provide mutual fire support to the other camp. To further complicate matters for the SAS, the camps were divided by the Rokel Creek which the WSB made good use of for transporting their supplies and ill-gotten gains.

As the SAS planners worked on a rescue strategy, the WSB's leader, 24-year-old Foday Kallay, a self-styled Brigadier and former NCO in the Sierra Leone Army, started to make political demands for the release of one his men, who was known locally as Brigadier Bomb Blast or Brigadier Papa. In addition to this demand he also wanted a safe passage out of Sierra Leone along with an education abroad, and ... an outboard motor for one of his dingies. Although the British tolerated these demands, it was becoming clear that matters were now coming to a head and fears for the safety of the hostages were growing. The WSB were now carrying out mock executions on the British soldiers quite openly; the SAS had seen enough and requested permission to mount a rescue

Assault Commander's orders

His job is to outline his plan by means of a warning order. This will outline assault tasks, infiltration/extraction routes, command structure and equipment levels to be issued.

His warning briefing will show air intelligence photos, maps, SF intelligence and OP reports. Prior to mission execution, SF are tasked with carrying out tactical reconnaissance on target location by means of covert OPS. They are to report on:

- hostage location and condition of detainees
- routes into, and out of, target location
- landmarks
- obstacles – both man-made and geographic
- landing zones – suitable for Chinook helicopters
- enemy OPS, listening posts and surveillance devices
- enemy strength
- enemy routines and hierarchy
- enemy weaponry – especially AAA and MANPADS – and where located
- enemy positions, defended areas and fixed arcs of fire
- likely ambush points – for both them and us
- lines of communication
- environmental issues, such as time of attack, weather and light conditions

Patrol Commander will also issue RVS, ERVS, FRVS, nicknames and code words, plus make a model of the target area.

Assault Force Briefing
This outlines:

- Ground: landmarks, obstacles, geography and orientation of target location
- Situation: enemy forces, routines, sentries, minefields and known arcs of fire
- Mission: define mission and its primary purpose, that being hostage rescue of friendly forces
- Execution: how the mission is to be carried out. General outline:
  - How many phases will there be and what will they be
  - Infiltration, assault, rescue, re-organisation, exfiltration
  - Who is taking part – RAF, Royal Navy, SAS, SBS and Parachute Regiment, plus attached personnel
  - Prep moves – drop-off points, timings, method of insertion/extraction, helicopter seating
  - Phase 1 – actions on ambush (RV or QRF) to be decided at time of contact
  - Phase 2 – route out to FRV point, plus actions if lost
  - Phase 3 – action in final RV
    On arrival:
    1. Occupation
    2. Action on ambush, extraction order and perimeter security
    3. Arcs of fire, signals to fire
  - Phase 4 – action on objective: cover, route, assault teams, arcs of fire, signals to fire, tasking, kill zone area, actions on separation, hostage rescue team tasking, Medevac and ambush drills
  - Phase 5 – withdrawal and action in final RV: signal to withdraw, sequence of withdrawal, headcount, POW extraction, hostage extraction, medical priority for extraction and actions if surprised
  - Phase 6 – route back: actions on helicopter loss, ERV point, signals, QRF call-signs and emergency exfiltration routes

Final Phase
Summary of mission execution.

To win a firefight you must have SAS: Speed, Aggression and Surprise, which is what the British had in abundance during Operation Barras.

the WSB opened fire on them with every weapon available, including captured heavy machine guns taken from the RIR's vehicles. In a highly co-ordinated movement the SAS opened fire on the rebels guarding the hostages, while the Paras made their assault after being inserted by the Chinooks.

Although taken initially by surprise, the WSB lost no time in getting into the defensive positions that surrounded both camps. As the Paras moved forward, their assault

Capture is always one of an operator's worst fears.

temporarily stalled after they got bogged down in a swamp located near to the Rokel Creek. From above the ground it looked like a flat field with long grass covering it, but in reality it was more like a paddy field. As a result the Paras were now wading through water up to chest level, making it very difficult for them to move quickly. The WSB spotted the Paras' predicament and opened fire on them with all of their heavy weapons inflicting many injuries; fortunately, however, none were fatal. The SAS spotted that the Paras were in serious trouble and directed their firepower at the WSB. In addition, the RAF Chinook pilots also noticed that the Paras had problems and risked their own lives by flying in front of the rebels' positions so that they could recover the injured soldiers. As they performed this brave act, other helicopters involved in the operation directed their weapons at the rebels' main defensive positions.

Within minutes the officers and NCOs of 1 Para began assaulting the WSB's main positions at Magbeni. As they did, the SAS launched their assault on Geri Bana and secured the building where the hostages were being held. During the short firefight a number of rebels were killed or injured, yet all the hostages were rescued unharmed. At Magbeni, the WSB were still putting up heavy resistance, despite the fact that a number of

them had fled when shooting started. To their credit the WSB were still fighting two hours later and only surrendered when the Paras brought in mortars and extra firepower from vehicle-based weapons. Among those taken prisoner was the WSB leader, Foday Kallay, and the WSB were to pay a heavy price for crossing the British. The number of confirmed dead was put at 25, but later investigations showed it was much higher. The WSB were now a spent force in Sierra Leone and never recovered from the devastating British operation.

The British also paid a price for their victory. During the initial assault at Geri Bana, Bombardier Brad Tinnion, who was serving with 22 SAS, was fatally wounded. Despite desperate efforts to save him, he died before reaching RFA *Sir Percival* which was berthed in Freetown. The Paras also suffered 12 casualties but all went on to make full recoveries from their injuries.

Operation Barras will go down in history as a textbook example of how to perform a hostage rescue in difficult conditions. It was a well-planned, well-executed operation that owed much to the bravery and professionalism of the British Armed Forces, especially the SAS who spent weeks gathering intelligence on the WSB while living and operating covertly in a hostile environment.

Cave Operators

Operators in Afghanistan

A British para gives Afghan Security Forces training in skill at arms – all highly necessary, as these men will be Afghanistan's future.

In our complicated lives, we take it for granted that our military forces are the best trained and best equipped for any type of conventional warfare, but this is not always the case.

Take, for example, Afghanistan. This is a landlocked country that has seen off the best of armies over the centuries – either by defeating them directly with the use of skilful tactics or in many cases just by allowing the foreign armies to wear themselves out in the mountainous and inhospitable terrain that makes up the majority of the country.

The Afghans have driven off Alexander the Great, the mighty British Empire and, in recent times, the ruthless Russian Bear. But there is one group of individuals who they simply couldn't suppress or defeat – or, for that matter, even wear down: our special forces and those of our allies.

For them, Afghanistan was merely another battleground in a faraway land – more difficult and demanding, yes; but at the end of the day it was just another mission. This is their story.

A British SBS operator covers up his face at the height of the Mazar-e-Sharif prison uprising in November 2001 – a bloody insurrection that left hundreds' dead and many wounded.

Searching out Terrorists

September 11, 2001 – a date that will be forever etched in our minds. It marks the day that terrorists perpetrated their biggest and most spectacular attack on the world's most powerful nation, the United States of America.

The attack began at 8.45am, US Eastern Standard Time, when an American Airlines Boeing 767 crashed into the giant North Tower of the World Trade Center in New York. At first it was assumed that it was just a dreadful accident; however, when 11 minutes later another Boeing 767, belonging to United Airlines, hit the South Tower, it was clear that something sinister was going on. As millions of people around the world watched the scene of carnage unfold on live television, the first of the two towers started to collapse in a horrific and violent way, then barely 20 minutes later the second tower imploded in a similar manner. As the giant clouds of grey dust filled New York's spectacular skyline, a cold reality dawned on the world that they had just

witnessed the worst terrorist atrocity in history. Thousands of innocent people from all walks of life and from many nations had been murdered in cold blood before their eyes.

It was a sickening scene. Then news came in of a further two incidents involving airliners. It was confirmed that an American Airlines Boeing 757 had crashed at 9.38am into the symbol of America's military power, the Pentagon. All 58 passengers and six crew members were killed along with 190 people on the ground. It was later announced that a fourth aircraft had crashed near Pittsburgh in suspicious circumstances. Fearing that more attacks were still to come, President George W. Bush was advised to take to the air in his personal aircraft, Air Force One. The theory was that while he was airborne he was safe from attack.

During the following days and weeks after the attack, it was revealed that the aircraft had all been hijacked by Arab terrorists under the

Looking more like Star troopers than soldiers, US operators respond to a stand-to-call at their Afghan base.

The Pentagon after 9/11. Of interest is the damage itself. Many believe that the damage was caused by a terrorist bomb or ground-launched missile, rather than an aircraft. The theory is that the aircraft was ordered to be shot down before it crashed.

alleged leadership of Osama bin Laden. The attacks had been meticulously planned and executed by a very sophisticated and well connected terrorist network, which caused great embarrassment to the US Intelligence agencies; they had failed to prevent them despite growing evidence of an intended attack on the US mainland.

As the political and emotional fallout began to mount over who was to blame for the events on 11 September 2001, which was now being referred to as Nine-one-one or 9/11, there was just one question to answer: what were the US and her allies going to do about it? Despite strong fears of a rash reaction from US President George W. Bush, he remained remarkably composed and rational in what was a highly charged and emotional period in US history.

As America considered its response to the attack, the world's media sometimes referred to the atrocity as America's alone, forgetting the other countries who had lost their nationals also. Yes, it was America's worst terrorist attack, but it was also Britain's, for example – until the horrific events of 7 July 2005 – despite over 30 years of terrorism from the 'Troubles' in Northern Ireland.

On 4 October 2001, British Prime Minister Tony Blair announced in the House of Commons that evidence had been produced linking Osama bin Laden and his Al-Qaeda (The Base) terrorist network to the attacks on the Pentagon and the World Trade Center.

Meanwhile, as the military operations were being considered, it was confirmed that Osama bin Laden was in Afghanistan under the protection of the Taliban regime.

Eyes on Afghanistan

There was now no doubt that military action was imminent, but what form it would take had yet to be decided. By sheer coincidence and good fortune, the British already had a massive force of air, sea and ground assets in the Gulf of Oman as part of Exercise Saif Sareea II (Swift Sword). The British put this entire force at the disposal of the US and basically invited them to help themselves to anything they wanted. Although this kind and generous offer was appreciated, there were only two assets that the US needed from Britain: tanker aircraft and the Special Air Service Regiment.

In late September 2001, George W. Bush issued an ultimatum to the Taliban: either turn Osama bin Laden and his Al-Qaeda supporters over or face the consequences. As the days ticked by, it became clear that the Taliban had no intention of complying with the US request and defiantly threatened a Jihad (Holy War). Although there was no deadline as such for the commencement of military action, the planners in the Pentagon were aware that they only had a short window of opportunity until the onset of winter in Afghanistan and then the weather conditions would became a serious factor in the execution of air strikes.

Counter-revolutionary warfare (CRW)

In the early 1970s, Western democracies suddenly found themselves under threat of attack from a plethora of terrorist organisations who were hell-bent on forcing their extremist viewpoint on anyone who would listen to them. Not content with breeding a culture of violence and intimidation in their own countries, many of these extremist groups wanted to take their grudges to the West and attack their values. Most of these organisations had sponsors in the Middle East and Communist Eastern Europe who were doing everything possible to undermine the West, and in September 1972 they showed the world just what they were capable of.

The event chosen by the terrorists to achieve maximum publicity for their cause was the Munich Olympic Games. On 5 September 1972, armed members of the Palestinian group 'Black September' took advantage of the low security at the Olympic village in Munich, and seized 11 Israeli athletes. They demanded the release of 234 fellow members of their group and a safe passage to Egypt or they would start executing the hostages. The German police had never dealt with a situation like this before and initially went along with the terrorists' demands and took the terrorists and hostages to the airport by helicopter. However, once they arrived at the airport, hidden snipers opened fire on the terrorists, killing two and wounding several others, including the helicopter pilots. In response the remaining terrorists took shelter in the helicopters, but came under attack

Probably the most famous special forces photo in the world, showing the storming of the Iranian Embassy in London in 1980. It was a major blow for terrorists around the world.

British SF operators practise a hostage rescue insertion alongside a Boeing 747 airliner.

again by German troops with armoured cars. A fierce firefight erupted between the terrorists and the troops, in which a helicopter exploded, killing several people. Shortly after, the terrorists executed five other hostages who were being held in another helicopter, before that, too, was blown up.

The rescue operation had been a complete disaster for the German security forces: five terrorists and every one of the Israeli hostages had been killed. But even in death, the terrorists had achieved a victory as the story dominated the world's headlines for weeks after.

In response, Germany set up a dedicated anti-terrorist organisation, which was given the name Grenzschutzgruppe 9, or GSG-9 as it was more commonly known.

After witnessing the events in Munich, virtually every country in the world was prompted to examine its ability to deal with a similar situation, should the need arise. Although many countries within Europe possessed special forces, none were trained for counter-terrorism. Munich was a painful wake-up call for many governments that terrorism was a growing problem and that

At the height of the 9/11 alert, President Bush took to the skies in Air Force One, as it seemed the safest place to be.

those countries who were least prepared for it were, on the balance of probability, the most likely to be targeted next.

In response to this threat, numerous CRW units were set up around the world, and although many of them were crude and rudimentary, they were at least a step in the right direction. As units worked hard to develop new tactics, techniques and procedures relevant to counter-terrorism, several CRW teams, such as the British SAS and German GSG-9, stood out from the rest as being highly adept at this new type of warfare, and in effect became the elite within the elite.

By the early 1980s, the standard of training within most CRW teams was good, regardless of whether they were regular army, special forces, paramilitary or police units. Essentially, most Western units are the same in their composition, structure, disciplines and weaponry, with many units modelling themselves on the British SAS and US Delta Force.

The days of the old ad-hoc CRW teams have long gone, as no modern, forward-thinking country can afford to be without some form of dedicated counter-terrorist unit. That said, even those who possess them are not immune from attack, as has been demonstrated on numerous occasions in recent decades. It would seem that just when you think you've seen the worst of what terrorism is capable of, along comes another attack that is bigger, more audacious and sadly, more often than not, more deadly.

To illustrate this point, we only have to look at the first decade of the 21st century to see what terrorists are capable of. First we had the 9/11 attacks on the US in 2001, which were without doubt the most daring and deadly mounted so far. Then in 2003, we had the outbreak of the Iraqi insurgency war, which to date is proving far more costly in lives than even 9/11. And in 2004, we witnessed the massacre of hundreds of innocent children in the Russian town of Beslan.

Terrorists and insurgents are the biggest threat we face today. Here, Palestinian gunmen engage Israeli forces – a day-to-day occurrence in this part of the world.

These attacks were, of course, not isolated as there were numerous others, such as the Madrid train bombing, the Russian airliner bomb, the Moscow theatre siege and the bombings in London in July 2005.

In all of these attacks there was a common denominator – they were all carried out by Islamic extremist groups, all operating without any sense of humanity and against the peaceful, honourable and respectful values that are generally associated with the Muslim faith.

It is important that a distinction be drawn between the two, as Muslims are every bit as vulnerable as anybody else and are just as likely to be targets of terrorism – take the indiscriminate targeting of innocent people of all faiths in the World Trade Center in September 2001, for example.

Underlining all this is the hypocrisy of certain situations. On one hand, you have Western born

Counter-terrorism units from around the world

ARGENTINA: Halcon
AUSTRIA: GEK; WEGA
AUSTRALIA: SASR
BELGUIM: ESI
BRAZIL: 1st Special Forces Btn
CANADA: Joint Task Force Two
CHILE: UAT; GOPE
CHINA: IAW
COLUMBIA: AFEU
CROATIA: Lucko
CUBA: CME; BE; PNR
CZECH REPUBLIC: SFB
DENMARK: Jaegerkorpset; PET
EGYPT: Task Force 777
ESTONIA: Special Operations Group
FINLAND: Osasto Karhusta
FRANCE: GIGN; EPIGN; RAID; GCMC
GERMANY: GSG-9; SEKS; KSK
GREECE: MYK; EKAM
HUNGARY: PSF
INDIA: NSG 'Black Cats'
INDONESIA: Kopassus
IRELAND: Army Ranger Wing; Garda Siochana
ISRAEL: Sayeret Mat'Kal; Mista' aravim; Ya'Ma'M

ITALY: GIS; NOCS
JORDAN: Special Operations Unit
MACAO: Special Duties Unit
MEXICO: Force F/Zorros; GAT
JAPAN: SAT
NORWAY: Beredskapstroppen
PAKISTAN: SSG Musa Co
NETHERLANDS: BBE; KCT; 7NL SBS
NEW ZEALAND: 1st SAS
PHILIPPINES: PNP SAF; PA A-20; PASCOM
POLAND: GROM
PORTUGAL: GOE
RUSSIA: Alfa/Beta Group; Naval Spetznatz
SINGAPORE: STAR
SLOVAKIA: 5PSU; UOU
SOUTH AFRICA: STF
SOUTH KOREA: 707th SMB; 868 Unit
SPAIN: GEO; UEI
SWEDEN: ONI; Special Protection Group
UK: SAS; D-11
USA: Delta Force; FBI HRT; DEVGRU; Army MP SRTS

An SBS **operator carries out a beach Close Target Recce (CTR).**

and raised Muslims fighting in Afghanistan and Iraq against the so-called Western Infidels, who represent all that is corrupt and wrong in the world – at least in their eyes. On the other hand, we have the bizarre situation when, once caught by our special forces, the same people scream about human rights abuses – to the very people who they are trying to wipe out. It's a crazy world.

The West doesn't help matters, either. Politicians constantly criticise our armed forces for the way in which they do their job, even when they get it right. For example, during the US-led assault on the Iraqi city of Fallujah, US forces were hammered by the media for using overwhelming and excessive firepower against the insurgents who were defending the place, stating that it was not the best way to deal with matters. What they never say, of course, is what is the alternative? Even Saddam Hussein, with all the might of his Ba'athist henchmen at hand, butchering and

killing the local populous en masse, couldn't pacify the insurgents in Fallujah. So how do they expect our forces to do it, bearing in mind they have to operate lawfully?

It is for these reasons that special forces are so vitally important. Unlike conventional forces, who are constantly under the glare of the media and therefore cannot move without attention, special forces are, for all intent and purposes, invisible. We only have to look at the much publicised movement of the Scottish Black Watch Battle Group, in support of the US Fallujah operation, to see a perfect example of this. Short of physically delivering an invitation to the insurgents to attack them, every possible detail was given. First, the media announced their route, the number of troops involved, their tactical concerns, details of their base and, more alarmingly, their timetable. As a result, they were attacked on a daily basis and sadly lost five of their number. Contrast this to the British special forces anti-insurgency operation mounted at the same time, of which there was no knowledge. And that's why the use of special forces is so critical in the war against terrorism – the insurgents never know when, where or how they are going to get hit.

If ever in modern times there was an example of how to fight a large scale military action against terrorists, then surely it must be that of Afghanistan.

Special forces operators can arrive by any mode of transport – some conventional and some not; one day it's by helicopter, the next it's on horseback.

Known terrorist organisations

Terrorism is on the increase throughout the world, hence the
growing need for more and more counter-terrorist units to
combat them. You only have to look at this list of known active
terrorist organisations to understand why this is necessary.

Terrorist organisation	National affiliation
Abu Sayyaf Group (ASG)	Philippines
Al-Gama'a al Islamiyya (The Islamic Group, IG)	Egypt
Al-Qaeda (The Base)	Afghanistan
Ansar al Aslam	Iraq
Armata Corsa	France
Armed Islamic Group (GIA)	Algeria
Aum Shnrikyo	Japan
Basque Homeland and Freedom (ETA)	Spain
Chukaku-Ha (Nucleus or Middle Core Faction)	Japan
Democratic Front for the Liberation of Palestine (DFLP)	Palestine
Fatah-Revolutionary Council (Abu Nidal Organisation)	Lebanon
Fatah Tanzim	Palestine
Fedayeen Saddam	Iraq
Force 17	Palestine
Hamas (Islamic Resistance Movement)	Palestine
Harakat ul-Mujahedin (HUM)	Pakistan
Hizbollah (Party of God)	Lebanon
Hizb-ul Mujahideen	Pakistan
Irish Republican Army (IRA) – ISSUED STATEMENT IN	Northern Ireland
JULY 2005 SAYING IT WAS CEASING TERRORIST ACTIVITY	
Jamaat ul-Fuqra	Pakistan
Japanese Red Army (JRA)	Japan
Jihad Group	Egypt
Kach and Kahane Chai	Israel
Kurdistan Worker's Party (PKK)	Turkey
Lashkar-e-Toiba	Pakistan
Lautaro Youth Movement (MJL)	Chile
Liberation Tigers of Tamil Eelam (LTTE)	Sri Lanka
Loyalist Volunteer Force (LVF)	Northern Ireland
Manuel Rodriquez Patriotic Front (FPMR)	Chile
Moranzanist Patriotic Front (FPM)	Honduras
Mujahedeen-e Khalq organisation (MEK or MKO)	Iran
National Liberation Army (ELN) Columbia	Columbia
National Liberation Front of Corsica (FLNC)	France
Nestor Paz Zamora Commission (CNPZ)	Bolivia
New People's Army (NPA)	Philippines
Palestine Liberation Front (PLF)	Iraq
Palestinian Islamic Jihad (PIJ)	Palestine
Party of Democratic Kampuchea (Khmer Rouge)	Cambodia
Popular Front for the Liberation of Palestine (PFLP)	Palestine
Popular Liberation Army (EPL)	Colombia
Popular Struggle Front (PSF)	Syria
Qibla and People Against Gangsterism and Drugs (PAGAD)	South Africa
Real IRA	Northern Ireland
Red Army Faction (RAF)	Germany
Red Brigades (BR)	Italy
Revolutionary Armed Forces of Columbia (FARC)	Columbia
Revolutionary Organisation 17 November	Greece
Revolutionary People's Liberation Party/Front (DHCP/F)	Turkey
Revolutionary People's Struggle (ELA)	Greece
Sendero Luminoso (Shining Path)	Peru
Sipah-e-Sahaba Pakistan (SSP)	Pakistan
The Return	Iraq
Tupac Amaru Revolutionary Movement (MRTA)	Peru
1920 Revolution Brigade of the National Islamic Resistance of Iraq	Iraq

As the tension mounted, reports started to
circulate that SAS units had been involved in
firefights with the Taliban in Northern
Afghanistan, but these were denied by the UK
MoD. Also around this time the Taliban made
claims that they had shot down a US spy aircraft
that had flown over their territory. It was, in fact,
a UAV, which had been lost due to control failure
rather than enemy action. This confirmed that
US forces (namely the CIA's SOG) were operating
close to Afghanistan and it was only a matter of
time before the shooting began.

Finally, on 7 October, the air war began
with multiple attacks on Taliban air defence
systems, command and control centres, and
fighter aircraft parked on airfields throughout
Afghanistan. Although much of the
intelligence for these initial air strikes came
from air-based assets, it was clear that some was
obtained by ground forces operating covertly
from a base in Uzbekistan. Both British and US
special forces were now operating in large
numbers within Afghanistan.

For the SAS, Afghanistan was an old hunting
ground. They had seen action before, during
covert operations in support of the
Mujahideen and their fight against the
Russians during the 1980s. At one point they
were even training Mujahideen fighters in
Scotland, until locals saw them and, assuming
they were illegal immigrants, called the police.
Although this put paid to their training
programme in the UK, the Mujahideen had
had access to Western weapons and military
intelligence which proved invaluable in
support of their cause. This experience also
proved to be advantageous when it came to
training the anti-Taliban force – the Northern
Alliance – as the SAS already had a good rapport
with many of their leaders.

Northern Alliance forces were based
primarily in north-western Afghanistan and
numbered around 15,000 men. Their enemy,
the Taliban, dominated the eastern part of the
country and fielded around 50,000 soldiers,
plus several hundred Al-Qaeda terrorists.
Although enthusiastic and well intentioned,
the Northern Alliance lacked military
knowledge and experience until the arrival of
the SAS and their US allies. It was noticeable
that before the involvement of Western
special forces, the Northern Alliance had
achieved very little in the way of military
success, yet within weeks of this Western

Australian 'diggers' take a break in Afghanistan after a routine patrol. However, their idea of 'routine' is quite different to yours or mine!

support, they had made substantial gains in territory and increased their numbers.

On one particular training exercise before a real operation, an SAS team had been instructing the Northern Alliance in standard British Army tactics for assaulting an objective while under effective enemy fire. While they moved towards the real target, a Taliban-held village, they suddenly and without warning abandoned the tactics and advice of their SAS instructors and proceeded to attack using dozens of horsemen as cavalry in a scene that would not have been out of place in a Rambo movie. As they charged, the rest of the force sat down on some rocks and watched the spectacle without firing any of their weapons at the defending Taliban forces. Fortunately, the Taliban fled on this occasion, but it did concern the SAS as to the reliability of their new friends. They quickly learned that to get the best from the Northern Alliance required patience and understanding, and that you merely advised them what to do.

The operations in Afghanistan meant the deployment of almost every available SAS squadron, as their mission tasking was growing by the day. The lack of roads hampered the speed at which mobility columns could move and even by SAS standards the going was tough. In one operation near Mazar-e-Sharif a number of vehicles got bogged down while operating off road. As they tried to extract themselves a group of Taliban soldiers opened fire on them from a distant ridge with heavy machine guns and rocket propelled grenades (RPGs). The SAS responded with their vehicle-mounted GPMGs

and 40mm grenade launchers, and a fierce firefight ensued in which many Taliban members were killed or injured before the SAS withdrew.

At this time the key task for the SAS was to identify Taliban troop positions for US bombers and, where possible, to provide intelligence on tank and artillery assets. These could then be hit by US Navy strike aircraft flying local support sorties or 'blat and splat missions' as the SAS teams called them. A further role was tasked to the SAS – a humanitarian one of vital importance. The US had promised to drop food aid packages from USAF transport aircraft to the starving Afghan people because it was virtually impossible to get sufficient aid in by truck. There was, however, a serious problem with the aid drops. Afghanistan is littered with millions of anti-personnel mines and these were killing dozens of people every day as they tried to reach the food packages. To reduce these risks, the SAS carried out surveys on suitable sites that were free from mines and marked them for the transport aircraft. It proved to be a successful mission and saved many innocent lives. The SAS squadrons were now active on several different fronts within Afghanistan, especially near to the lower slopes of the southern Hindu Kush Mountains and around Bagram airfield, near Mazar-e-Sharif.

As the combined air and ground operations gathered pace throughout Afghanistan during the latter part of 2001, the SAS began direct attacks against Al-Qaeda and Taliban training camps as part of a combined allied operation

An AC-130 Spectre gunship engaging a target during a firepower demonstration. Such aircraft are invaluable during counter-terrorist operations.

involving British and US ground forces, as well as the Northern Alliance. These camps were generally well hidden and often featured cave complexes that were virtually impossible to attack effectively from the air. One tactic that the SAS used to great effect in the mountain regions involved a combination of Sabre Squadrons and US AC-130 Spectre gunships. They would identify a training camp and keep it under surveillance for a few days. Once satisfied that it was an important target, a strike would be summoned to deliver deep penetration bombs straight into the mouths of the cave entrances. Once this mission was completed a Spectre would be called in to hit the dazed survivors of the first attack by strafing the ground with its deadly armament of mini-guns, 40mm cannon and howitzers. After this attack, the SAS recce team would plot the predicted escape route of the enemy forces and arrange for the rest of the squadron to mount an ambush against them. If planned well an enemy force could be totally decimated before they realised what was happening. This highly effective tactic was based on the Russian 'Hammer and Anvil' concept, developed during the Soviet occupation of Afghanistan for use against the Mujahideen.

The SAS were also able to draw on their operational experiences in Aden and Oman for tactics, techniques and procedures that would be relevant in this conflict. This was to be of great importance, because during the first few weeks of deployment in Afghanistan, the US special forces were finding it difficult to operate as they had little comparable combat experience in an environment like this. As a

result a small number of four-man SAS teams were assigned to them as advisors.

Mazar-e-Sharif episode
It was during one of these combined operations that the US suffered its first combat casualty while operating near Mazar-e-Sharif. After weeks of fighting between the Northern Alliance and the Taliban over the strategically important airfield of Bagram, it finally fell, with many Taliban soldiers taken prisoner. Those who were captured found themselves in the stronghold of the Qala-e-Jhangi fortress – an impressive collection of mud-walled compounds located just outside Mazar-e-Sharif. As prisoners were being interrogated by the CIA, a revolt broke out in which a CIA operative was killed along with many soldiers from both the Northern Alliance and the Taliban. It took several days of heavy fighting, including calling in air strikes, before order could be restored by both the SAS and US special forces who were acting as advisors to the Northern Alliance. At the height of the revolt a number of SAS soldiers were seen on live television arriving at the fortress in white Land Rovers. The soldiers quickly put on masks to protect their identities and wore a mixture of camouflaged combats and local Afghan dress. After the rebellion had been subdued, the SAS troopers withdrew to resume other tasks in the local area and were lucky to escape without taking casualties. It had been a ferocious and bloody action in which hundreds died.

By now the Taliban were in retreat and had few strongholds left in which to take sanctuary; all of the towns they had once occupied had fallen and were now in the hands of the Northern Alliance. The priority now was to find Osama bin Laden and the remaining Al-Qaeda terrorists who were still putting up resistance, despite intensive US bombing on their known positions. One report stated that bin Laden was holed up in an Al-Qaeda training camp near to Kandahar in southern Afghanistan. This could not be confirmed, so the SAS were given the task of attacking it. After observing the camp for a few days it was decided that a ground assault would be more appropriate than an air strike, as part of the camp was underground and would be difficult to target from the air. Even by SAS standards this was going to be a tough mission as the terrorists had sworn to fight to the death.

The SAS carried out the attack with two full squadrons, comprising about 100 well-armed men who were highly experienced in this type of warfare. As they fought their way through the Al-Qaeda defensive positions they met with fierce resistance from a number of well placed machine guns on a ridge set into the side of a gully. As the SAS tried to work their way around the position, they were attacked by a large number of Taliban and Al-Qaeda fighters who sprang out from an underground bunker via a cave entrance. This attack caught the SAS by surprise and they were in danger of being outflanked. The SAS advanced forward in a classic charge which saw them come face-to-face with their enemy at close range and involved hand-to-hand combat. As the fighting continued, SAS soldiers who had been manning the communications base saw what was happening and raced to the aid of their fellow troopers who were now fighting for their lives. After several minutes of intense fighting the SAS turned the Al-Qaeda and Taliban fighters back and the action ended. Although they had been heavily outnumbered, the SAS only suffered four casualties during this entire operation but left 27 enemy dead and 35 wounded.

Facing the future

After this action, SAS involvement in Afghanistan was limited to supporting the Northern Alliance rather than leading them in further operations. This was deliberately done so that they did not upstage them in front of the Afghan people and cause a confidence issue in their ability to defend the country from further insurrection.

The last operation of any significance for the SAS in Afghanistan involved helping the Northern Alliance to sweep the cave complexes of Tora Bora, which were located just south of Jalalabad, bordering Pakistan. This was the last known hiding place of Osama bin Laden. Even though the caves had been bombed for many weeks, there were still survivors who posed a considerable threat. The SAS showed the Northern Alliance how to clear caves and bunker complexes from their past experience in this type of warfare.

Despite extensive searches for Osama bin Laden throughout Afghanistan, no trace was found of him and it was widely assumed that he had been killed during the bombing campaign. As there was no positive proof of this, America and its allies vowed to continue searching for him and the remains of his Al-Qaeda network. It is now known that he survived the attacks and continues to pose a considerable threat to the West.

The Special Air Service Regiment can be proud of the part they played in the war against terrorism, as they were able to achieve so much with so little. As US Defense Secretary Donald Rumsfeld said of the SAS, 'They are among the best soldiers in the world and are truly exceptional men.'

An SAS operator at the height of anti-Al-Qaeda operations in Afghanistan. His eclectic mixture of clothing and weaponry is especially tailored for purpose.

Nintendo Operators

Action in Iraq

At the time of writing, over 10,000 special forces personnel have seen action in Iraq, with seemingly no end in sight. This is the story so far.

On 19 March 2003, US President George W Bush gave Saddam Hussein a warning: leave Iraq within 48 hours or else face the consequences. Anticipating that Saddam would defy him and hold a council of war with his fellow Ba'ath party regime members, President Bush gave the go-ahead for a pre-emptive 'decapitation attack'. The idea was to terminate the top Iraqi leadership in one precise, surgical strike, thereby negating the need for a war. The decision was certainly a gamble, as it altered months of meticulous military planning that had been in place since November 2002 – the original preferred date for a war against Iraq. But nonetheless it was a risk deemed worthy of taking, as it would save lives, both friendly and enemy alike – assuming, of course, that Saddam was going to be in the location that was about to be targeted. President George W Bush, however, was not acting on a hunch or indeed a piece of satellite imagery to justify his confidence; he was acting on a solid and extremely reliable intelligence tip-off provided by a member of the CIA's super-secret Special Operations Group (SOG). This unit, although largely unknown prior to Operation Iraqi Freedom, had a good reputation for getting its hands dirty quickly in times of tension and hostility, and was there on the ground in Baghdad, operating covertly for many months before the outbreak of hostilities with Iraq. Its role was to gather intelligence and encourage insurrection. Within

military circles, such an operation is referred to as a 'stake through the heart' mission: its effects can be awesome if successful, but disastrous if poorly planned and executed.

To accomplish such complex mission tasking required massive special forces resources, both from the UK and the US. Bearing in mind that ongoing counter-terrorist operations post 9/11 were still taking place in Afghanistan, Yemen, Somalia and the Philippines, at the same time as those being carried out in Iraq, this was no easy task.

Following on from the supposed end of the conventional war in 2003 was the insurgency war, which, to date, is still ongoing, despite the capture of Saddam Hussein and most of his fellow regime members; the death of his two sons, Uday and Qusay; the restoration of utility services throughout most of the country; and the first free democratic elections in 50 years.

This is the operators' story of Operation Iraqi Freedom.

A statue of Saddam Hussein is hit, following a ground attack.

Operation Iraqi Freedom

On 20 March 2003, at approximately 05.30am local time (02.30 GMT), cruise missiles launched from ships and submarines deployed in and around the Gulf region began impacting on the city of Baghdad. As large as it first appeared to be, this was not an attack on the scale originally billed as part of the much-heralded 'Shock and Awe' campaign, which boasted of hitting Iraq with an initial strike of some 3,000 cruise missiles.

By early morning, as the smoke wafted across Baghdad from the carcass of the building that was supposed to be Saddam's tomb, word quickly spread on the streets that Saddam had been mortally wounded in the precision strike the night before – his personal ambulance had been spotted arriving at the scene shortly after the missiles had stopped falling. However, sources later confirmed that he had survived the attack and was now in an unknown hiding place.

While President Bush contemplated this news, Coalition ground forces from the US, UK, Australia and Poland began invading Iraq by land, sea and air. However, there was one group of individuals whose war had begun long before this. It was, of course, the covert war fought by the special forces.

It is now known that some elements of the British SAS entered Iraq via Jordan in August 2002, some eight months prior to the official commencement of hostilities; their mission was to overwatch main supply routes (MSRs) for troop movements and to gather intelligence on possible targets. For cover, they passed themselves off as oil smugglers and drove around in battered old fuel tankers that had been hollowed out to allow the carriage of both personnel and equipment. It proved an excellent ruse, as the Iraqis turned a blind eye to oil smugglers, especially if they paid good bribes. During their time in Iraq, the SAS were able to link up with various agencies operating in the region, such as MI6, the CIA and 'Gray Fox', the US Army's covert intelligence arm.

For the special forces, there was much work to be done before the Coalition forces' military campaign. Operations carried out included:
- Tactical, strategic and close-target reconnaissance
- Target identification
- Reconnaissance of routes of ingress and egress
- Troop observations
- Reconnaissance of military road traffic movement
- Identification of friendly indigenous forces and hostile enemy forces (both conventional and unconventional)
- Sabotage of transportation and communications systems and networks
- Reconnaissance of beaches, landing points, bridges and lines of communication, defended positions (including minefields) and suspected weapons of mass destruction (WMD) research sites

Special forces were instrumental in bringing down the conventional Iraqi forces, in this case by means of a precision guided munition.

British Special Forces

This is a personal account of a counter-insurgency sweep and clear operation mounted near Basra, at the height of tensions between British forces and local Iraqis. The operation involved Royal Marines, regular British and TA soldiers, as well as elite members of the newly formed Iraqi National Guard.

A Royal Marine scans the horizon for possible enemy activity – his .50 cal HMG (heavy machine gun) is perfect for long-range firepower.

It was a normal Iraqi summer's evening. The flames of the oil flare pipes lit up the horizon, casting fiery shadows all around. Little did I know, but this seemingly routine day was about to mark the beginning of a rocket and roadside bombing campaign that would be aimed at my base.

Just after I had received my patrol tasking from the Ops room, a call came over the net: 'Large group of men in Iraqi Guard uniforms seen stopping traffic near MSR – go and investigate.' I gathered my patrol together and my interpreter, Ali. Just as we were leaving camp, we heard a sound like a fast train. I shouted, 'Mortar attack, take cover!' and we ran for the control centre. As we waited, a second whoosh broke the silence and the radio crackled into life.

I awaited further orders, but there were none. I was still to investigate the suspect Iraqi National Guards as first briefed. We drove out of camp, knowing that somewhere there were insurgents who had just rocketed our base. Out on the MSR, we spotted the suspect VCP [vehicle checkpoint] and slowly moved towards it. I ordered my rear vehicle to stop short, to provide a fire base should anything happen. In the distance, we spotted torches waving on the road and slowed down. I ordered my 2I/C to dismount and provide cover, while I approached a group of around 15 men wearing balaclavas and carrying AK47s. We approached on foot, almost casually to alleviate any tension.

We started talking to them, asking who was in charge. A man stepped forward and identified himself as a Major. He explained they were on an anti-smuggling operation. They had heard the explosions, but thought they were miles away.

Meanwhile, another Iraqi Guard, who spoke English, told me they wore balaclavas out of fear, as they could be murdered if identified by insurgents. As we spoke with the Iraqis, further orders were received, requiring us to investigate a suspect launch site. We went there and found nothing – these people don't usually hang around.

Returning to our base, we encountered another VCP, but this time it was an Iraqi Police Service's permanent checkpoint located along the MSR. We stopped to talk to them and exchanged cigarettes. Our time with them was well spent, as we gleaned good intelligence that was to pay dividends in the morning.

After leaving the VCP, we carried out more searches, until at 3am we heard a series of shots. As my patrol returned to camp, we were invited to stand down, but my answer was no way: I wanted to find the launch site.

At about 9.30am, we received a tip-off regarding a possible mortar site that was being prepared for firing. We scrambled our patrol, along with a QRF [quick reaction force].

As my patrol neared the target location, I spotted four rockets, but no insurgents. We checked the rockets over and confirmed that, although in an advanced state of preparation, they could not be fired. We were ordered to secure the area. As we did so, the Iraqi National Guard Major from the night before turned up and wanted to blow the rockets up, until I pointed out how dangerous that would be.

As we talked, a local farmer approached from behind the rockets and mentioned that other rockets had been fired from behind his farm. At this point, one of the Iraqi National Guard personnel warned me to be careful of some his fellow countrymen, as they could not be trusted.

Eventually, the Army bomb disposal team turned up and removed the rockets and associated equipment. Military intelligence believed we may have disturbed the insurgents during the night.

A week later, I found out that one of my top cover had seen something suspicious on the night of the attack, but had said nothing. I was angry: his inaction could have cost lives. I also learned that a Marine sniper team was only 500m away at the time of the attack, and again never saw anything! Catching insurgents is not an easy business.

The two Gulf Wars

US Vice-President Richard Cheney described Operation Iraqi Freedom as one of the most extraordinary military campaigns ever conducted, when asked to give brief details of what led to success in Iraq.

The campaign that US and Coalition forces launched on 20 March 2003 followed 'a carefully drawn plan with fixed objectives and the flexibility to meet them', he said in a speech to the US Heritage Foundation in Washington.

Vice-President Cheney noted that Operation Iraqi Freedom displayed vastly improved capabilities over the first US-led war in the Persian Gulf in 1991. In Operation Desert Storm, 20 per cent of the nation's air-to-ground fighters employed laser-guided bombs. In Operation Iraqi Freedom, all US air-to-ground fighters were capable of employing laser-guided bombs.

'As a result,' Mr Cheney said, 'with only two-thirds of the attack aircraft deployed in Desert Storm, we could strike twice as many targets.'

Ground forces also employed improved combat power, he said. In Operation Desert Storm, US Marines had M-60 tanks. In Operation Iraqi Freedom, they had the Abrams M-1, equipped with a thermal sight and a 122mm gun that 'increased their range by 50 per cent and enabled them to engage the enemy before they could even fire a single round'.

He said that in Operation Desert Storm, Bradley armoured vehicle crews estimated the range of their targets, often missing on the first round. In Operation Iraqi Freedom, improved laser rangefinders enabled the crews to hit their targets first time.

Only one type of UAV was available to locate enemy targets in the early 1990s, Mr Cheney continued. In 2003, there were ten types, 'ranging from a tactical system that would allow our soldiers to look over the next hill, to strategic systems that operate at 65,000ft (20,000m) and could provide images the size of Illinois'.

US forces had also dramatically improved their ability to use targeting photos, he continued, and command and control systems had become more flexible and effective. Where in the past only air component commanders had a near real-time picture of the air campaign, in Operation Iraqi Freedom, all US component commanders shared a real-time computer display of Coalition air, land and sea forces.

'These advances in command and control allowed us to integrate joint operations more effectively than ever before, thereby enabling commanders to make decisions more rapidly, to target strikes more precisely, to minimise civilian casualties and to accomplish missions more successfully,' Mr Cheney concluded.

Operation Iraqi Freedom was also conducted differently from Desert Storm, he noted, highlighting the expanded role of special operations forces.

Close support aircraft, such as these F-14 Tomcats, are always a welcome sight for operators.

The 1991 war began with a 38-day air campaign, followed by a brief ground attack. This time, the ground war began before the air war. Unlike in 1991, when Saddam Hussein had time to set Kuwait's oil fields on fire, special operations forces went in early to defend 600 oil wells to protect the environment and safeguard a vital resource for the Iraqi people.

During Desert Storm, Saddam's forces fired Scud missiles at Israel and Saudi Arabia. This time, special operations forces seized control and prevented missile launches.

'US, British, Australian and Polish special ops forces played a much more central role in the success of Operation Iraqi Freedom than they did 12 years ago,' the Vice-President said.

An operator jumps clear of a helicopter during a routine training exercise. Such helos are capable of creating near hurricane gusts through their downdraft, so there is little room for error.

How does Operation Iraqi Freedom compare with Operation Desert Storm?

It would be easy to write off Operation Iraqi Freedom as an extended version of Desert Storm, but that would not be the case. Yes, there are some similarities, but there are great differences, especially when it comes to special forces. In the first Gulf War, special forces were viewed as a sideline act, whereas in Iraqi Freedom they were the main event – only the public didn't get to hear too much about their activities. To start, there were the Scud-hunting teams and the road-watch teams – same modus operandi (MO) as Desert Storm, but different players. Secondly, there were the intensive tactical reconnaissance and targeting missions that proved critical to the success of Operation Iraqi Freedom, greatly increasing operational efficiency and effectiveness, and thus minimising collateral damage. Finally, there were the special forces support operations that were designed to encourage insurrection and to reduce Saddam's military forces and their will to fight.

By all accounts these missions went to plan, but the enemy resistance experienced was greater than originally anticipated, especially in the case of post-war Iraq. In the case of military hardware, most of the weaponry used in the recent conflict was the same as that used in 1991, but the efficiency and targeting of it was vastly superior, especially in the case of precision guided munitions (PGMs).

Operation Iraqi Freedom also saw the deployment of low risk munitions, such as the cement bomb – an air-dropped weapon that is designed for use in built-up urban areas where there is a high risk of collateral damage; its preferred method of targeting is courtesy of special forces' operatives. In one well documented incident, a British SAS soldier targeted an Iraqi tank located near a school and requested that it be knocked out by means of a cement bomb – or a Blue Circle, as the SAS would say. The RAF, keen to oblige, dropped the first cement bomb, but it failed to destroy the tank, prompting the SAS soldier to say: 'That was really impressive, but next time can we have one that goes bang please.' The point is that not all technology deployed in Operation Iraqi Freedom worked to plan, despite the best intentions of its user. But one thing that did work well was the use of the operatives themselves. In a deployment that was truly massive in terms of its size and scope, special forces played a critical role in every dimension – especially in southern, western and northern Iraq, where their presence was most keenly felt.

Essentially, the Australians operated primarily in western Iraq, but had elements of their forces in central and southern locations. The Americans, on the other hand, operated throughout Iraq, but were particularly strong in the southern, central and northern areas of the country. The British operated very strongly in the south, north and western regions of Iraq, and the Polish operated solely in the south of Iraq, primarily around the port of Umm Qasr, on the Al Faw peninsula.

1: Special Forces at War in Iraq

Although Australian forces were not mentioned much by the world's media during the conflict, this lack of coverage belies the fact that Australian forces played a significant part in this war and their efforts deserve to be recognised.

Australian special forces activities were performed under the umbrella of Operation Falconer. The main element of the SF Task Group deployed to the Middle East in mid-February under the auspices of Operation Bastille; their aim was to acclimatise and prepare for possible roles in the war.

At the same time, an Australian Special Operations Forward Command element set up in theatre to command all SF operations in the Middle East. The SF Task Group was manned by personnel from Headquarters Special Operations, the Special Air Service Regiment (SASR) in Perth, 4 Royal Australian Regiment (RAR) Commando, the Logistics Support Force, the Incident Response Regiment, the 5th Aviation Regiment, plus support personnel from the Army and the RAAF (Royal Australian Air Force). SF

Members of 4 RAR carry out a sweep-and-clear search in a former Iraqi facility – always dangerous work because you never know what's around the corner.

Headquarters was part of a clearly defined command chain which ensured that Australian special forces were always commanded by Australians.

The Headquarters not only commanded the SF Task Group, but provided an important command link to Headquarters Australian Theatre in Sydney and the Australian National Command Headquarters. It was also linked closely to the equivalent Special Operations Command element for the US and was co-located. This was critical to ensure a full observation and transparency of Coalition special forces activities and, from all reports, the relationship worked exceptionally well.

By early February 2003, Coalition planning had evolved to give a clearly understood role for the Australian special forces during Operation Falconer. In accordance with clear government guidance, it was agreed that if there was an eventual Australian commitment, the Task Group was to conduct special operations in western Iraq as part of a Coalition effort to defeat the WMD threat.

Specifically, their job was to deny Iraq the ability to launch theatre ballistic missiles in the west. Other missions included harassing operations, destruction of critical command and control nodes, and operations to prevent the freedom of movement of the Iraqis in the theatre. When the main contingent first arrived in the Middle East in early February, it started training on the premise that it was likely to be committed – to think otherwise would certainly have risked failure. Consequently, the Task Group conducted what is known as Full Mission Profile Exercises by day and night, stepping through the full range of contingencies that it could expect, if committed to Iraq. This intensive, realistic training period enabled the soldiers to acclimatise to the environmental conditions that they might expect and to hone their skills.

This acclimatisation and work-up period proved to be of immense value in the war that

Interoperability is key in SF operations, because you may need to hitch a ride from one of your allies during high tempo missions, especially when all is committed.

followed, as Australian special forces had to interoperate regularly with other special forces units such as those of the British SAS and the US Delta Force. In relation to air operations this was critical. The Australians relied heavily upon British and American close air support and any doubt or confusion about location is a recipe for disaster, especially on today's fast-moving battlefield where the possibility of friendly fire incidents can be only seconds away.

While the acclimatisation training was taking place, the Task Group established a logistic support infrastructure to support the forces once deployed on operations. Known as the Combat Service Support Group, this group consisted of 77 people drawn from nine different regular Australian army units. It had the pivotal role of providing communications support, ordering stores, warehousing, managing freight distribution and providing resupply, which was normally by air. They also had the job of servicing the wide range of vehicles used by the SASR. This was no easy task at the best of times, but during a sandstorm where winds could gust at anything up to 50km (30 miles) per hour – well, that was something else. Indeed, it was not uncommon for tents to be blown away, leaving equipment, food and personnel exposed to sand and fine dust; not a good situation.

On the plus side, however, communications and computer networks held up well under the same conditions.

On the transport side, Australian CH-47 Chinooks provided critical combat service support in the rear areas to free up both US and UK aircraft for combat tasks, where the pilot's vision is virtually always obscured during landings due to the perpetual sand and dust.

One of Australia's key assets during this war was The Incident Response Regiment (TIRR), co-located with the Commando Alert Force. Its task was to deploy into Iraq at short notice to assist in the detection of WMD associated with materials that may have been discovered by the SAS. All personnel operating within TIRR are highly skilled, as their role is extremely dangerous and demanding. On one occasion during Operation Falconer, they deployed to a giant military complex at Al Asad to conduct a search mission. This was to be a demanding task for them. The facility was covered with abandoned buildings, bunkers and massive amounts of military hardware, all requiring meticulous attention. After several days of hard searching it was declared safe of WMD, with nothing incriminating found there.

Although somewhat disappointed with this result, the fact that the Task Group could undertake this sort of mission without relying on Coalition support was a major boost to their confidence and clearly justified the robust stand-alone capability that Australia had deployed to this region.

Within the Task Group, the Commando element was regarded as the cavalry of the

Australian forces – always ready and willing to be deployed at a moment's notice should anyone need them. To achieve this they established an alert force capability which could be activated in the event of an emergency, such as a downed aircrew. However, it could equally be used for the recovery of wounded personnel or to provide assistance to threatened SAS patrols. The alert force also included helicopter assets, medical support and TIRR detachment. It was reassuring for the SAS to know that if they got into trouble they had an alert force manned by the commandos, all Australians, of course, who could come in and support them. While the alert force was never activated in anger, the commandos were tasked, towards the end of the campaign, to assist the SAS in clearing the large Al Asad airbase, to secure the Australian mission in Baghdad and to further provide support for the medical teams involved with Operation Baghdad Assist.

For most Australian special forces operating in Iraq, the western desert was their primary area of operation – an inhospitable place that is open and bare with few places to hide. This alone makes daylight movement almost impossible, as the detection risk is just

Account from an Australian SASR operative

In all there were around 80 of us operating in western Iraq, but to the Iraqis it must have seemed like 800. Our primary role was to stop weapons of mass destruction from being launched from the 1991 'Scud Line' in the western Iraqi desert, while our secondary role was to raise merry hell – 'Digger style'! Basically we were like an enormous itch that the Iraqis could not scratch, as we were everywhere and anywhere. One day we were in the desert, the next in a giant cement works – in this case, the one at Kubaysah, about 60km (36 miles) north of Highway One between Baghdad and Amman and 20km (12 miles) south of the huge Al Asad airbase. This massive civilian infrastructure was nicknamed 'The Temple of Doom' by us and was captured, along with 40 prisoners as well, without us firing a single shot.

However, it was not always like this, as in several contacts we engaged enemy forces on an ongoing basis for a number of days, fighting running battles with them that were as good as any I experienced in Afghanistan. Along the way we even treated wounded enemy, fed and watered prisoners, and then sent them home with a simple message: 'The war is over for you.' During our 42-day excursion, we took on more than 2,000 Iraqis, including elite Republican Guard troops and counter-special forces troops – not at the same time – and suffered no casualties. That's got to be a ripper result.

During our mission we found no Scuds, but we left our own calling card – 46,000kg (100,000lb) of bombs and missiles in the first week of combat alone to be exact. The overwhelming success of the SAS mission to deny the enemy any ballistic missile launches was down to technology, training and superior communications. The fact that the squadron suffered no casualties did not surprise me, as we minimised the risks to our own people and to the Iraqis. Despite the lack of casualties and the string of victories this was no picnic; the Iraqis were well organised and well equipped.

The first SAS patrol to cross into Iraq by night spent 96 hours in open desert terrain without being spotted by anyone, including local Bedouin herdsmen and enemy forces. For them not to get compromised in that dead flat terrain was a significant effort. Although we never saw any Scuds during our deployment, the fact that we were operating as if they were there made a real difference, because the Iraqis were always trying to second guess us. It is called manoeuvre warfare and is designed to put pressure on the enemy and to unmask them. We were a small-force element creating quite a disproportionate effect by means of shock and surprise. We were also completely unpredictable in our actions, which was the key component of our tactics. In addition, we had to deal with an unpredictable enemy, who would on occasion raise his hands in surrender yet resume firing as we approached. We even have one of their flags that bears proof of this as it has both powder burns and bullet holes from being fired through. Adding to our operational experience we also had the weather to contend with. Temperatures often ranged from –5°C (23°F) to 43°C (109°F). All in all it was a magnificent effort, and a great achievement!

An Australian F/A-18 Hornet pilot prepares for another close support mission over Indian territory.

- Insertion phase
- Combat phase
- Interdiction phase
- Security phase

Firstly, the insertion. This in itself was quite an achievement. The force inserted by night by vehicle and helicopter into areas remote from friendly conventional forces. The intent was to insert clandestinely and get deep into the assigned area before the sun came up. The vehicle insertion involved breaching an earth berm and trench system, and negotiating a network of Iraqi Guard posts undetected. This was achieved successfully, however, 30km (20 miles) inside Iraq, the force bumped into a number of enemy vehicles. These were engaged by fire and then detained. As they later found out, this was one of the first contacts of the war and one in which SAS medics rendered first-aid to a couple of wounded Iraqi soldiers. Due to the need to continue the mission, the enemy was released and the force moved on, arriving where they planned to be just on first light without further mishap.

Helicopters played a key role in special forces operations in Iraq, but the difficulty and risk of their usage under certain conditions should not be underestimated. In one mission, US helicopter forces carrying Australian SAS operatives flew over 600km (370 miles) from the SAS staging base deep into Iraq, by night and in poor weather with much of it at very low altitude. During the flight, they had to conduct a difficult air-to-air refuelling activity, as well as negotiate an extensive enemy air defence system. After landing, they were the closest Coalition ground elements to Baghdad and they remained so for a number of days.

While the troops may have thought the insertion was demanding and exhilarating, there was a lot more to come and what followed certainly set the tone for the campaign. The intention of the commander on the ground was not to sit back and wait for the enemy to come to him or wait for him to deploy his Scud missiles. Rather, he undertook to commit to aggressive operations to unmask the enemy in terms of his intent, his location and his strength. This involved high-tempo offensive patrolling in a controlled sequence across the area of operations. At the same time, he needed to

too great on account of the Bedouins and local Iraqis.

Just like the British SAS in Desert Storm, the SAS Task Group experienced all the extremes that a desert can offer. Early in the conflict the temperature dropped to −5°C (23°F) – and that's not taking into account the wind chill factor, while later in the war, temperatures exceeded 40°C (104°F). On one occasion, sandstorms blew constantly for two days with winds averaging 30km (20 miles) an hour, reducing visibility to 10m (33ft). On another occasion, it rained so heavily that the Task Group's weapons systems were being clogged and jammed by wind-blown mud; but apart from that, it was perfect weather.

Essentially, SAS operations comprised four elements:

An Australian
commander briefs
his men prior to
deployment in
Iraq.

The attack used carefully placed cut-offs and a sequenced assault to clear the facility, followed by close air support to destroy the tower. Surprise was achieved and a sharp but one-sided firefight ensued with a significant number of enemy casualties; the net result was the destruction of the facility. This operation immediately decreased the Iraqi theatre ballistic missile capability and sent a strong message to the Iraqi leadership in Baghdad.

As expected, this activity stirred up a hornet's nest and on the following morning an SAS element was involved in a running firefight for a significant number of hours. They were engaged by five or six armed vehicles, but the SAS used superior tactical manoeuvres and an application of heavy weapons to destroy most of the force. The enemy, in disarray, eventually withdrew through a number of buildings, but they were pursued by well directed close air support and were ultimately defeated.

Throughout this and other firefights the enemy was engaged by the SAS using a significant number of weapons. They included Javelin rocket launchers, heavy machine guns, Mark 19 grenade launchers and sniper rifles. This heavy lay-down of firepower, coupled with the aggressive front-foot approach of the SAS and extensive use of close air support, was enough to break the spirit of the most demanding enemy assault.

On a separate occasion in the first few days, another small element was confronted with a force of about 50 enemy mounted in civilian four-wheel-drive vehicles and trucks. This force aggressively assaulted the Australians using rocket-propelled grenades, mortars and machine guns, but to no avail. The SAS held their ground – a remarkable feat considering that their weapons systems had suffered numerous stoppages at the height of the firefight. Within minutes of the contact, the Iraqi vehicles were destroyed, forcing their occupants to dismount and fight on foot, which made them extremely vulnerable.

Seeing their plight, the SAS pushed forward aggressively and routed them. One soldier, due to a weapon stoppage, used all four of the available weapon systems mounted on his long-range patrol vehicle. 'Systematically moving from weapon system to weapon system, he was able to engage the enemy targets at vastly different ranges in different

maintain a static surveillance on the main access roads down which the enemy could deploy his Scuds or the main larger conventional reaction forces.

This phase coincided with an exceptionally heavy period of activity in the first week of the war, during which time the SAS were in heavy contact with the enemy on virtually a daily basis. This was no accident. The enemy was clearly seeking out the Australian force in a co-ordinated and well drilled fashion, yet at the same time the SAS were intentionally meeting the enemy head on with unpredictable shock engagements. However, the enemy couldn't keep pace with this high-tempo shock activity and were ultimately beaten in this phase. On the second night in Iraq, a good proportion of the SAS force was involved in a raid on what turned out to be a well defended radio relay station. This was a carefully co-ordinated activity, conducted by night and involving a methodical ground and airborne surveillance process which collected as much information about the site as possible before the attack phase of the operation.

circumstances. Certainly testament to the skill of the SAS soldier,' said Special Operations Command chief of staff Col John Mansell.

There were a number of other engagements similar to this in the first three or four days, which set the enemy on the back foot from the outset and from which they didn't recover. The intensity of this phase was such that the SAS were on full throttle without any real sleep for 96 hours. In contrast to the frantic pace, another SAS element had been concealed in observation positions overlooking Highway Ten. As a testament to their skill, they remained undetected throughout the period. This was a significant and equally demanding task, given the environmental demands, the numbers of enemy around and also the nomadic Bedouin who move around in this area. The contrast was striking. 'On the one hand, there were elements of the SAS moving at a million miles an hour, daily engaging the enemy with aggressive firefights. And, on the other hand, we have a separate force operating with equal skill, equal daring, but with great skill and great stealth,' said Col Mansell.

In the early stages of the campaign it was apparent that the Kilometre 160 feature, which is essentially a crossroads and a truck stop just west of Ramadi, needed to be neutralised. At one stage upwards of 200 Iraqis defended the feature. The SAS, using high-powered optics standing off from the target, called in air support to pinpoint targets over a 48-hour period to destroy the facility. They then assembled a large vehicle-mounted force to assault and clear the installation.

'Unfortunately, but as expected, the remaining enemy had withdrawn under cover of a sandstorm,' said Col Mansell.

'The SAS standoff capability as agents for air power was critical to provide pinpoint guidance against targets which were indistinguishable from the air. Just as importantly, the SAS were also able to confirm that targets had indeed been neutralised. The enemy's pro-active and co-ordinated counter special operations tactics that could have worked so well against an ill-prepared force were largely ineffective in the face of such an exceptionally aggressive and well equipped force who fought a high-tempo war at a high-tempo pace,' said an Australian Army officer.

At this point it was clear that the enemy's ability to launch theatre ballistic missiles from the west had been neutralised. The psychological impact was also significant upon the Iraqis. Quite clearly they were unhinged. It was the special forces' tactic to achieve this and they did it in a highly effective manner.

About a week into the campaign the area quietened down and the SAS became more and more involved in highway interdiction tasks. The task was to deny the enemy any form of escape route, be it for high value mobile targets or regime personnel, while at the same time being mindful of the suicide bomber threat. To achieve operational effectiveness, they had to constantly change their locations and methods so as not to set a pattern.

'They experienced success on a number of occasions, culminating in the capture of a

An operator zeros in his weapon.

Australian operators scan for trouble in the dark, cold deserts of their enemy.

significant number of likely Fedayeen and Ba'ath Party members, along with considerable amounts of cash, as they tried to exit the country. They also apprehended convoys carrying communications equipment and gas masks. Also during this period they established links with the local sheiks from the enemy-occupied town of Ar Ramadi, which helped facilitate the capitulation of the enemy in this location,' said Col Mansell.

The last significant activity involving the SAS was the capture of the massive Al Asad airbase – one of Iraq's largest airbases. The SAS found it defended and occupied by a large force of approximately 100 men, along with armed looters, so requiring comprehensive and forceful operations to secure it.

'The operation, therefore, required both boldness and cunning for such a small number in the SF Task Group to take a large airbase manned by a large number of forces. In one engagement, to avoid unnecessary casualties and despite being engaged by the looters' heavy weapons, the SAS Commander had ordered his snipers to place well aimed shots quite close to the looters to scare them away. Fortunately, it had the desired effect,' said Col Mansell.

Upon securing the base, they conducted a lengthy and potentially highly dangerous room-by-room clearance of the facility. There was always the danger of mines and booby traps, and when the size of the base was taken into consideration, it is little surprise that it took some 36 hours to clear.

'The facility contained in excess of 50 MiG jets and 7.9 million kg of explosive ordnance. While the SAS were operating to secure the airbase, RAAF F/A-18 fighter jets provided overwatch. Shortly afterwards, the Commandos and TIRR came in to assist securing and searching the base.

'Over the following days the task group cleared and repaired the runways to allow an air link to be established and the first fixed wing aircraft into Al Asad was an Australian 36 Squadron C-130 aircraft,' said Col Mansell.

At this point, probably the largest gathering of Australian Special Operations Forces ever deployed into hostile territory was gathered at Al Asad, with appropriate support provided by RAAF fighter and transport aircraft. This was a proud moment for the SF Task Group and the Australian Defence Force, as they had both performed superbly.

Australian close support mission in progress, courtesy of a brace of F/A-18 Hornets.

2: Special Forces at War in Iraq

Killing the Hydra

Following the fall of Baghdad in April 2003, and the supposed ending of hostilities, coalition forces embarked on a series of operations to find Saddam Hussein and his sons Uday, Qusay and Ali, as their demise was seen as being critical to the long-term stability of Iraq.

These were tough operations, as US forces were being subjected to numerous attacks each day by radical elements such as the Fedayeen Saddam and the terrorist group 'The Return'. As each day went by during May and June 2003, US losses increased in central and northern Iraq. There were now serious concerns as to how long the US could continue with its casualty rate, which was now virtually one fatality per day. Desperate for a result, the US set up a reward system similar to that in Afghanistan: $25 million for the whereabouts of Saddam Hussein, and $15 million for his sons, Uday and Qusay. Shortly after the reward was posted, US forces in the region began receiving numerous bogus and unreliable reports of possible Saddam sightings. Many innocent Iraqis longed for Saddam to be caught, as they were being arrested on account

of their facial likeness to him. Ironically, the most arrested man in Iraq was Saddam's distant cousin, an impoverished petrol pump attendant from Tikrit, who hated Saddam with a passion. Saddam had had him jailed in the past for refusing to be one of his many doubles.

However, in July 2003, a piece of information arrived in the hands of the US Army's Gray Fox unit. The informant was a relative of Saddam, Nawaf al-Zaidani, a sheikh of the Bu Issa tribe. In his statement to Gray Fox, he eluded to them that he had unwanted guests in his villa that needed removing. They were Saddam's sons: Uday, a psychopath and reviled member of the Ba'ath regime, and his brother Qusay, Saddam's successor.

The Americans wasted no time in deploying forces to the region where the villa was located. The forces chosen for this dangerous mission were drawn from the elite Task Force 20.

The villa itself was located in the northern city of Mosul, 450km (280 miles) north of Baghdad, just outside the 'Sunni triangle', an area where Saddam still enjoys strong support.

On 22 July 2003, some 200 members of the 101st Airborne Division, together with elite SEAL and Delta operatives, surrounded the

Below: The final hiding place of Saddam's sons.

Above: Saddam Hussein poses with his two sons, Uday and Qusay.

Account by a Royal Marine at Al Faw

My personal war with Iraq started in the early hours of the first night of the invasion phase, but nearly ended that night due to a minefield. It was a really weird experience for me and all the lads. The insertion phase had gone well enough, but when we landed that's when it went tits up. It was pitch black where we were, and apart from some lights in the distance there was nothing to see.

Some of the lads had NVGS [night vision goggles], which is just as well as they were the ones who spotted the mines near us. The boss shouted at us not to move, as he wanted us to wait until first light. It made sense to me as I couldn't see anything at all. I found a spot to lay up in, which was on a beach with a small raised bit. It would give me some cover if we had a contact, but if we were mortared, then I knew it was curtains. For me it was the longest four hours of my life, I can tell you, but we all got through it.

If the Iraqis didn't know we were here now, then they never would. As daylight slowly broke, we could see where we all were and more importantly where the mines were. I could see three of them in and around our location, but there were more further down the beach. After a long night I just wanted to push on, but we were told there was to be no move until later in the morning as we were to await other units.

Eventually, we began to move out of our position and forward towards a distant column of smoke that was rising up on the horizon. By now we had helicopters and aircraft flying over us all the time. As I looked around me I felt proud. All I could see everywhere was military activity – loads of it and all ours thankfully. At one stage we saw a large column of US troops moving forward towards an urban area that was west of us and obviously under attack.

We continued our move forward, and were joined by other commandos and some of us Marines. Our first engagement didn't occur until late in the evening of the first day, but it was worth the wait; everything I had ever trained for was to come into play. The attack was against a group of buildings near an old port facility. The boss told us that it been attacked earlier in the day, but was still active. In support we had no armour and no artillery, as everything was committed elsewhere. However, we did have a US Marine Cobra gunship that was on hand in case things got a bit hot.

As my section moved forward to the side of the road, out of sight of the target buildings, the shooting started. It was heavy at first, then went

Special forces operators often wear conventional uniforms and insignia to blend in when on deployment. Can you tell the difference between this and standard issue gear?

quiet, then started up again, but seemed to have no cohesion. What didn't help was the dust blowing in front of our position, but it must have been the same for them [the Iraqis] as well, as their shooting was rubbish. We had a sniper with us who was a bit tasty, and he was put up to try to spot for us. Just as he was getting into position, a number of Iraqis ran out of one building and over towards another, shooting as they went. As they did so, just about everyone opened fire on them. They were now really in trouble, as they couldn't move forward or back without being slotted. Overhead the Cobra buzzed them, but didn't fire, as we were all too close to where the Iraqis were.

Eventually, one of the lads shouted that they were surrendering as they had thrown their weapons out onto the open area, but there was no white flag. As we waited out, one of them got up with his hands above his head and began walking slowly towards us. He was quickly followed by the others and with the help of the Yanks who were with us, we took their surrender. Looking at them, they were scared and probably conscripts – their weapon handling skills were abysmal. Once documented, we moved forward towards the buildings in arrowhead formation. Inside the buildings we found stuff ranging from RPG [rocket propelled grenade] rounds to mortar shells, but no more Iraqis. My guess is that the ones we captured were not the same as those who had attacked the Yanks earlier in the day – those ones were good and these ones weren't. So that's my war story for you.

A forward air controller (FAC) calls in an A-10 Thunderbolt II during a training exercise. Such skills are in high demand both in Afghanistan and Iraq.

suspect villa, following confirmation from Gray Fox that it was the correct target. Anticipating some form of resistance, Task Force 20 set up a defensive perimeter. Their assessment of the situation was proven correct after a small team of US soldiers tried to gain access to the building via the front door but were met with a fusillade of automatic gunfire, wounding four of them. As Task Force 20 took stock of the situation, A-10 Thunderbolt close support aircraft and Apache helicopter gunships began buzzing the villa. They elected to pulverise the villa with intense firepower, minimising casualties and collateral damage. The villa had been heavily fortified prior to Task Force 20's arrival and the occupants put up fierce resistance. So much so that serious consideration was given to calling in an air strike. The idea was rejected, forcing Task Force 20 to resort to the use of anti-tank missiles instead. Once employed against the villa, the occupants' guns soon fell silent and an all-out assault was mounted on the burning

building by members of the special forces. In all, the villa seige had lasted six hours. Once the charred bodies had been dragged from the wreckage of the stone-columned villa, an autopsy confirmed that two of the bodies were indeed those of Saddam's sons Uday and Qusay, while others were later identified as those of a bodyguard and a young boy, believed to be Qusay's 14-year-old son, Mustafa.

According to Lt Gen Ricardo Sanchez, head of Coalition Forces in Iraq: 'We are certain that Uday and Qusay were killed today. We've used multiple sources to identify the individuals.' He later added that the US expected to pay out the $15 million reward that the Bush Administration had offered for information leading to the death or capture of each of Saddam's sons.

At the time of writing, the majority of the 55 most wanted regime members have either been killed or captured, including Saddam Hussein. And as for his sons, they were buried in a pauper's grave in northern Iraq.

3: Special Forces at War in Iraq

From the time the war first started, I was on the move virtually 24-7. With our own guys at first, but then later with the British Royal Marines, as they needed us to ride shotgun for them. This tenure of deployment stemmed from a policy of mutual support, where they provided artillery support to our marines, and in return we provided Cobra gunships, fast patrol boats and, of course, our good selves!

It was an arrangement that worked real well for us, as the Royal Marines are A-1 guys who know their stuff – and know how to fight. Why they are not classed as special forces is beyond my comprehension, as they are each worth ten men – well, that's my opinion.

Essentially, our role supporting the Royal Marines kept us pretty much down in the south of Iraq for most of the war. Although we never really engaged the Iraqis in any serious firefight, we still had a few interesting experiences. On one occasion we were moving up a waterway towards Basra, when we came across a small building that was too small to be a house, yet too big to be a shelter. It got our attention due to the enormous number of footprints that were around it. Why does an insignificant building like this have so many visitors, especially those who wear military-style footwear? We mounted an extensive search operation in the nearby vicinity, both on the bank that the building was on and the other side of the waterway, as we suspected the presence of an underground facility. As we moved slowly towards the building, the Royal Marines took up position behind us should things go wrong. My partner in crime jumped out of the boat first, while we provided cover by means of the '.50' and the Mk 19. As he slowly moved up the bank to the left of the building, I jumped out of the boat and moved right, performing a pincer movement. For a few seconds it was pretty tense, but once we were happy that nobody was at home, we relaxed and

US **Navy SEALs and British Royal Marines work well together in Iraq by respecting each other's unique capabilities.**

A Polish GROM operator surrounded by SEALs brings in an Iraqi suspect for interrogation.

From the distance these suckers looked like rust-buckets, but they still had weaponry onboard that looked remarkably serviceable. After satisfying ourselves that everything was hunky-dory, we boarded them and carried out a thorough search operation that again yielded nothing. While on board the boats, our Royal Marine friends decided that the rockets and munitions that were everywhere on the deck and below needed to be dumped as they could still be used against us. I helped them throw the main bulk of the weapons into the water.

Finally, after we were done there we came across yet another boat, which looked like a Staten Island ferry tug but again yielded nothing. My personal opinion for this lack of action stems from the fact that we were just too big a force to take on, especially if you wanted to live afterwards. Yes, there were occasional pot-shots, but nothing more serious. Ironically, the biggest firefight of my tenure with the Royal Marines arose out of a Blue-on-Blue incident (friendly fire) that no SEALs were involved in; the result being one Marine killed in action and several wounded. When I heard what had happened, it left a bad taste in my mouth; potential incidents like these are always on your mind and no matter how careful you are, it can happen. It just hurts more when they are guys that you know and respect.

From a personal perspective, my time on Al-Faw was interesting, albeit uneventful from a combat point of view. But I guess if we had not been there, then things may have been a darned sight hotter for everyone else concerned.

had a mosey around, but found nothing incriminating. We eventually put the footprints down to the fact that this may have been a crossing point before the outbreak of hostilities.

Days later and it was the same old thing; as we moved further up river, lots of little huts, wrecked buildings and abandoned boats, but no enemy. One day we decided to push further north, as we were simply finding no trade down here to speak of and things were becoming a tad tedious. On board our boat we had a micro UAV, which enabled us to survey the area in front of our line of advance. The Brits often teased us about this gizmo, as they had seen nothing like it before. On one patrol, however, it came in real useful when it spotted a number of abandoned Iraqi gunboats that had been tied up together close to a fork in the waterways.

An alert SEAL scans for possible trouble.

4: Special Forces at War in Iraq

Unlike the rest of the guys who were hard at it in western Iraq, we were – for our sins – on a covert recce mission in the middle of nowhere. At least that's how it felt at first. Basically, our team was a road-watch team, but to call what we were doing simply 'observing a road' would be an insult – this was no M1.

Our mission tasking was to watch, report and target, but with the type of traffic we had to observe, targeting would have been a waste of time, as the munitions would cost more than the target itself. For the best part of the day, all that moved down there were smugglers and their ill-gotten gains. They carried oil, tyres, satellite dishes and just about anything else that would bring in a buck – or in this case a dinar. But for us this was good news, as the Iraqis tended to turn a blind eye to this sort of activity, making movement for us easier should we be compromised. Military traffic seemed limited to troop, artillery and armour movements, but no Scuds. Even at night, little changed apart from the volume of traffic. We certainly never saw any target of value that would justify compromising our position here. As boring and unexciting as our traffic was, it told us where Saddam's forces were moving to.

During our time here nothing really threatened our security as we were on a high embankment that only goats or idiots like us would climb and visit. The only time we had a concern was when a camel caravan traversed across the side of our embankment about 80m (87yd) away. However, the herders had

Account from a British special forces operative

From the time the balloon first went up we were busy. We were initially deployed close to Basra and had the job of targeting Iraqi forces, both conventional and unconventional. Our position was such that we had a good field of view over the main urban area that led to the river and as such we could observe everything that moved along the main line of communication. This vantage point gave us the ability to recce or target an area as circumstances dictated. On several occasions this vista provided us with good intelligence on Iraqi troop and armour movements, as we were able to predict their routes out of the city, thus enabling an intercept by friendly forces or a target mission.

Our team was one of several that had infiltrated the city of Basra and between us we had all routes covered. In one action we spotted a small convoy of armed Toyota pick-up trucks heading for a warehouse complex that was located near to a bridge controlled by British and US forces. As we observed it, a group of Iraqis set up a mortar on the back of one of the vehicles and began bracketing the bridge with effective fire. Seeing the danger, we were able to provide target information on the convoy via our forward air controller (FAC) and within a short time the threat was eliminated.

In another action, we spotted a large force of some 20 Iraqi APCs and tanks heading for our forces surrounding the city. But our concern was short-lived, as the force was quickly destroyed by a squadron of Challenger tanks. This must have been an extremely frustrating time for the Iraqis, as they could not move anywhere within the City without SF spotting them. Essentially, we acted as a barometer for our own forces, gauging the right time for them to attack and gauging the right time for them to withdraw. Only when we felt that the time was right did they advance. I believe that our actions saved many lives – both British and Iraqi alike – and I am proud of what we did.

Snipers are great force multipliers, so it's no surprise that more and more are being trained up in this deadly art.

Many of the most successful tactics in use today against the insurgents in Iraq were developed in Northern Ireland. Here, we have an 'Eagle Patrol' in progress.

Operations still continue in South Eastern Afghanistan with a village patrol by 45 Commando Royal Marines as part of Task Force Jacana.

other things on their mind, as they were trying to transport the carcass of a luxury car downhill without losing it off the camels' backs. For the others in my team it was a great laugh, as it helped break the monotony of the situation, but I had seen this stunt performed before in Afghanistan.

Once the herders had moved on, normality returned to the OP, but things were about to change. The war was well underway by now and the military movements on the road were intensifying by the hour – first one way and then another, but still no Scuds or anything else that could pass off as a high threat. There were certainly no WMD here. Barely a week later and there was clearly an exodus of Iraqi headsheds, as the pressure was mounting and they knew it. I had no beef with the rank and file Iraqi Army. They were as much victims of Saddam's regime as anyone else. It was the Republican Guard and the Fedayeen who I despised, as they persecuted their own people.

The only time that our lives were ever potentially threatened was during an overflight by American close support aircraft, which just happened to be in our vicinity as a convoy was passing through. They lined up for an attack, but thankfully broke off. I say thankfully because we probably would have been malleted as well as the Iraqis, as we were very close to the road. If things had really gone tits up we could have tried calling them off by way of the TACBE, but then we would have risked being compromised. And I personally did not fancy trogging off into the Ulu, with half of Saddam's cousins on my tail – as they just might be a little miffed.

Action in Iraq   79

Rescue Mission

She joined the US Army to earn money for college and dreamed of eventually becoming a kindergarten teacher. But nowhere in her plans did she ever figure on being captured and held as a POW, only to be rescued in a spectacular manner by her fellow countrymen on 31 March 2003 during Operation Iraqi Freedom.

Like many Americans, Jessica Lynch joined the army as a stepping stone to something else and, as her truck driver father, Gregory Lynch, recalled: 'They offered a good deal.' The 19-year-old from Palestine, West Virginia, joined the army as a supply clerk and was assigned to the 507th Maintenance Company at Fort Bliss, Texas – a unit comprising of welders, repairmen and clerks.

In the early hours of 23 March, the 507th convoy crossed the Iraq–Kuwait border and headed north on the road to Baghdad, following behind the US Marines. The 507th's mission was to support the frontline troops. However, in the confusion of battle, the convoy took a wrong turn and rolled into the southern Iraqi city of Nasiriyah, where they were ambushed by a larger force of Iraqi irregular forces.

The 507th were both outnumbered and outgunned, and stood little chance against the enemy force's overwhelming firepower. After some 15 minutes of intense combat, the guns fell silent, leaving nine US soldiers dead and six captured, one of whom was Jessica Lynch.

By the end of the day, the soldiers were officially posted as missing. A few days later, five of the US soldiers that were feared either killed or captured appeared on Iraqi television, but there was no Jessica Lynch. For a while, nothing more was heard, until one day an Iraqi lawyer, identified only as Mohammed, approached a US Marine checkpoint and told them that he had seen an American woman in the Saddam hospital at Nasiriyah.

Mohammed, whose wife was a nurse, told the Marines: 'I went to the hospital to visit my wife. I could see much more security than normal.' He then asked one of the doctors, who happened to be a friend of his, about the extra security. 'He told me there was a woman American soldier there.'

Together, the two went to see her. Peering through the hospital room window, Mohammed watched as an Iraqi colonel slapped the injured woman, first with his palm and then with the back of his hand.

The lawyer said: 'I knew then I must help to save her. I decided to tell the Americans.' Later that day, after walking for several miles, he came across a US checkpoint. Worried that he would be mistaken for an attacker in civilian clothes, he approached the Marines with his hands high above his head.

When challenged, Mohammed told the Marines: 'I want to help you. I want to tell you important news about Jessica.' What he told them was immediately passed on to senior officers. After talking with the Marines, Mohammed returned to the hospital to obtain more information about the security

PFC Jessica Lynch pictured here during happier times.

The faces say it all – being captured is a terrifying experience, but if you have the world's best operators available, then there's always hope for you.

arrangements, such as where they sat to guard the injured American soldier, and where they ate and slept.

Mohammed said that as he watched what was happening at the hospital, the notorious regime death squad paid an unexpected visit to his home. His wife and six-year-old daughter fled to a nearby family. The squad took his car and other belongings.

Back at the hospital, Mohammed and his friend went into the room where the injured American lay. She was covered up to her chin in a blanket and her head was bandaged. A wound on her right leg was in a bad condition.

Mohammed said that the doctors wanted to amputate the leg, but he and his doctor friend argued with them and managed to persuade them to delay the surgery. For two days, Mohammed observed what was going on at the hospital and was able to wish the American 'Good morning' in English.

When he reported back to the Marines on 30 March, he took five different maps that he and his wife had made. He was able to point to the exact room where the captured soldier was being held. He also gave details of the

security layout, and the times that shift changes occurred. He had counted 41 Iraqis involved in guarding the American woman.

Meanwhile, US forces had spent two days planning an operation that was based around the information that Mohammed had provided. The rescue operation began on the night of 31 March, and involved US Army Rangers, Delta Force, US Navy SEALS, USAF pilots and controllers, and for perimeter security, a force of US Marines.

The hospital was on the other side of the river, in relation to the disposition of the US forces, so therefore a diversion was needed. On a given signal, elements of the US Marines opened fire on known Iraqi positions on the opposite side of the river, while other units sped across the river by means of both helicopters and ground vehicles.

As the main assault force moved in to secure the hospital grounds, special forces landed nearby and began entering the hospital building where Jessica was being held. As they moved through the building, the SF rescue team came across a sympathetic doctor who led them straight to Jessica's room. In conversation, he mentioned that there were remains of US troops nearby, either in the morgue or buried outside.

As the special forces entered Jessica's room, they called out her name. 'She had been scared, had the sheet up over her head because she didn't know what was happening,' said USAF Major General Victor Renault, when describing the operation five days later. 'She lowered the sheet from her head, but didn't really respond.'

The general said that one team member repeated: 'Jessica Lynch, we're United States soldiers and we're here to take you home.' The general said: 'Jessica seemed to understand that. And as he walked over and took his helmet off, she looked up at him and said "I'm an American soldier, too".'

A Ranger doctor evaluated Jessica's condition and the team evacuated her. She seemed in a fair amount of pain. The general said: 'Jessica held up her hand and grabbed the Ranger doctor's hand, held on to it for almost the entire time and said "Please don't let anybody leave me." It was clear she knew where she was and didn't want to be left in the hands of the enemy.' One helicopter transported her to another nearby waiting aircraft, which took her to a field hospital.

Other parts of the rescue team were led to a site where 11 bodies were buried, some of them thought to be American. 'The rescue team did not have shovels so they dug up those graves using their hands,' said the general. 'They wanted to do that very quickly so that they could be off the site before the sun came up.'

The team recovered the bodies of eight US soldiers and three other people. The American soldiers who were killed had been with Jessica when the convoy was attacked. On Thursday, 3 April, Jessica was flown to the US Ramstein Air Base in Germany and was taken to the nearby US Landstuhl Medical Centre. Her injuries included fractures to her right arm, both legs, right foot and ankle and lumbar spine, as well as a head laceration. Doctors initially said that she had not been shot or stabbed, but a few days later, the medical team said that Jessica had been wounded by a low-velocity small calibre weapon.

On Sunday, 6 April, Jessica's family arrived at the hospital to see her, having flown from their home in Palestine, West Virginia. On 11 April, Jessica and 49 other wounded soldiers arrived at the Andrews Air Force Base outside Washington D.C. and were taken to a nearby military hospital.

Commenting on the rescue operation afterwards, USAF Major General Gene Renuart said, 'It's a great testament to the will and desire of our forces to bring their own home.'

Combat report from Northern Iraq: Soldier D

As dawn broke over our position, the morning after our night insertion, I was fascinated by our surrounding area as it reminded me of Afghanistan. Apart from the birds flying over the valley in front of us, and squawking every now and again, it was totally quiet. There was just no way that you would believe a war was taking place barely spitting distance from the position we were occupying. The week before we'd been just north of Mosul, where there was intense Iraqi Army activity, but for us no contacts. Our general mission was to see and report, nothing else. For us it was just a question of finding targets, reporting them and then observing them to see if anything interesting was happening.

One night, just a few clicks from our position, an almighty firefight developed on a ridgeline opposite our OP. At first we couldn't tell if the fire was for us or someone else, but after a while it became apparent that the Iraqis were shooting at each other. We later learnt that some had deserted their positions and fled towards the Kurdish enclaves, and that the firing was designed to deter others who had the same idea.

I found this area a bizarre place to operate in as there was something of a phoney war taking place. By that I mean there was no all-out fighting, yet there was no peace, either. It seemed that the Iraqis were resigned to the fact that they were going to lose this war and they didn't want to fall foul of the Kurds, especially with Saddam gone.

Operation Red Dawn

On Sunday, 14 December 2003, America's most senior administrator in Iraq, Paul Bremer, called a press conference and began his speech with the words: 'We got him.' He was, of course, referring to the capture of the world's most wanted 'dead man walking', Saddam Hussein – or HVT (high value target) No 1 as he was known within US military and intelligence circles.

The capture of Saddam was the result of an intelligence tip-off, gleaned from intensive military operations in and around the former dictator's home town of Tikrit in northern Iraq. With a bounty of $25 million on his head, Saddam made for an attractive target – the payment would be made whether he was found dead or alive. In part, his capture was due to intelligence gained from distant relatives and members of the Kurdish PUK

US special operations aircraft pictured here prior to a mission. Such aircraft carry out myriad support roles on behalf of special forces, most of them classified.

(Patriotic Union of Kurdistan), but the role of the special forces in this operation should not be underestimated as they were the ones who captured him ... ironically, without a single shot being fired. This was in contrast to the operation that killed his two sons, Uday and Qusay. A battle raged for almost a day before they were eventually overcome, but as for Saddam, he came out without so much as a wimper. Here is the timeline to the remarkable operation that led to his capture.

10.50am Saturday (7.50GMT): Coalition forces received intelligence on the possible location of Saddam Hussein, the target area being the small village of Ad-Dawr, some 18km (11 miles) from Tikrit. Two suspect sites were identified as possible hiding places; they were designated under the codename of Wolverine 1 and Wolverine 2.

Two US Army Black Hawks ride shotgun over a ground mission – highly dangerous work for all concerned.

The operation was to be known as 'Red Dawn', and only the senior commanders knew the intended target, 'HVT No 1'. For all others concerned, it was a routine HVT operation.

6pm: Under cover of darkness and at high speed, some 600 US soldiers, including elements of Task Force 20, deployed to the target location by helicopter and vehicle. The main force was commanded by Col Jim Hickey and comprised the 4th Infantry Division, supported by Humvees, light armour, artillery and Apache helicopter gunships. The smaller special forces element of the force operated under the command and control of Lt Gen Ricardo Sanchez, the most senior US military commander in Iraq.

The force commander was given the mission, 'Kill or capture HVT No 1'.

8pm: US forces surround and secure the village of Ad-Dawr and commence 'sweep and clear' operations. After an initial sweep, which revealed nothing, the soldiers cordoned off an area of land, about 1.6km (1 mile) square, and began a thorough and detailed search. After a

short period, a suspicious location was found to the north-west of Wolverine 2. It was a small walled compound with a metal lean-to and a mud hut.

As operators from Task Force 20 made their approach to the target, two Iraqis fled the location; they were later identified as Saddam's bodyguards. Now pensive and apprehensive of what lay within the compound, the operators began a finger-tip search of the area, until a rug was found covering a fake rock bed of bricks and earth that was built into a block of polystyrene – its purpose being to act as a hatch cover.

8.26pm: As the special forces cautiously removed the hatch, a spiderhole was discovered that led to a shaft some 2.5m (8ft) deep. Now pointing their weapons into the shaft and illuminating it with their torches, they discovered a figure lurking within. It was Saddam Hussein. Looking dirty, haggard and dishevelled, the once feared and arrogant dictator was now reduced to a pathetic figure. He appeared 'tired and resigned', said Gen

Stay low and no bullets will show – that's the theory, anyway.

Sanchez, while Maj Gen Ray Odiero stated, 'He was caught like a rat. He was disorientated as he came up, then he was just very much bewildered; then he was taken away. He said hardly anything at all. There was no resistance of any sort. We got him out of there very quickly once we figured out who it was. The

Right: A dishevelled Saddam Husseln shortly after capture.

Below: The moment Saddam is discovered.

soldiers were extremely happy and extremely excited, but very professional. It is rather ironic that he was in a hole in the ground across the river from one of these great palaces he built where he robbed all the money from the Iraqi people.'

9.15pm: Saddam is extracted by helicopter and flown to a secure location for medical examination, DNA testing and interrogation.

The lair Saddam left behind was a purpose built bolt hole, 2.5m (8ft) in length and just large enough to allow a man to lay down flat. It had a small pipe and a fan for ventilation, but no communications equipment. Therefore, Saddam could not have orchestrated attacks on Coalition forces from here. Above the bolt-hole within the hut, two AK-47 assault rifles and a green metal case with $750,000 in $100 bills was discovered, while within the hole itself a pistol was found. Nearby were two small boats, possibly used for transportation and resupply via the Tigris river, while an old battered taxi parked in the grounds served as Saddam's limousine. It was a major comedown for a man who once lived in opulance and splendour beyond most people's wildest dreams. At the time of writing the people of Iraq have still to see him tried for the decades of suffering he inflicted upon them.

Although the capture of Saddam was a major boost for Coalition forces, it was unlikely to bring about total peace and reconciliation. But hopefully it brings it a step closer.

Airborne Operators

Hell from Above

Many books on special forces lack any information on the people who make it possible for SF operators to operate – the aircrews that bravely and skilfully insert and extract special forces as they go about their business. Without them, most SF missions would be doomed to fail before they had even started.

These days, helicopters play a critical role in SF operations and are the preferred method of transportation. Their ability to operate in all weathers, both night and day, means that special forces can also operate around the clock, without any fear of mission compromise.

Helicopters have, of course, been used by special forces for decades, with the first intensive use made of them in combat during the Korean War. After that, the British made extensive use of them in Malaya and Indonesia, where they proved invaluable for jungle-based operations. From there, it was the US's turn to show the world what could be done with the helicopter. This they did spectacularly during the Vietnam War, performing amazing feats such as the Son Tay raid and the Koh Tang Island hostage rescue mission.

For all intents and purposes, modern helicopter warfare is based largely on the tactics, techniques and procedures developed during this period, but with new refinements and adaptations.

Highlighted in this chapter are some of the missions and operations that have shaped current US thinking on helicopter-based warfare. There will also be a present-day account of helicopter operations in Iraq, as seen through the eyes of Maj Gen David H. Petraeus and his unit, the mighty 101st Airborne Division (Air Assault).

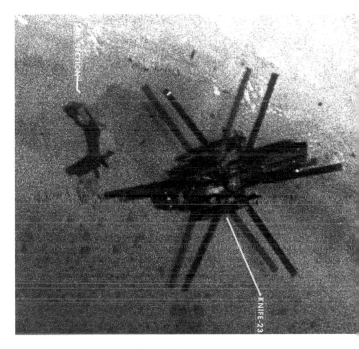

The wreckage of US CH-53 helicopter Knife 23 lies on the beach of Koh Tang Island shortly after being shot down by enemy AAA fire in the Vietnam War.

Helicopter-based Operations

Operation Eagle Claw was executed in 1980 following the kidnapping of US Embassy staff in Tehran in Iran in 1979. The rescue mission itself was a failure, following a number of catastrophic events that were impossible to overcome. For example, the worst sandstorm in living memory; multiple helicopter malfunctions; and finally, a collision between a refuelling aircraft and a helicopter at an RV point, known as 'Desert One'. Although a failure, and a major setback for US Special Forces at the time, Operation Eagle Claw was an extremely brave attempt to do the right thing, and the courage, flying skills and tenacity of the aircrews involved cannot be faulted.

Following on from Eagle Claw, America expanded its use of helicopter special

American students celebrate their rescue in 1983 as they board a US transport aircraft on the island of Grenada.

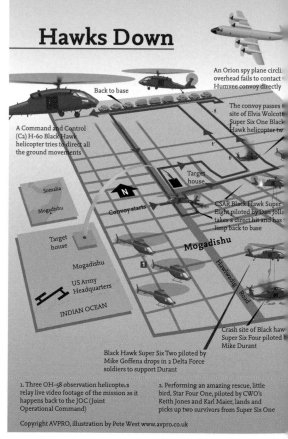

Hawks Down

An Orion spy plane circli overhead fails to contact Humvee convoy directly

Back to base

The convoy passes site of Elvis Wolcott Super Six One Black Hawk helicopter tw

A Command and Control (C2) H-60 Black Hawk helicopter tries to direct all the ground movements

Somalia
Mogadishu

Convoy starts

Target house

CSAR Black Hawk Super Eight piloted by Dan Joll takes a direct hit and has limp back to base

Target house

Mogadishu

Mogadishu

US Army Headquarters

Hawlwadig Road

INDIAN OCEAN

Crash site of Black haw Super Six Four piloted Mike Durant

Black Hawk Super Six Two piloted by Mike Goffena drops in 2 Delta Force soldiers to support Durant

1. Three OH-58 observation helicopters relay live video footage of the mission as it happens back to the JOC (Joint Operational Command)

2. Performing an amazing rescue, little bird, Star Four One, piloted by CWO's Keith Jones and Karl Maier, lands and picks up two survivors from Super Six One

Copyright AVPRO, illustration by Pete West www.avpro.co.uk

Above: The real story of how the Black Hawk helos went down. (Avpro Aerospace)

A us **Black Hawk of the 16oth** SOAR **prepares to go downtown over Mogadishu in Somalia.**

Scott O'Grady arrives on board a us **carrier after being rescued by** us **Marines. His face says it all.**

operations, culminating in the heavy usage of helicopter-orientated special forces units in both Grenada in 1983, during Operation Urgent Fury, and Panama in 1989 during Operation Just Cause. us Special Forces now had USAF's SOG and the Army's 16oth SOAR in their ORBAT – both highly potent, combat-proven units and both the envy of the world.

Their finest hour came in 1991 when they participated in Operation Desert Storm, as part of the Coalition force that liberated Kuwait from Iraq. As part of that operation, MH-53s from USAF's SOG acted as Pathfinders for the us Army's Apache gunships. The Apaches could not navigate accurately at night, whereas MH-53s had state-of-the-art navigation systems.

Mission mishaps

An artist's portrayal of Operation Urgent Fury as seen from the us **Marines' point of view.**

Unfortunately, disaster struck during the 1993 UN humanitarian operation in Somalia. Several us Black Hawks were lost following a snatch raid against a known warlord in Mogadishu. This story has been told already,

in books such as *Chariots of the Damned* and *Black Hawk Down*, which eventually became a film.

If nothing else, Somalia taught the us special forces community a valuable lesson: if you have a tried and tested modus operandi, then stick to it and don't be bullied into changing it.

Having elite units within a military ORBAT also breeds its own problems. This became apparent in 1995, following the downing of a USAF F-16 fighter over Bosnia. The unlucky pilot was Captain Scott O'Grady, who found himself the centre of attention both from the Serbs, who wanted him as a war trophy, and his fellow us brothers in arms, who were competing as to who was going to rescue him first. The competition was between USAF's SOG, who favoured a night rescue, and the us Marines, who preferred a daylight one. In the end, it was the Marines who got to him first, after mounting an amazing rescue.

From Bosnia onwards, both the SOG and the 16oth performed superbly in all operations, with Operations Enduring Freedom and Iraqi Freedom the most demanding to date. These operations are currently the most intensive since Vietnam and have resulted in heavy platform losses, primarily from the harsh and demanding flying conditions in Afghanistan and Iraq rather than from combat.

US 101st Airborne Division (Air Assault)

The 101st Airborne Division (Air Assault) is the biggest air cavalry unit in the world today and played a key role in Operation Iraqi Freedom.

From the time the 101st Airborne Division first left its forward operating base in the Kuwaiti desert, right up until its arrival in the northern Iraqi city of Mosul – a distance of some 1,200km (750 miles) – it was in the thick of the action, firing an incredible 3,500 rounds of artillery along the way.

During a briefing in May 2003, the Division's commander, Maj Gen David H. Petraeus, described the Division's drive north: 'Our soldiers had a number of very tough fights in southern Iraq, liberating An Najaf, Karbala and Al Hillah, and then clearing al Mamadia, Escondaria and south Baghdad, as well as Hadithah in the western desert.

'We then air assaulted 500km (300 miles) further north to secure and clear Mosul, Tall Afar, Qaiyara and other cities in Nineveh Province. Three of the Division's soldiers were killed in combat and some 79 were wounded.

'Mosul had been the scene of some stiff firefights. We came in with a tank battalion, an Apache battalion, a Kiowa squadron and several battalions of infantry, a brigade, and a lot of other combat multipliers, artillery and so forth.

'We immediately secured the city, establishing a civil military operation centre in the former governance building in the centre of the city with its leaders to ensure that there weren't repeated instances. We did have several firefights in our first week here, but we took no casualties.'

As an example of the sheer intensity of the

A soldier of the 101st Airborne Division looks through the sights of a TOW missile launcher at a building in Mosul suspected of harbouring Saddam Hussein's sons Qusay and Uday.

A Black Hawk is readied for another mission. Note the weapon hardpoints and long-range fuel tanks.

combat in which his units were involved, Gen Petraeus stated that as well as the 3,500 rounds of artillery, they had fired nearly 1,000 2.75in rockets and Hellfire missiles, 114 tactical missiles and over 40,000 rounds of machine-gun ammunition from Apache and Kiowa attack helicopters. They also flew some 150 sorties of close air support and used 'tons of everything else in our inventory', he said.

'Our Apaches did a great job for us,' said Gen Petraeus. 'We did, in fact, change our tactics from night-long deep attack operations for two reasons. Following a successful deep attack, but one in which we crashed a helicopter in a night dust landing on return and also had problems on take-off, we now had two problems.

'One was that night dust landings were very, very difficult, despite having experienced soldiers who had flown in Afghanistan, spent quite a bit of time with environmental training in Kuwait and had no problems there.

'The other problem was that the Iraqis dispersed very early on and moved their tanks and fighting vehicles and artillery away from the avenues of approach that the 3rd Division, in particular, was going to use. And so they weren't massed in the way that we usually want for Apache operations. We did, as I say, have one quite successful deep attack operation and had a reasonable battle damage assessment (BDA). But it was not the kind that we had hoped to see with the 100-plus tanks, tracks, artillery and air defence systems.

'Following that, when we could not get the target definition that we needed, we went to daylight, deep armed reconnaissance operations and conducted a number of very successful missions of that type. We packaged these operations with ATACMS missiles and called for 114 of these. Each of these clears an entire grid square; they're massive munitions. We had those in a direct line between the shooters and the Apaches. We also had JSTARS supporting them, to direct them; AWACS, EA-6 jammers and close air support all packaged together with HARM shooters. And that package went down range; we could identify the target at up to 8km (5 miles).

'And then, depending on how much fuel the Apache had, if the pilot had a lot, he would bring in close air support – ATACMS – and save his missiles and rockets for later.'

The general said they also had considerable success with attack helicopters operating in close support of infantry soldiers. 'The one operation in which we actually ran into a substantial fight with the Republican Guards, and one of the few cases that I'm aware of where the Republican Guards employed combined arm operations, was the morning that the V Corps attacked with an armed recon [reconnaissance] by our

Air-to-air refuelling is routinely practised by all US SF pilots, enabling long-range missions deep behind enemy lines.

A 101st Airborne Division casualty evacuation (CASEVAC) chopper on QRF standby in Iraq.

Apaches to the north-west of Karbala, the lake,' said Gen Petraeus.

'The 3rd Infantry Division attacked into the Karbala Gap, both in the west and the east of the city; and then, of course, never really stopped from there. We attacked into south Al Hillah, where we encountered a dug-in Republican Guard battalion with a tank company, artillery and air defence. We had a very heavy fight there and lost our first soldier.

'The Apache company in that operation fought very hard and took some degree of fire. All of them made it safely back, another sign that the Apache can get hit and keep on flying, as it showed in Afghanistan as well, in close combat.

'In that fight, we destroyed that Republican Guard's battalion. We destroyed the tank company. We destroyed two artillery battalions, an artillery battery and a number of other systems. We never again saw a Republican Guard unit stand and fight and employ combined arms like that.'

General Petraeus also went on to mention that the Division often employed its Kiowa Warrior cavalry squadron attack helicopters directly over cities.

'The Kiowas were hard targets to hit generally. You could take the [Kiowa] doors off, lean out and look directly down through the palm trees and into the city streets where the regular army, militia and Fedayeen were hiding their systems; we would then use the Apaches around the edge of the city and occasionally bring them in for really robust attacks. That worked quite successfully.'

UK Helicopter Special Operations

Although the UK does not have a direct equivalent to the US 160th SOAR, it does have an equal to the 101st Airborne (Air Assault) Division, albeit a smaller one. This is 16 Air Assault Brigade. The UK simply does not have the helicopter assets of the US, but on the first night of Operation Iraqi Freedom, it certainly created the illusion of a massive air armada.

'The air assault on the Al Faw peninsula was unique – I've never seen helicopters used so aggressively in a plan,' said Wing Cdr David Prowse, officer commanding 18 Squadron, after he had led the first wave of Boeing Chinook HC2s through fierce sandstorms during the opening hours of the invasion

phase. Their mission was to land Royal Marine Commandos on strategically valuable oil facilities; this was made all the more difficult by the fact that the landing zones were being bombarded by both mortar and artillery fire. In part, this counter-action had been anticipated in advance by Coalition special forces, who had taken steps to neutralise their effect. In one such mission, a CH-46E Sea Knight returning from Al-Faw was lost in a non-combat-related accident, resulting in the loss of four crew and eight British soldiers (some of whom were believed to be from the SBS – Special Boat Service).

Cdr Prowse further stated: 'We have been used in so many roles, over a large area of

An RAF gunner, complete with GPMG, prepares for a mission over Iraq.

southern Iraq, that we felt fully involved. When I first briefed my inner circle on the plan, there was stunned silence; after two months' training, everyone was ready for it. The plan changed very little. We knew the risks and that gave us a high confidence level.' His confidence was understandable as the Coalition forces had little fear of the Iraqi Air Force; their operational capability had been heavily degraded prior to the outbreak of hostilities. In total, the UK deployed some 97 helicopters on Operation Telic, a large force that was split down into three distinct force packages:

- Package 1 was deployed with a tailored air group embarked on the HMS *Ark Royal* task group
- Package 2 was deployed to Jordan to support British, Australian and US special forces operating in western Iraq
- Package 3 was deployed to Kuwait to support the main land force, after Ankara turned down a UK request to base its forces in Turkey for operations against northern Iraq.

All helicopters for this force, except for those operating from Royal Navy warships, were provided by the Joint Helicopter Command (JHC) which is based at Wilton in Wiltshire. They were delegated to operate with the three British Brigades deployed in the Middle East and were organised as follows: 3 Regt Army Air Corps (AAC) was to operate under 16 Air Assault Brigade's tactical control, while RAF Chinooks and Puma HC1s were to support 7 Armoured, 3 Commando and 16 Air Assault Brigades.

'We are a brigade-level force – 1,500 people – making it the biggest thing for RAF support helicopters since the last Gulf War,' stated JHC HQ commander Group Capt Andy Pulford. He went on to say, 'The Al Faw operation was the largest helicopter assault since Vietnam. There were 42 helicopters in the air at one point. It was the first time since the Falklands that we had to use the complete helicopter force (except for the RAF's Merlin HC3s) at the same time. The whole fleet has been out doing its job.'

During the war itself, UK helicopters performed just about every possible mission, from air assault to stores replenishment. They were extremely active around Al Faw, Basra and the western desert, where they supported special forces operations in difficult and demanding conditions. Other roles included POW transportation, anti-

Royal Marines prepare to move out of their hangar as 'H' hour approaches for the invasion of Iraq in 2003.

Brown-out conditions play havoc with man and machine, but it's the same for the enemy.

armour and Eagle patrols – a well tried and tested method of suppressing insurgents by means of air power.

For the British, this special operation was a remarkable success because it enabled them to deploy the main combat elements of 3 Commando Brigade on heavily defended enemy coastline in hours rather than days, as would have been the case if they had chosen to rely on landing craft. Later in the war, as British forces stormed the Iraqi city of Basra, helicopters were used for attacking buildings, vehicles, armour, artillery, gunboats and troops.

Mission possible

However, their finest hour took place on the Rumailah oil fields, as British and US forces secured the key critical oil wells that Saddam had threatened to blow up as part of his scorched earth policy.

Despite the Iraqis best attempts to destroy the wells, they failed. The British and Americans were too quick for them. In part, this agility was down to the services of the RAF's Pumas and the AAC's Lynx helicopters, enabling British forces to deploy rapidly from location to location when tasked with providing mobile vehicle checkpoints and security patrols.

Flying helicopters at low level and at night is demanding enough at the best of times, but in sand and dust storms it is something else. To the eternal credit of the pilots, they overcame

these problems admirably, performing with great skill and tenacity in conditions that were at times utterly appalling.

Despite being targeted by Iraqi gunners on numerous occasions, no British helicopters were lost to enemy fire. Two Chinooks were badly damaged, though; one after it ran out of fuel en route to Baghdad and the other after it was shot up while flying reinforcements into Al Majar Al Kabir, following the ambush of a Parachute Regiment patrol. Overall, the Chinooks performed superbly during Iraqi Freedom, prompting one senior officer to comment, 'In the first wave on to Al Faw, we delivered 220 Marines in four aircraft; it would have taken 22 Sea Kings to deliver them. When the assault was delayed, the Sea Kings with us had to go into a holding pattern and then go back to a forward arming and refuelling point or ships to refuel.' One other officer, Wing Cdr Paul Lyall, OC 33 Sqn, said: 'This operation proved you need varying sizes of helicopters. In vehicle checkpoint operations, we carried eight to 12 troops. That is insignificant for the Chinook but right for a Puma. Its simplicity and ruggedness made the Puma ideal for this environment. It is a risk judgement: do you have 50 troops in one target or spread them around four or five targets? You need more smaller helicopters alongside the big helicopters. The Puma is good for covert tasks – the Chinook is a larger, noisier beast.'

Global Operators

Special Forces Worldwide

A question often asked is which country has the best special forces? It's a simple enough question, but the answer is rather more difficult. Every country puts together the best possible force that it can with the resources available.

Of course size is not always an indication of strength. And there are many countries whose soldiers are designated special forces only because they are better trained than the conscripts who make up their regular armed forces. The opposite is also true, where countries have soldiers who are the envy of the world, yet in their own countries are only deemed elite.

The truth is that every country looks at each other's SF capabilities and either tries to copy it, or better it if possible.

Some countries throw money at the armed forces to mass produce lots of operators, but special forces cannot be mass produced; it simply does not work. Instead, capability has to be built up and refined until it serves a purpose – and that takes time. At present, the US has the best equipped and balanced SF capability in the world, but of course still has room to improve.

Still, there are many countries whose operators train in the US, as it has a lot to offer in terms of support and first-hand practical experience.

In recent years, Europe has tried to standardise its SF training so that interoperability and combat efficiency is increased. There have been some rising stars in unexpected places, such as Poland, where its GROM unit performed superbly alongside British, American and Australian special forces in the recent Iraq conflict. Further afield, the Russian special forces showed admirable courage and determination in action against Chechen rebels, even if their tactics and techniques were somewhat lacking.

Following is a directory of the world's current special and elite forces and, while it's by no means comprehensive, will give you a good insight into who is out there – and what exactly they are capable of.

US Navy SEALs practise insertion techniques following the terrorist attack on the USS *Cole* in Yemen. All kit is for practical reasons – including the ice hockey-style helmets.

Algeria

Algeria has a long and bloody history of internal turmoil that has kept its armed forces, and indeed those of the French, extremely busy for many decades, until France granted Algeria its independence in July 1962. Since then the country has struggled to keep terrorist factions in check. There have been numerous bombings and attacks on government forces in recent years, which prompted the formation of a dedicated counter-terrorist unit.

Although little is known of its strength or capabilities, the counter-terrorist unit is part of a new airborne special forces division within the Algerian Army and replaces the 1st, 2nd and 3rd parachute commando battalions which were first formed in 1962. Algeria's first special forces unit was the 19th Algerian Parachute Battalion, which was formed by the French Army in 1954.

After being granted its independence, Algeria turned to the Soviet Union for its training and equipment, and much of its new airborne operational doctrine is now based on Russian practice, rather than French. The Algerian special forces have been involved in combat outside Algeria. They are known to have deployed a battalion to Fayid in Egypt for raids across the Suez Canal against the Israeli Defence Force (IDF) during the War of Attrition.

Since 9/11, Algeria has found itself in an extremely difficult position; many of Al-Qaeda's current members originate from within the country and are keen to continue the fight against the West from there. Against this background, Algeria has sent its special forces into action against known terrorist strongholds and enclaves, but they have their work cut out – the terrorists often have the backing of locals sympathetic to their cause. There is also the ongoing Israeli–Palestinian issue, a perennial thorn in the side of any moderate Algerian government that tries to convince its people of the virtues of peace and democracy.

Marines from Argentina line up alongside US Marines during the largest amphibious assault exercise in Latin America, UNITAS, in 2003.

Argentina

Argentinian special forces regularly train in the US, particularly with the US Marines and Navy SEALS – a relationship that caused some concern to the UK during the Falkland's War.

Brigada del Ejercito 601 and 602

Argentina first set up a special forces capability with US assistance in the 1960s, forming a commando brigade which was modelled along US Ranger lines. Known as Brigada del Ejercito 601 (Army Brigade 601), this force quickly gained respect among the Argentine armed forces, which led to the formation of a second brigade, the 602nd.

All members of the brigade undergo parachute training at the Catamarca Airborne School and cross train with other SF units. The 601st saw action during the Falkland's War on Mount Kent where they fought running battles with the British SAS. Standard equipment includes sniper rifles, assault weapons fitted with high quality night-vision devices and high quality combat clothing.

Brigada Halcon

Formed in 1986 to combat terrorism, the Brigada Especial Operativa Halcon (Falcon Special Operations Brigade) is a police unit directly under the command of the Buenos Aires police department. Its make up is very similar to that of a military CRW team and consists of 75 operators, who are then sub-divided into five 15-man teams.

Each team consists of two snipers, eight assaulters, one negotiator, one intelligence specialist, a communications specialist, a medic and an EOD specialist. Training comprises three two-month courses, which cover shooting, parachuting, offensive driving, sniping, intelligence gathering, use of explosives and helicopter insertion. In addition to its anti-terrorist role, Halcon also provides bodyguards for VIPs.

Brigada Halcon uses both local – and foreign – manufactured clothing and protective gear. Weapons include the Franchi SPAS 12 shotgun, Glock 17 pistol and HK G3 GS/1 for sniping.

Soldiers from 1LI boarding an Argentinian Huey (of the UN flight from Nicosia) during the damping down operations that followed after a fire at Episkopi Garrison.

Australia

Based at Campbell Barracks, Swanbourne, the Australian Special Air Service Regiment (SASR) has an operational strength of around 600 men and is made up of six squadrons – three Sabre, one signals, one support, one base – and a Regimental Headquarters (RHQ). To ensure maximum operational efficiency at any given time, the three Sabre squadrons work on a three-year cycle, which provides both training and operational experience.

A typical squadron cycle would, in its first year, process new recruits and work them up, while at the same time the more experienced troopers within the squadron would develop new skills and attend refresher courses. The second year would see the squadron train for its overt military responsibilities, which includes special operations in conventional warfare. This provides a good contrast for the third year, which involves training for covert operations.

The Base Squadron provides logistical and administrative support, while the Operational Support Squadron evaluates new equipment and provides specialist training for new tactics, techniques and procedures. In addition to this support, the SASR also has 152 Signals Squadron, which provides a highly capable communications network.

The SASR has a long and proud history dating back to the Second World War when the first Australian SAS squadrons were formed to fight the Japanese behind their own lines – a task they performed with great success. After the war ended they were disbanded in the same way as the British SAS and had to wait

An operator from the 4th Battalion Royal Australian Regiment guards a captured Iraqi MiG fighter at the Al Asad airbase in Iraq.

Australia's Special Operations Command

Established in May 2003, and headed up by Major General Duncan Lewis, SOC comprises:

- A joint HQ with offices in Canberra and Sydney
- The Special Air Service Regiment (SASR)
- The 4th Battalion the Royal Australian Regiment (Commando)
- The Tactical Assault Group (West) and (East)
- The 1st Commando Regiment
- The Incident Response Regiment

The Special Operations Service Support Company is a unit that comprises logistics, communications, heavy weapons and a special forces aviation support element, and is operated and manned by 330 highly trained personnel who are available to supplement Australia's existing Special Forces ORBAT in an emergency.

Operators from the 4th RAR cautiously approach a well-camouflaged Iraqi fighter at Al Asad

TAG/OAT Special Forces

The Tactical Assault Group (TAG) was formed in 1978 in response to the Sydney Hilton Hotel terrorist attack. The TAG is known as B Squadron within the SASR and all of its members have to undergo the same selection and training as troopers in the regular SASR. The selection phase lasts for three weeks and is then followed by almost a year of intensive training before the successful troopers are allowed to wear the coveted sand-coloured beret. The TAG's training facilities include sniping ranges, aircraft mock-ups, CQB ranges and an urban counter-terrorist (CT) complex.

The Offshore Assault Team (OAT) is basically an off-shoot of the TAG and specialises in maritime operations. The unit regularly practises its skills on ferries, small boats and oil rigs, and is viewed as a separate but equal element of TAG.

Both the TAG and OAT have a considerable arsenal of weaponry at their disposal. Favourites include M16A2s, F-88 5.56 Austeyr assault rifles plus the entire family of MP-5s. Other weapons include the 7.62 Galil, HK PSG 1, Parker Hale 82, Finnish Tikka.223 plus a variety of Beretta and Remington shotguns. Pistols include the Browning HP 9mm and SIG-Sauer P228.

All TAG/OAT operators are HALO/HAHO qualified and are highly proficient in heliborne operations. They frequently cross-train with other countries and have a very close relationship with the US Delta Force and Navy SEALs. During the Sydney 2000 Olympic Games, both the TAG and OAT played a key role in protecting international athletes against possible terrorist attacks.

until 1949 before being reformed. For three years the unit was known as the 1st SAS Company and operated out of Swanbourne. In 1951, they were incorporated into the Royal Australian Regiment (RAR) as an airborne platoon, but this was far from ideal and in 1957 they broke away and became the 1st Special Air Service Company.

This unit quickly grew in size and capability and in 1964 became the 1st SASR, a title that is current to this day. The SASR mirrors the British SAS in many ways, having worked together over many years both in combat and training. The strength of this special relationship was ably demonstrated in the jungles of Borneo from February 1965 to August 1966, where British and Australian SAS troopers fought side by side against Indonesian forces in difficult and demanding conditions. This experience was of immense value to the SASR, as it soon found itself involved in another difficult operation in Vietnam, fighting in support of the US armed forces.

The SASR had originally deployed to Vietnam in 1962 as part of the Australian Army Training Team. However, as the war dragged on it became necessary to raise another squadron in July 1966, which brought the SASR up to an operational strength of three Sabre squadrons. Up until 1971 each squadron rotated after completing two tours of

Vietnam. SASR troopers gained a reputation for being tough and tenacious fighters who never quit during their time in Vietnam.

After Vietnam the SASR was forced to disband one of its Sabre squadrons, but this was reformed in 1982 following a terrorist bomb attack on the Sydney Hilton Hotel on 13 February 1978. Within days of the attack, the SASR was formally designated as the national counter-terrorist unit and immediately set up the TAG/OAT groups as a reaction force.

From 1982 the SASR rapidly expanded and soon found itself needing a dedicated Signals squadron. In response, 152 Signals Squadron was formed and set about providing each Sabre squadron with a signals troop to enable better communications while on operations. The Gulf War in 1991 led to the deployment of one SASR squadron in support of the Allied Coalition force. This force of 110 men joined up with the New Zealand SAS to form the ANZAC SAS Squadron, which worked alongside British and US special forces against Iraq.

In recent years the SASR has been involved in operations in East Timor, Afghanistan and Iraq, where they performed superbly.

Essentially, the SASR draws upon the best of British and US SF doctrine, and combines and adapts it to fit Australian military requirements, which are in many areas unique.

During Operation Iraqi Freedom in 2003, the SASR deployed with specialist troops from the newly established Incident Response Regiment (IRR) based at Holsworthy, New South Wales. Its mission: to combat Iraq's WMD.

Other roles included direct support of Australia's quick reaction support force – 4RAR Commando unit; covert reconnaissance; hit and run operations; and deep strike.

Uniforms and equipment of the SASR
The SASR wear standard Australian army combat uniforms with only their sand-coloured beret, cap badge and wings differentiating them from any other conventional Australian Army unit. Standard weapons include the F-88 Austeyr assault rifle, M16A2, M249 Minimi SAW and various 40mm grenade launchers. As with the British SAS, the SASR makes good use of its Land Rover long-range patrol vehicles and operates a large fleet of specially developed vehicles, which are 6×6 rather than 4×4 in configuration. Known as the Land Rover Perentie within the SASR, this excellent vehicle is ideal for operating in Australia's vast and varied landscape, and has proved very successful in supporting the SASR in operations in Afghanistan and Iraq.

Australian operators played their part in the 2003 invasion of Iraq, known to Australians as Operation Falconer.

Austria

Austria's Gendarmerieeinsatzkommando (GEK) 'Cobra' history dates back to 1973, when a unit known as Gendarmeriekommando Bad Voslau was formed. This was in response to Palestinian terrorists who posed a threat to Jewish immigrants both living in and travelling through Austria. The unit was deployed on several occasions when terrorists seized a number of hostages and demanded millions of dollars for their safe return. In one incident, the infamous Carlos the Jackal received a large multi-million dollar ransom in exchange for the safe return of a number of ministers who had been taken hostage during a meeting of OPEC countries.

With terrorism then on the increase within Europe it was felt the current unit was inadequate for its role and that a new force was needed. In 1978, GEK 'Cobra' was formed to replace Gendarmeriekommando Bad Voslau. Its first commandant, Oberst Johannes Pechter, had close ties with Germany's GSG-9 and Israel's Sayeret Matkal and cross-trained with both of these units to ensure that his force was up to the standard of some of the best in the world.

Not content to copy everyone else for ideas, GEK has developed other skills in certain areas of anti-terrorist operations, such as ropework and building assaults. Typical weapons include the Glock 17 pistol, Steyr 5.56 AUG

Working under water is just as important as being able to operate on it, so scuba work is essential in today's special forces world.

assault rifle and Steyr 7.62 police rifle for sniping work.

Jagdkommando

The Jagdkommando is located in Wiener Neustadt, just south of Vienna, and is manned by highly motivated volunteers rather than national service conscripts. To join this elite force, volunteers must be both physically and mentally fit, with no criminal convictions. Aptitude training requires a candidate to undergo a 24km (15 mile) march in three and a half hours with a 10kg (22lb) pack and personal weapon, a 5km (3 mile) run in under 24 minutes and a suspended traverse along a 30m (100ft) sloping rope, a dive from a 10m (30ft) tower and a 30 minute non-stop swim.

After passing the initial assesment, potential commandos have to complete basic military and preparatory cadre training prior to undertaking a 22-week commando course. During this training, they learn parachuting (including free-fall), close-quarter combat, alpine operations, demolitions, sniping, amphibious warfare, first aid and survival techniques.

After completing this course, the newly qualified commandos can look forward to working with other special forces, such as their own GEK 'Cobra', the German GSG-9 and the US Delta Force.

An Austrian operator surveys a possible target through the 1.5× magnification sight on his futuristic Steyr 5.56 assault rifle.

Belgium

ESR (Specialised Reconnaissance Teams)

Although the Equipes Specialisés de Reconnaissance (ESR) were officially disbanded in June 1994, they warrant a mention as many of their former members are now assigned to the Para-commandos as instructors for future Belgian Long-Range Recce Patrol (LRRP) teams.

ESR were first formed in 1961 for the demanding role of deep reconnaissance behind enemy lines. Their primary mission was to gather intelligence data and transmit it back to their operational HQ for evaluation. The Belgian government always denied the existence of the ESR even when 12 of their members defended the Belgian Embassy in Kinshasa, Zaire, from rebel attacks. The ESR also deployed to Sarajevo as a close protection force to the Belgian General Briquemont, who was Commander-in-Chief for the 'Blue Helmets' in Sarajevo. In Somalia, 28 ESR were discreetly deployed to monitor Somali

warlords, in particular General Muhammad Said Hersi. The final operation the ESR performed before being disbanded took place in Rwanda, where they took part in Operation Silver Back – a rescue mission set up to secure the safe evacuation of European nationals.

ESI (Specialised Intervention Team)

The Escadron Special d'Intervention (ESI) was formed after the terrorist attack on Israeli athletes in Munich during the 1972 Olympic games. Originally called Le Group Diane, this was changed to ESI in 1974 to reflect the unit's operational role as an anti-terrorist force. However, despite the name change, the Belgian press still refer to the unit as 'the Diane'.

ESI doctrine is proactive rather than reactive and as a result the unit is used in an agressive way, performing both anti- and counter-terrorist roles. Not only do they take active measures to prevent terrorism they also seek out potential terrorists before they have a chance to strike within the country.

Service within ESI is voluntary and all potential candidates must undergo a tough process before they can be considered for active service. The initial selection process lasts for two weeks and has a high failure rate, with almost half the candidates failing to reach the end of the course. Those who pass the selection phase move on to three months of intensive training before they become qualified operators. ESI also allows females to serve in the unit, but only in observation and undercover roles. This operational flexibility allows the unit to perform other duties such as fighting narcotics traffickers and their criminal gangs.

ESI training involves making tactical use of high-speed vehicles in both defensive and offensive modes. Current vehicles include Mercedes sedans, unmarked vans and 4×4 Range Rovers. Weapons used include the HK MP-5, Remington 12-gauge shotguns, Sako TRG-21 7.62 sniper rifles, Glock 17s and Browning 9mm pistols.

Belgian paras take part in a NATO Reaction Force exercise in Turkey.

A Belgian commando unit practises insertion techniques during a deployment exercise.

1st Special Forces Battalion

Brazil

Rio de Janeiro is home to the 1st Special Forces Battalion, Brazil's leading special forces unit. It was formed in 1953 following the hijacking of an aircraft on an internal flight over the Amazon. In 1983, a detachment from the 1st Special Forces Battalion was assigned to anti-terrorist duties, a role that it still maintains to this day. All members of the unit are volunteers and undergo a 14-day selection course, which has a failure rate of almost 90 per cent. Those who pass then go to a 13-week counter-terrorist (CT) training course, which is held at a secret base near Rio de Janeiro.

The training undertaken is similar to that of the US Delta Force and includes parachuting, heliborne insertion, fast roping, marksmanship and close quarter combat. Teams within the CT Detachment tend to be large as they will often be required to carry out long-range patrols deep within the Brazilian rainforest. In some cases these patrols can have as many as 24 men.

Although Brazil needed US assistance to set up its original parachute training school and special forces unit, it operates independently of outside help but maintains an association with the US 1st SFOD-D, 7th Special Forces

Jungle warfare is demanding for all concerned in two ways – from the enemy and also the environment.

Group and the Portuguese GOE.

Within Brazil, the 1st Special Forces Battalion trains with other elite army units that have a counter-terrorist capability. They also work closely with the federal and state police, as well as the Brazilian Navy's GRUMEC unit.

Weapons used include the HK MP-5, M16A2, Remington M870, ENARM Pentagun, HK PSG 1 and Colt .45 pistol. In addition to firearms, the CT Detachment also practises unarmed combat with knives and machetes.

Marines from Latin America, including Brazil, often train alongside their US counterparts during multinational exercises.

Both pictures: Canadian troops and special forces, backed by the US 101st Airborne Division, US special forces and Afghan troops, recheck bombed-out cave networks in the mountains of the Tora Bora region in Afghanistan during a military operation in 2002. (Reuters/Corbis)

JTF-2 (Joint Task Force Two)

Canada

JTF-2 was set up in April 1993 following the disbandment of the Royal Canadian Mounted Police's (RCMP) Special Emergency Response Team (SERT). Reliable and accurate information about this unit is hard to verify because the Canadian Armed Forces (CAF) are reluctant to discuss its existence. This is understandable as the greatest enemy of the CAF has been constant defence cuts by its anti-military politicians. The CAF's attitude is the less known about its armed forces the better, especially special forces and their activities.

JTF-2 is secretive about its size, training, operational roles and even its location. Its estimated operational strength is around 200 operators plus support personnel, making it self-sufficient and independent. The role of JTF-2 would seem to be that of recce and counter-terrorism as the RCMP and Canadian Security Intelligence Service (CSIS) carry out all intelligence gathering both in Canada and overseas. JTF-2 works closely with the British SAS and US Delta Force, having operated with both of them in Kosovo and Afghanistan. Although JTF-2 is a relatively new unit compared to other more established Western SF organisations, there is no doubting their dedication and professionalism. Many of its operators have come from disbanded units such as the Canadian Airborne Regiment, a once proud and highly respected regiment.

Weapons used include the Colt M4, M16A2, HK MP-5, 40mm grenade launcher and Browning 9mm HP pistol.

UAT and 1st Battalion Airborne Forces

Chile

1st Battalion Airborne Forces

Chile's first involvement with special forces began in 1965 with the opening of the Parachute and Special Forces School at Peldehue. This facility had American instructors who helped form Chile's first SF unit, the 1st Battalion Airborne Forces, on 2 April 1968. It is both a special forces unit and a paratroop battalion, with a rigorous selection process. Those who pass can look forward to more training in other South American countries as well as the US.

The unit played a major part in the overthrow of the Allende regime in 1973 and then went on to fight Communist insurgents in the Andes. One parachute battalion is under Air Force control, while the Boinas Negras SF Commando Battalion is under Army command.

Weapon used include the M16, HK MP-5, Remington M870 shotgun, Colt .45, M203 40mm grenade launcher and, for close quarter combat, the Corvo (a curved jungle knife).

Unidad Anti-Terroristes (UAT)

Located near Tobalaba Airport in Santiago is Chile's UAT, a unit primarily tasked with anti-terrorist and hostage rescue duties. It has 120 operators who are sub-divided into seven-man teams. All potential recruits must undergo and complete the Chilean Army's Commando Course, which is extremely demanding.

Operators move on to advanced training, including CQB, marksmanship, unarmed combat and parachuting. Further training includes exercises with other South American special forces, as well as specialised training in the US.

Weapons used include the M16, Colt .45, 40mm grenade launcher and a variety of foreign sub-machine guns.

Special Warfare Units

China

6th Special Warfare Group
8th Special Warfare Group
12th Special Warfare SF Detachment

China has the largest armed forces in the world with approximately two million men and women serving with the People's Liberation Army (PLA) alone. They also have a large number of special forces at their disposal, who are organised into spearhead units for large-scale assaults prior to the arrival of conventional forces. These units are known in China as the 6th and 8th Special Warfare Groups. Although they are not as experienced or refined as Western special forces units, they are learning the value of such units and their role in modern warfare.

The first Chinese special forces were disaffected members of the Kuomintang Army who decided to remain on the Chinese mainland following the Nationalists' defeat and departure to Taiwan. Having been parachute-trained by US forces they quickly set about building up an impressive airborne capability of three full divisions. First seeing action in Korea, this massive force went on to oppose the Nationalist threat that prevailed during the 1960s, their primary role being key point defence and the protection of the Party elite, who greatly valued their services.

Modern Chinese special forces perform a variety of operational missions which include counter-terrorism, counter piracy,

long-range reconnaissance, sabotage, hostage rescue, hit-and-run operations and deep penetration warfare. China also has a large number of combat divers at its disposal who specialise in both inshore and offshore maritime warfare.

It is also highly probable that China has a fleet of mini-submarines for covert insertion, such as those operated by North Korea, as China's long-range airborne special forces capability is limited.

Although China is secretive about the role of its special forces and their operations over the past few decades, they have mounted a number of low-key operations in neighbouring countries for reconnaissance and intelligence gathering. Units of the Special Warfare Group were also tasked with guarding the US Orion spyplane that was forced to land in China following a collision with a Chinese fighter aircraft in 2001. This incident led to a serious political crisis, which at one stage bordered on possible military action, because China refused to release the captured US aircrew. The crisis was eventually resolved following intense diplomatic negotiations, which secured the release of both the aircraft and its crew.

Chinese nationals have also been seen in Afghanistan observing British and US forces. When questioned, they stated that they were journalists reporting on the war. However, the general opinion at the time was that they were members of a Chinese special forces recce unit sent to gather intelligence on Western forces in the region. This sort of operation was no different from that carried out by British and US special forces during the Russian occupation of Afghanistan in the 1980s. Although China procures military hardware and services from many countries, it is reluctant to discuss what equipment is purchased for its special forces. However, during its Olympic Games bid for 2008 it did seek advice from a number of Western

Chinese SF capability is rapidly expanding, much to the alarm of the West.

A 'terrorist', played by a Chinese soldier, is surrounded by special forces during an anti-terror exercise in Beijing in June 2004. (Wilson Chu/Reuters/Corbis)

governments on CT tactics, techniques and procedures for its 12th Special Warfare SF Detachment.

Weapons used include licensed copies of the Kalashnikov AK-47, AK-74, AKS-74 and Dragunov sniper rifle SVD. China has also illegally copied and produced a number of modern Western weapons, however their build quality is questionable.

Colombia

Lanceros

Colombia's special forces unit, the Lanceros, was formed in December 1955 during the 'La Violencia' civil war. The initial cadre for this unit was made up of army officers from the Colombian Army who volunteered for special forces training. These men were then sent to the US Army's Ranger School for special training in mobile warfare and counter-insurgency operations.

Having completed the training course, the officers set up an elite force of paratroopers who had the job of finding and wiping out the guerrilla fighters who were terrorising the country. This was a difficult task as Colombia's terrain is vast and varied with many natural obstacles, such as mountains and jungles, to hinder progress. The Lanceros quickly became adept at fighting in the jungle against the guerrilla forces, however they could never defeat them as, numerically, they were outnumbered.

Essentially there are three main insurgency groups active in Colombia: the ELN, EPL and FARC (*see page 56*). These groups have a combined strength of almost 5,500 guerrillas at their disposal plus some 15,000 supporters. The biggest problem for the Lanceros is narcotics traffickers, as they are well equipped with modern weapons and are seen by many of the poverty-striken Colombians as good employers. This in turn makes it hard for the Lanceros to acquire intelligence on the guerrillas operating within the Colombian drug cartels' controlled areas – the locals are well aware of what happens to anyone who opposes the drug barons.

Fortunately for the Lanceros, help is

Colombian SF operators work in highly dangerous environments and are never off duty, thanks to the drug barons who control their country. Help is often sought from the UK and US, as both these countries have a vested interest in stopping narcotics trafficking at its source.

offered from the British SAS and US special forces who provide training and equipment for them. They also mount combined operations against the drug cartels, because much of their product will end up in the UK or the US; it therefore serves their own interests as much as it does the Colombian government's.

All volunteers for the Lanceros are sent to the Escuela de Lanceros school for a ten-week course that involves marksmanship, martial arts, forced marches and training in airborne operations. In addition to this course, all candidates are trained to operate in mountain environments, as well as attending a three-week jungle course.

Although their prime mission is counter-insurgency, the Lanceros also carry out intelligence gathering operations against the drug cartels, as well as search-and-destroy missions on the well camouflaged cocaine plantations that are scattered around Colombia. Their job is not an easy one as they are small in number and have a vast area to patrol and cover.

Weapons used include the M16A2 with 40mm M203 grenade launcher, M249 Minimi SAW, HK MP-5, Glock 17, Remington M870 shotgun and Colt Commando.

AFEU

The Agrupacion de Fuerzas Especiales Urbanas (AFEU) was formed following a major terrorist attack on Bogota's Palace of Justice in November 1985. This attack involved 30 heavily armed members of the 19th April Movement (M-19) terrorist group, who decided to storm Bogota's main Criminal Court and seize over 500 hostages as an act of protest. Within this group of hostages were members of the Council of State and Supreme Court, as well as ordinary Colombian citizens. Without any warning, elements of the Colombian Army assaulted the Palace and fought a fierce gun battle with the terrorists, killing almost 20 of them in the process. However, there was a high price to pay for this operation as over 50 hostages had been killed (11 were members of the Supreme Court), as well as 11 soldiers. In response, the AFEU was formed and tasked with hostage rescue and VIP protection.

The AFEU is a small unit with around 100 operators who are drawn from various elements of the armed forces and police. It is organised into six 15-man squads, with each squad consisting of two officers and 13 operators. These squads are all under the direct command of the Commandante de las Fuerzas Armadas.

Selection for the AFEU lasts seven days and those who are accepted for operator training move to Facatativa, near Bogata, where they learn hostage rescue from aircraft, ships, buildings, buses and trains. In addition, all candidates train in sniping, EOD, fast-roping, heliborne operations and high-speed driving.

Weapons used by the AFEU include the HK MP-5, M16A2 assault rifle, M60 light machine gun, Beretta 92F pistol and Browning HP pistol.

Cuba

Cuba's Comando de Misiones Especiales (CME) is tasked with performing special operations both in Cuba and overseas. They are well trained and highly motivated operators who owe much to their former Soviet Spetsnaz instructors. CME operates under the control of the Ministry of the Interior department and has many links with subversive groups around the world.

The CME is believed to have been involved in supporting regular Cuban forces in Grenada during the 1983 US invasion. This has always been suspected because the resistance experienced by the US Armed Forces was well co-ordinated and highly effective. Since Grenada, Cuba has tried to improve its political relationship with the US, but there is still major distrust between them.

Following the terrible events of 11 September 2001 and the subsequent US operations in Afghanistan, all Al-Qaeda and Taliban forces captured in Afghanistan were sent to an infamous holding facility in American-held Cuba, known as Camp X-Ray. No doubt the CME takes great interest in this facility as it is right on their doorstep.

Weapons used by CME include the AK-47, M16, Colt Commando and AK-74.

Cuban forces undergo special training to counter terrorist attacks and are especially adept at close combat fighting.

Jaegerkorpset

Denmark

Based at Aalborg Air Base in Northern Jutland is Denmark's Jaegerkorpset (Ranger Corp LRRP – long-range reconnaissance patrol), an elite unit that is responsible for most of Denmark's counter-terrorist capability. It has a reputation for being highly skilful and capable despite its small size.

The Jaegerkorpset's operational strength is estimated at around 100 men plus support personnel and is effectively an elite Ranger-type force, which has strong links with British and US special forces. The unit was established in 1961 after a number of Danish Army Officers had passed the US Army's Ranger training course. After completing the course they went on an operational attachment with the British SAS before setting up their own training centre at Aalborg in Northern Jutland.

Candidates for the Jaegerkorpset have to undergo an eight-week patrol course, which then leads them on to further advanced training that includes parachuting, diving and airborne sniping from moving helicopters. Since Denmark has no large support helicopters of its own, it is not uncommon to see British helicopters flying over Denmark on training exercises with the Jaegerkorpset, as both countries' special forces have a good working relationship.

Although the Jaegerkorpset is small, it is no paper tiger – elements of the unit have been deployed on operational tours, some even seeing action in Afghanistan during Operation Anaconda.

Weapons used by the Jaegerkorpset include the HK MP-5, HK PSG-1 7.62 sniper rifle, HK G41, HK 13E and Remington M870 shotgun.

Whether it is SWAT (Special Weapons and Tactics) duties or calling down a helicopter, the Jaegerkorpset is ready for anything.

Egypt

Based near Cairo, Task Force 777 (TF 777) was formed in 1977 following a number of terrorist incidents that gave Egypt cause for concern. The initial force consisted of three officers, four NCOs and 40 operators who had little idea or experience of counter-terrorist operations, having previously only fought against conventional military forces.

Egypt's terrorist troubles began in 1972 when President Anwar al-Sadat ordered the expulsion of 30,000 Soviet advisors because he wished to make peace with the Israelis and, in turn, the West. This decision caused outrage among Arab terrorist groups who then saw Egypt as an enemy and vowed to attack its people.

There were two Arab terrorist groups who particularly gave Egypt cause for concern. They were the Abu Nidal Faction and the Popular Front for the Liberation of Palestine (PFLP). In 1978, TF 777 was dispatched to Cyprus following the hijacking by the PFLP of a Cyprus Air passenger aircraft en route from Cairo to Nicosia. With only an hour to prepare for such an operation, nobody had thought to notify the Cypriot Authorities of TF 777's imminent arrival; a simple mistake that was to have devastating consequences.

As the operators of TF 777 made their way across the tarmac towards the hijacked aircraft, local police units mistook them for terrorist reinforcements and opened fire. The ensuing firefight lasted for almost 80 minutes and cost the lives of 15 TF 777 operators and several Cypriots.

As bad as this incident was for TF 777, there was worse to come. The second disastrous operation occurred in 1985 when Palestinian Abu Nidal terrorists hijacked Egypt Air Flight 648 at Athens Airport and ordered the aircrew to fly to Luqa Airport in Malta. The aircraft had been hijacked as an act of revenge for Egypt's failure to protect terrorists who had seized the cruise liner Achille Lauro. Ironically, the aircraft hijacked had been the

very one used to transport the Achille Lauro terrorists in the first place.

This time around, Egypt made sure that the Maltese government was aware of TF 777's involvement and that they were on their way in a C-130. Upon arrival at Luqa Airport, TF 777 made a number of fatal mistakes. First of all, they failed to carry out any surveillance on the aircraft prior to assaulting it. Second, they failed to interview any of the hostages who had survived an attempted execution by the terrorists. Third, they failed to study blueprints of the hijacked Boeing 737 aircraft. And fourth, they had no stun grenades available for disorientating the terrorists during the initial assault phase. Instead, their plan was to use a higher charge than normal to blow a hole in the aircraft's roof, the theory being that it would create an entry hole for the operators and at the same time stun the terrorists.

The reality, however, was completely different. As the explosives were detonated, the force of the blast was so powerful that it blew six rows of seats out of their mountings, killing 20 passengers in the process. When the operators then stormed the aircraft they fired indiscriminately, killing several more passengers and injuring a number of other passengers. To escape the carnage, the remaining passengers understandably ran out of the aircraft and were cut down by snipers positioned on nearby emergency vehicles, who mistook them for terrorists. In all 57 hostages were killed, making it the worst special forces blunder ever.

Needless to say, after this incident TF 777 was temporarily disbanded pending an enquiry, but following a major change in its ranks and organisation it was allowed to reform. The new TF 777 prefers to maintain a low profile for understandable reasons and operates within Egypt as a counter-terrorist unit. In recent years, it has been involved in Egypt's civil war against the Muslim

Brotherhood and has lost a number of operators. TF 777 now trains with the US Delta force, SEALS, France's GIGN and a number of other Western units.

Equipment used by TF 777 includes Mil-8 and Westland commando helicopters, unmarked vehicles for internal police support, as well as a small number of boats. Weapons used include the HK MP-5, M16A2, Remington M870 and the AK-47.

Egyptian SF members prepare to board a US transport aircraft during a routine training exercise involving US paratroopers.

Estonia

Based in Tallinn and comprising some 30 operators is Estonia's small but highly efficient CRW force, the Special Operations Group (SOG). Although only formed in the mid-1990s, the SOG displays great determination and professionalism. Whatever it may lack in terms of operational experience is more than made up for by the enthusiasm and willingness of its members. Their desire is simple: they want to be the best SF unit in Europe. Although Estonia was a Russian satellite state up until 1991, most of its current training is provided by US special forces (usually Green Berets) under the US military assistance programme.

Candidates wishing to join SOG must be extremely fit and speak at least one foreign language. Before being considered they must first complete a one-year conscription period, which is then followed by nine months' rigorous training in disciplines such as marksmanship, rappelling, climbing, parachuting, scuba diving, unarmed combat and close protection. Parachute training commences with the Soviet static line D-5 and advances to freefall, with some candidates going on to attend courses in the US to become HALO/HAHO qualified. On completion of these courses, candidates can volunteer to undertake further specialised training in sniping, explosives and hostage rescue.

Estonian forces patrol a street in Baghdad, alongside US soldiers, as part of Multinational Corps Iraq to secure a 15km (9 mile) section of road in western Baghdad.

Weapons used by the SOG include the HK MP-5, Uzi sub-machine gun, Steyr AUG assault rifle, SIG-Sauer sniper rifle, Remington M870 shotgun and the entire range of Makarov and Tokarev combat pistols.

Finland

Although a small country, Finland is proud of its conscript military forces and wants to involve them more in peacekeeping operations as a means of providing operational training.

In 1996, the Finnish Defence Forces embarked on a new strategy that would better prepare them for any possible conflict situation. This requirement specifically identified a need for a dedicated special forces unit that would be unique within the West, as it would be the first force to feature conscript volunteers rather than regular volunteers.

Volunteers undergo psychological as well as physical tests prior to being accepted for SF training. Successful candidates undergo parachute and commando training before being declared operational. Those who volunteer for Ranger-type roles go on further courses in reconnaissance and survival, skills that the Finnish Army is renowned for.

France

Special Operations Command (Commandement des Operations Speciales – COS)

France's combat experience during the Gulf War highlighted a number of operational deficiencies in its military capabilities such as tactical assets, organic transport assets, operational procedures and command, control and communication (C3) structures.

In response, France set about creating a unified command structure that would bring Army, Navy and Air Force special operations forces under one roof, answering only to the Armed Forces Chief of Staff. The new command – COS – became operational in 1992 with a mandate: 'To plan, co-ordinate and conduct at the command level all operations carried out by units that are specifically organised, trained and equipped to attain military or paramilitary objectives as defined by the Armed Forces Chief of Staff.'

GIGN

The Groupe d'Intervention Gendarmerie Nationale (GIGN) was formed in 1974 and is one of the most active police counter-terrorist

---

Commandement des Operations Speciales

Based at Taverny, operating under the command of a Major General or an officer of equivalent rank, COS is composed of the following units:

- **1er Regiment Parachutiste d' Infanterie Marine (1er RPIMa)**
  A French Army unit that carries on the traditions of the Free French SAS units of the Second World War. Although only a battalion-sized force, it is France's primary special operations unit and is tasked with conducting SAS-type missions such as LRRP, light strike and counter-terrorism (along with GIGN). Note: despite its title it has no connection to naval infantry units.
- **Detachment ALAT Operations Speciales (DAOS)**
  The French Army's special operations aviation unit (comparable to the US 160th SOAR) and comprises two special operations helicopter squadrons. The first squadron operates Cougars and Pumas, while the second squadron operates armed Gazelles (soon to be replaced by the Eurocopter Tiger).
- **Groupement Speciale Autonome (GSA)**
  1er RPIMa and DAOS form a separate subcommand within COS known as GSA. GSA operates in a very similar manner to the US Army's Special Operations Command.
- **Commandement des Fusiliers Marins Commandos (COFUSCO)**
  The naval component of COS.
- **Goupement de Combat en Milieu Clos (GCMC)**
  A 17-man force tasked with conducting maritime counter-terrorist operations.
- **Commando Hubert CASM (Commando d'Action Sous Marine)**
  The French Navy's combat diver unit (similar to the British SBS and US Navy SEALs).
- **Division des Operations Speciales (DOS)**
  Equipped with C-130 Hercules and C-160 Transall transport aircraft.
- **Escadrille des Helicoptères Speciaux (EHS)**
  Performs special operations and Combat Search and Rescue (CSAR) missions in support of French and allied forces.
- **Commando Parachutiste de l'Air No 10 (CPA 10)**
  Provides a link between air and ground assets, for example CSAR, FAC, laser target designation and combat air traffic control.

In addition to these units, COS also has a research and development branch, an administration support staff and a sizeable group of reservists who specialise in conducting civil affairs operations.

French marines board a local fishing dhow in the Gulf of Oman as part of the war on terror to support Operation Iraqi Freedom.

French special forces prepare to seize control of *Bobo*, an MSC ship moonlighting as a suspected arms smuggler during a multi-national military exercise.

units in the world today. Consisting of only 87 operators, this small but highly efficient unit carried out over 650 operations between 1974 and 1985, freeing over 500 hostages, making over 1,000 arrests and eliminating dozens of terrorists in the process.

One of its most successful operations in recent times took place on 26 December 1994, after a group of Algerian terrorists hijacked an Air France airbus in Algiers and ordered it to fly to Marseilles. GIGN operators had hoped for a peaceful ending, but following the murder of three hostages, they had no choice but to storm the aircraft. During the successful rescue operation which freed 173 passengers unharmed, four terrorists were shot dead and nine GIGN operators wounded.

They later discovered that the terrorists had in fact planned to crash the aircraft into central Paris, a plan that thankfully failed because of GIGN.

GIGN recruits exclusively from the ranks of the Gendarmerie. Volunteers must have an exemplary record and a minimum five years' experience before being considered a potential candidate. However, even with these high standards, only seven per cent of all applicants are accepted. After entering GIGN, the new candidates attend a ten-month training course before being declared operational within one of the four 15-man groups that make up GIGN. In addition to these teams there is a command and support group, and a special hostage negotiation cell.

Although GIGN is a police unit, it operates all over the world and has seen action in Djibouti, Lebanon, New Caledonia, Sudan and the island of Comoros. To help prepare operators for such diverse deployments, GIGN trains in alpine, desert and urban conditions on a regular basis. Typical training involves parachuting, combat shooting, unarmed combat, fast driving, sniping, scuba diving and mountaineering.

Weapons used include the HK MP-5, HK-G3 assault rifle, French FAMAS assault rifle, Beretta 92F pistol, .357 Magnum revolver, Remington M870 shotgun and the Barrett .50 long-range sniper rifle.

French Foreign Legion

Based in Corsica, the Legion Etrangère (Foreign Legion) was formed in 1831 to help maintain control of the French colonies in North Africa. However, after a series of major actions it soon became clear that this highly effective force had much more potential to be exploited in other regions around the world.

US Marines and commandos of the French Foreign Legion fire each other's weapons during a live-fire training exercise at the French Commando Training Centre, Arta Beach, Djibouti.

French Foreign Legion

The Foreign Legion operates the following combat units:

- **1er Regiment Étranger de Cavalerie (1 REC)** Based at Orange, it is part of the French 6th Light Armoured Division. It consists of three armoured car companies and a mechanised APC infantry company.

- **2eme Regiment Étranger d'Infanterie (2 REI)** Based at Nîmes, it has served in virtually every French colonial campaign since its formation.

- **3eme Regiment Étranger d'Infanterie (3 REI)** Based at Kourou, in French Guiana. This unit is the Legion's jungle warfare specialist and is also responsible for the defence of the French missile launching site that is located there.

- **5eme Regiment Étranger (5 RE)** Based on French islands located in the Pacific, this unit is responsible for the French nuclear weapons test site situated on Mururoa Atoll.

- **6eme Regiment Étranger de Génie (6 REG)** Based in Plain d'Albion, this unit was formed in 1984 and provides engineer support for overseas detachments. In addition the unit also has combat swimmers and underwater EOD teams that are part of Detachment d'intervention operationnelle subaquatique.

- **2eme Regiment Étranger de Parachutistes (2 REP)** Based at Calvi in Corsica, this airborne commando regiment is a rapid deployment unit that comprises six companies who all have different combat specialities.

- **13eme Demi-brigade Legion Étranger (13 DBLE)** This half brigade is based at Djibouti in Africa and comprises an armoured car squadron, an infantry company and a support company armed with heavy machine guns, mortars and MILAN anti-tank missiles.

- **Détachment de Legion Étranger à Mayotte (DLEM)** This detachment is responsible for the island of Mayotte in the Indian Ocean.

Until 1962 its headquarters were located at Sidi Bel Abbes in Algeria, but after Algeria was granted its independence it moved to its current location in Corsica. The Foreign Legion is largely made up of foreign mercenaries and French citizens who are commanded by French officers. The only langauge allowed to be used within the Legion is French.

The Foreign Legion fought with great distinction in both World Wars and later in Indo-China. Although the Foreign Legion is not part of France's special forces ORBAT, they have been used for special forces operations around the world on behalf of France. In 1991, the Legion fought in the Gulf War as part of the Allied Coalition Force assembled against Iraq and received considerable praise for their knowledge of and expertise in desert warfare.

The Foreign Legion has also had its fair share of controversy. The most famous incident is the Algerian mutiny in 1961, which occurred after a Legion regiment mutinied in support of Algerian settlers who tried to prevent independence. Despite having an excellent combat record the regiment was disbanded in disgrace as an example to others.

In 1988, the French Army was reduced in size as France wanted an all professional army similar to the British, rather than a conscript army. As part of these cutbacks, the Legion was reduced in size to 7,500 men and withdrew from a number of its overseas bases.

The Foreign Legion carries out its own recruiting and training at Aubagne, near Marseille, by two of its regiments: 1er Regiment Étranger (1 RE) at Aubagne, which is responsible for all new recruits, and 4er Regiment Étranger (4 RE) at Casteinaudar, which is responsible for recruit and NCO training.

Aubagne is the new spiritual home of the French Foreign Legion, where its band and museum are located.

Selection and training

The Foreign Legion accepts volunteers from all over the world and currently has soldiers from over 100 different countries. In theory there are no French members, except for officers, but many get around this by stating they are French Canadian, Belgian or Swiss.

Most enlist under an alias if they are running away from something or someone, and there are always those who have a naïve romantic vision of the Legion and what they think it represents.

Once enlisted, recruits attend a demanding three-week induction course. During this period recruits are free to leave or can be discharged if found to be unsuitable. Those that survive induction have to serve for at least five months before embarking on further training with 4 RE. Here, they concentrate on physical training as well as marksmanship. There are also opportunities for specialist training in signalling and engineering.

However, for those who wish to become potential NCOs, they must attend a demanding eight-week course before promotion to corporal and a 14-week course for potential sergeants.

Weapons used by the French Foreign Legion include the FAMAS assault rifle, M249 Minimi light machine gun, Uzi SMG and HK MP-5.

Special Autonomous Group (Groupement Speciale Autonome – GSA)

Based at Pau, the GSA is an independent Army command within COS. The unit consists of the DAOS special operations aviation unit, the 1er RPIMa and three support units, research and development, personnel, training and logistics. GSA is commanded by a Brigadier General and operates under the direct control of COS.

GSA is tasked with acting as a link between the French Army and COS, and is responsible for sourcing and developing new equipment for French Special Forces. It plans training exercises, provides admin support, helps develop joint special operations doctrine and ensures that new equipment is compatible with that already in use with other services.

French Foreign Legion in the Ivory Coast.

Germany

KSK

Based at Calw in Baden-Wurttemberg, the Kommando Spezialkrafte (KSK) was initially formed in 1995 to protect or rescue German nationals at risk in overseas conflicts. At present the unit is currently working up to its Brigade status strength of 1,000 fully trained operators, but still has some way to go before achieving this figure.

The impetus for forming the KSK dates back to 1994 when Germany found itself unable to rescue 11 of its nationals who were trapped in Rwanda during the civil war because it had no suitably trained force available. Fortunately for the Germans, help was at hand in the shape of Belgian and French paratroopers who were able to rescue them. The German government was highly embarrassed over this incident and

appointed a senior Army Brigadier to oversee the formation and development of a new special forces unit that would have an operational capability similar to that of the British SAS or US Delta Force. The Brigadier recognised that his force would have to be capable of rapid deployment anywhere in the world at a moment's notice and that it would have to be capable of operating in any terrain, be it arctic, desert or jungle. He also understood that forming such a unit from scratch would be no easy task, so where possible he used existing soldiers who were mature and experienced.

Even though KSK is trained for hostage rescue operations it is a military unit, trained for military operations, and not another GSG-9 type counter-terrorist force (*see pages 123–5*).

Members of the KSK carry out a boarding against a suspect vessel in the Arabian gulf.

Although GSG-9 is an excellent unit, it is a Federal Border Guards unit, restricted by German law from operating overseas on military-type missions. It did, however, break this law in 1977 when it carried out a spectacular rescue mission in Mogadishu, Somalia. This restriction also applies to other elite German police units such as the SEKs (SWAT type units). KSK was initially formed from soldiers of the army's two Long Range Scout Companies which were part of the three Cold War-era West German airborne brigades' commando companies. The unit comprises an HQ, four commando companies, an LRRC, a communications company and a logistics company. Each fighting company has four platoons, one of which specialises in hostage rescue within Germany and overseas. Platoons also specialise in different areas such as airborne and amphibious operations, ground infiltration, and arctic or mountainous warfare.

As with many other special forces units, KSK operates on the tried-and-tested four-man team principle, with the LRRC operating as many as 40 four-man teams at a given time, each capable of operating independently of each other.

Should an emergency develop overseas involving German nationals or interests, KSK would deploy and operate under the control of the German Crisis Section and would be capable of conducting missions such as deep penetration raids, strategic reconnaissance, hostage rescue, counter-terrorist operations, peacekeeping, rescue and recovery of downed pilots, military crisis deterrence operations and defence of German or NATO territory.

Although KSK has the means of attacking high value targets such as enemy airfields, HQS and lines of communication, its main operational priority is to protect German citizens in war or conflict zones, and hostage rescue.

Even though KSK is not fully up to strength, it still has more than enough trained operators to undertake low-level operations, as demonstrated in 1999, when a detachment from KSK deployed to Kosovo as a close protection detail for high-ranking German officials. In 2001 a small force was deployed to Afghanistan following the abduction of a number of German nationals by the Taliban. They were, however, released unharmed after intense diplomatic pressure was brought to bear on the Taliban rulers before they were deposed. KSK is also known to have provided protection for German government officials taking part in the G8 summits, as these meetings involve high-level VIPs and are seen as possible terrorist targets.

When KSK declares itself fully operational, it will be organised according to the box (left).

Weapons and equipment used by the KSK include HK-G36 5.56 assault rifles, HK MP-5 SD3 9mm SMGs, HK-G8 assault rifles, HK-512 12-gauge shotguns, G22 sniper rifles, P8 9mm pistols, HK PII underwater pistols, HK-21 5.56mm LMGs, HK-23 7.62mm LMGs, MG3 7.62mm GPMGs, MILAN and Panzerfaust 3 anti-tank weapons. Operators also have access to night vision sights, tactical lights and laser aiming devices.

Vehicles used by the KSK include Mercedes Benz G wagons, unmarked cars and Unimog 2 tonne trucks. Operators also practise insertion and extraction techniques using German Luftwaffe Bell 212s and Sikorsky CH-53s.

KSK ORBAT

- **HQ and Signal Company** – HQ Platoon, 3 Signal Platoons, Long Range Recon Signal Platoon (all operators are trained in SATCOM, HF, LOS communication).

- **Commando/Long-Range Recon Company** – HQ element, Long Range Recon Commando Platoon, Long Range Recon Platoon.

Each Commando Company consists of the following:

- HQ Platoon
- Four Commando Platoons, each specialising in different operational areas:
1st – Land Infiltration
2nd – Air Infiltration (HALO capable)
3rd – Amphibious Operations

4th – Mountainous and Arctic climate operations

Each platoon consists of four teams of four men each. Each of the four men specialise in one of the following areas: communications, medical, explosives or operations and intelligence, with one of the men acting as team leader. One of the four platoons is trained in conducting hostage rescue and counter-terrorist operations, with some operators trained in high-speed defensive and offensive driving.

Support Company – Logistics Platoon, Parachute Equipment Platoon, Maintenance and Repair Platoon, Medical Platoon and Training Platoon

KSK selection and training

Unlike many special forces units, the KSK are remarkably open about their selection criteria considering most of their training courses were developed in consultation with the UK, France and the US.

To become a KSK operator takes about three years and includes HALO/HAHO and scuba training. The initial selection process and basic training phase for new recruits lasts for three months and is broadly based on the British SAS and US Delta Force system.

Before a potential recruit can undergo KSK training he must meet the following criteria:
- Officers must be under 30 years of age and NCOs under 32
- Candidates must be airborne qualified
- Candidates can come from any part of the army
- Candidates must volunteer for at least six years of service with the KSK
- Combat officers and senior NCOs must successfully complete Einzelkaempferlehrgang 1, an advanced training course

The selection process takes place at the KSK's Blackwood training centre, which is located at Calw, and involves:
1. 1-day psychological test (which involves a computer assisted process)
2. 1-week selection phase
3. 2 days of physical fitness testing (1 minute maximum situps, 1 minute push-ups, 3 × 10m sprints, stand jumping and 12-minute run); a 500m swim in under 15 minutes; complete a standard German military assault course in less than 1 minute 40 seconds; complete a 7km (4 mile) field run with 20kg (45lb) backpack in under 52 minutes
4. Additional psychological tests (3 days).

Candidates who successfully pass the basic screening and selection course then go on to more advanced specialised training courses such as:
- Basic Commando Training
- 1 week of Survival, Evasion, Resistance and Escape (SERE) training under extreme and demanding conditions which require the candidate to complete a 100km (60 mile) march in 4 days with full combat kit. During this march candidates will be required to carry out abseiling, river crossings, map reading by day and night, and contact drills
- Further psychological screening
- Basic Commando Training II
- 3-week combat survival course at the International Long Range Recon Patrol School, which is located at Pfullendorf.

Once this training is completed candidates are then assigned to an operational KSK team, where they will have many opportunities to work with other special forces units such as the British SAS and US Delta Force.

A KSK machine gunner sights his weapon during a training exercise. Note how effective his flectarn smock and helmet are in this type of foliage.

GSG-9

Grenzschutzgruppe 9 (GSG-9) was formed in response to the Munich Olympics massacre in 1972. The tragic loss of so many lives was put down to the German police and their lack of preparation and training for dealing with hostage rescue situations, prompting the creation of GSG-9, a dedicated counter-terrorist force.

At its peak GSG-9 had an operational strength of almost 250 operators. However, this figure has now reduced down to some

200 regular personnel as Germany now has the additional resources of KSK and local police SWAT teams.

The formation of these new units has given GSG-9 great cause for concern as it has meant their future has been in doubt on a number of occasions. Some Germans take the view that GSG-9 is simply not needed anymore, as KSK can handle hostage rescue and counter-terrorist operations both in Germany and overseas, and have the legal mandate to do so. And members of GSG-9 are legally forbidden from deploying overseas on counter-terrorist operations (although they have been allowed to break this law on a number of occasions, as witnessed by their spectacular Mogadishu operation).

For GSG-9, Mogadishu was their finest hour. On 18 October 1977, GSG-9 operators stormed a Lufthansa airliner at Mogadishu airport, killing three Palestinian terrorists and wounding one other without any losses to their own operators or the hostages on board the aircraft. The operation had been well planned and executed, and had taken the terrorists completely by surprise. In part, this success was also down to the British SAS, who provided two highly trained operators. These SAS operators were equipped with stun grenades and various assault weapons (one, in fact, shot and wounded a female terrorist during the assault).

The success of this operation also led to a very close relationship being formed with the British SAS, a relationship that is still strong to this day.

A GSG-9 operator sights his weapon during a training exercise. His HK features a short magazine rather than a 30-round one because GSG-9 are a police unit as opposed to a military one.

The many faces of combat training, practised by all until they are second nature. Members of GSG-9 can come from the military police, so live firing practice (below) is vital.

Members of the unit are all volunteers, either from the German Army or border police and undergo six months of arduous training before being declared operational. In addition to the physical training, operators are expected to have a good knowledge of both police and legal matters, with great emphasis placed on further academic studies. The failure rate of potential candidates is high, with only 20 per cent of each intake being accepted. These demanding standards have made GSG-9 an outstanding counter-terrorist force in the world today, and although their future path is uncertain they have many friends around the world who greatly admire and respect their capabilities.

Weapons used by the GSG-9 include the HK MP-5, SIG SG 551-1P 5.56mm special operations assault rifle, HK 7.62mm G8 assault rifle and HK PSG-1, Mauser SP86, Mauser SP66 sniper rifles. Pistols include the Ruger .357 magnum revolver, 9mm Glock 17, HK P7, P9, P9S, Walther P5 and P88 models.

GSG-9 also operates a large fleet of both marked and unmarked vehicles such as the Mercedes 280, which have special modifications that allow operators to fire through the windscreen while the car is on the move. In addition to vehicles and small boats, GSG-9 has its own aviation group, the Bundesgrenzschutz-Fliegergruppe, which has some of Germany's best pilots in its ranks.

Greece

Greek special forces are among the most modern in the world and are capable of mounting land, sea and air operations on an impressive scale. Although not in the same league as the British and American special forces in terms of operations carried out in recent years, they do have the longest recorded history of unconventional warfare, their first mission being the Trojan Horse operation.

The Hellenic special forces organisation was formed in Egypt, following the Battle of Crete in May 1941, which forced the Hellenic Government to flee Greece and reform elsewhere in the Middle East. In order to retake Crete, the Hellenic Army formed a number of new military units that were capable of operating in a commando-type role against the occupying German and Italian forces. One of these units was the 'Company of the Chosen Immortals', which

was established in August 1942 under the command of Major Stephanakis. Although only 200-strong when formed, this unit operated in North Africa with the British SAS and quickly gained a fearsome reputation for its raiding techniques.

The unit was later renamed the 'The Sacred Company', a title that has been used on four prior occasions within the Greek Army. After their success in North Africa, 'The Sacred Company' redeployed to Italy and the Dodecanese where they fought many succesful actions until their disbandment at the end of the Second World War.

During the 1945–50 Greek civil war, many ex-members of the Sacred Company fought as a raiding force in a manner very similar to that of the British SAS and SBS. In 1946, a Mountain Raiding Warfare Company was formed to deal with armed communist

A Greek SF soldier familiarises himself with the Spanish G36E rifle as part of a multi-national exercise to enable different NATO countries to train to use each other's weaponry.

A squad of Greek Marines disembark from a Spanish UH-1 helicopter during a training exercise.

groups that were active in the mountain areas. Eventually their operational strength grew to 40 companies which remained active until the end of the revolt in 1950.

After the civil war ended the Greeks decided to retain a special forces capability and, with American help, they set about creating a Parachute School at Aspropyrgos in Attica near Athens. In addition to airborne forces, the Greeks also set up specialist maritime units that operate under the command of the Special Forces Directorate in Thessaloniki.

During the Turkish invasion of Cyprus in 1974, Greek special forces fought running battles against Turkish forces until a ceasefire was negotiated by the UN which eventually led to the partitioning of the country. It was a costly war both in political and human terms with 33 Greek special forces losing their lives for a conflict that could have been avoided.

The Greek special forces are an all volunteer force and are organised as follows:

- The Special Forces Directorate
- 1 Ranger Regiment
- 1 Marine Brigade
- 1 Parachute Regiment
- 1 Special Operations Command

Although Greece and Turkey have entered dialogue over the future of Cyprus, there have been a number of incidents in recent years that have almost taken the two countries to the brink of war again. The Greeks are very mindful of Turkey's military capability and have spent a lot of time and effort in recent years expanding and modernising their special forces in preparation for any possible threat.

In 2004 they mounted their biggest operation to date, after they were charged with the task of providing security and protection for the Olympic Games when Greece was the host nation. This was a considerable undertaking as there were serious concerns over a possible terrorist attack by Al-Qaeda, who had already struck Madrid just a few months earlier.

Although their caution was well justified, they were also mindful of the need not to panic or alarm the athletes or visitors entering the country, as they were the key to the success of the event. The Greek special forces had worked tirelessly with other foreign units to perfect their tactics, techniques and procedures during the months that preceded the event, and the Olympics passed off without incident.

Weapons used by the Greek special forces include the M16A2 assault rifle with M203 grenade launcher, Colt M4 assault rifle, M249 light machine gun and HK MP-5.

India

India's Special Rangers Group (SRG) is a combination of military and police units. Its members are tasked with mounting anti-terrorist operations throughout India and its border areas near Kashmir.

It is a massive force consisting of some 7,000 personnel who are drawn from a variety of military and police backgrounds and reflect India's ethnic mix.

The SRG has been involved in numerous actions in recent years, including the seige of the Golden Temple at Amritsar in 1986 by Sikh militants, and on-going counter-insurgency operations against terrorists and drug traffickers. In addition to these roles, the SRG also provides protection for VIPs during high-level state visits.

An Indian–US special forces team races to board an Indian Air Force Mi-17 helicopter for combined heliborne operations.

India's temples are often the subject of attack, so India's Special Ranger Group is regularly tasked with their protection.

Iran

Iran's original special forces unit, the 25th Airborne Brigade, was set up with American assistance in the early 1970s and operated as part of the Iranian Imperial Armed Forces. However, following the fall of the Shah of Iran in 1979, the unit was disbanded with many of its former members forced into exile in the West.

Those who stayed behind in Iran helped form a Special Forces Division comprising several new units. Some operated under the command and control of different elements of the Iranian Armed Forces, such as the regular army, the Bassidjis (irregular forces) and the Pasdaran (Islamic Revolutionary Guards).

During the Iran–Iraq War, elements of the special forces supported the Revolutionary Guard in offensive operations but achieved little success as their skills were wasted on large-scale assaults, rather than small surgical actions. Since the war's end, Iranian special forces have operated in Lebanon (training Hizbullah guerrillas), Bosnia (gathering intelligence on US forces) and Sudan (training soldiers in sabotage and infiltration techniques).

At present, the Iranian special forces are working up their capabilities, in anticipation of a possible attack against their country, vis-à-vis their nuclear research facilities which have alarmed the West. Matters are not helped by Iran's perpetual support of terrorist groups – operating both in Afghanistan and Iraq.

Weapons known to be used by the Iranian Special Forces Division include the M16 assault rifle, AK-47 assault rifle, AK-74 assault rifle, SVD sniper rifle and RPG-7.

Iranian special forces are often unaware of US spy planes flying high above them.

Iraq

Among all the world's special forces there can be few that expose themselves to as much danger on a daily basis as that endured by the newly formed Iraqi National Guard Special Forces Unit.

Created after the fall of Saddam Hussein, the Iraqi special forces have taken on a job that precious few in the West would ever contemplate. Born out of the Iraqi National Guard, which was itself only formed in 2003, following the disbandment of the Iraqi Army, the Special Forces Unit is essentially made up of the best recruits who have passed the National Guard's selection and training process – which is very basic to say the least.

Compared to Western special forces, these troops are not in the same league from a training or equipment point of view, but in terms of enthusiasm, attitude, determination and sheer courage, they are certainly on a level playing field.

Life expectancy within the Iraqi special forces is short and dozens of Iraqi police officers and National Guard personnel are killed or injured every week by terrorist insurgents.

The role of the Iraqi special forces is to spearhead operations in advance of other forces. They clear routes, carry out house-to-

An emerging elite unit within the Iraqi security forces, the SWAT team plays a key role in restoring security and stability in Northern Babil province.

house searches, protect VIPs and provide assault troops during British and American military operations, the most infamous so far being the assault on Fallujah.

Typically, they wear old-style US desert battle dress uniforms (BDUs) or blue urban combats. It is also not uncommon for them to be seen wearing face masks, as these help disguise their identity – extremely necessary as they, and indeed their families, are high priority targets for terrorists.

It has often been argued within the US military that the Iraqi Army should have been kept intact, until the Ba'athist members within its ranks had been routed out, thereby leaving a viable force available to fight the Sunni and foreign terrorists before they had a chance to gain a hold. But equally it can be argued that, had they done this, the Shi'as would have risen up; they despised the Iraqi Army with a passion when it was under the command of Saddam. It is for this reason the National Guard Special Forces Unit was created, as they are generally perceived by most Iraqis as being neutral.

At present, weaponry is limited to AK-47 assault rifles and RPK light support weapons, occasionally they get more exotic Western weaponry, but this is rare.

US **Marines train Iraqi Security Force soldiers in marksmanship as part of the Combat Leaders Course.**

Army Rangers Wing

Ireland

Based at the Curragh Camp in County Kildare, Southern Ireland, is the Irish counter-terrorist and special operations unit, the Sciathan Fianoglach an Airm (Army Rangers Wing). Although small in number (100–125 operators) this unit more than makes up for its personnel deficiency by having high quality operators who are professional and extremely well trained. The Army Rangers Wing was first formed in the early 1970s, after a cadre of around 25 suitable candidates from the Irish Army were sent over to Fort Benning, Georgia in the US for special forces training. Once it had been set up this unit made contact with a number of other police and special forces units to exchange ideas on hostage rescue and counter-terrorist operations.

Although the UK has a close relationship with the Republic of Ireland and provides specialised military training to the Irish Armed Forces in a number of key areas, this excludes contact and operational training with the SAS as the political situation in Northern Ireland is still too sensitive.

Operational roles set out for the Army Rangers Wing include counter-terrorism, sabotage, VIP protection, counter-insurgency operations, raiding, hostage rescue and covert reconnaissance. Despite the small size of the Irish Armed Forces (18,000 regular and 22,000 reservists), the Army Rangers Wing plays an important part in supporting the UN on peacekeeping operations throughout the world and are on short notice to deploy, should a crisis develop.

Potential recruits for the Army Rangers Wing are required to pass an arduous four-week selection course before being considered for the Rangers' six-month basic skills course, which includes weapons and explosives, hostage rescue training, combat medicine, CQB, survival training, mountaineering, long-range patrolling and basic parachuting.

After completion of this course, candidates can volunteer for more specialized training courses such as HAHO/HALO operations, fast-roping, EOD, combat diving, boat handling, amphibious operations and sniper training.

Weapons used include the Austrian 5.56 Steyr AUG, M16 with M203 grenade launcher, SIG P-226 pistol, Remington 870, Accuracy International AI 96 sniper rifle and HK MP-5.

A sniper of the Irish Rangers shows off his ghillie suit – effective but cumbersome.

Israel

Israel's special forces are amongst the most active and proficient in the world, and they have to be as Israel lives under a perpetual cloud of bloodshed and violence. The roots of Israel's special forces history can be traced back to the 1930s, after Captain Charles Orde Wingate formed special night squads to fight an anti-guerrilla war against Arab intruders.

During the Second World War, Palestinian Jews fought against the Axis forces in Eritrea as part of the British 51st Middle East Commando and the Special Interrogation Group in North Africa. After failing to defeat the Israelis in the 1948–49 war, the Arabs changed their tactics and began mounting covert infiltration operations into Israel. The Arab guerrillas usually entered the country through the large and open Negev desert as it was very hard for the Israeli forces to defend it with their limited resources.

To help combat these infiltrations, Israel formed a number of special units, among them Unit 101, a small formation of some 60 volunteers who trained for night fighting. However, after less than four months the unit was disbanded and its members were incorporated into the first Israeli Defence

Force (IDF) regiment, the 890th. This regiment eventually became the 202nd Parachute Brigade, a unit that greatly distinguished itself during the Battle of the Mitla Pass in October 1956 and subsequent spearhead actions.

Despite Israel's numerous successes against the Arab marauders, raids still took place that caused confidence and safety issues among Israeli citizens, prompting the formation of special anti-guerrilla units. One of the most effective units was the Shaked (Almond) reconnaissance unit, which became the first mobile Sayeret (Reconnaissance Company).

The Sayeret consisted of six teams, each manned by five soldiers, a driver and an officer as commander. Shaked became the first Sayeret to pursue terrorists through the desert using helicopters, however these operations were reactive rather than proactive. To stem the raids, Israel formed a special hit squad known as Shefifon (Rattlesnake), which performed missions on behalf of IDF Intelligence.

After the Six Day War in 1967, Israel formed several Sayerets, one for each of their territorial commands. These Sayerets included Shaked, Carob (specialising in unconventional warfare

Israeli operators move forward cautiously against a known terrorist position, with all weapons made ready in case of a contact.

Israeli operators hard at work during a typical day. Many are Palestinian Israelis rather than Jewish Israelis, but that often makes no difference to the terrorists.

in the Jordan Valley) and Walnut which was based in the north. During the 1968–70 War of Attrition, the Sayerets carried out numerous deep penetration raids against the Arabs, while in the 1973 Yom Kippur War they fought in a more traditional manner carrying out both reconnaissance and anti-commando missions.

After the war ended most of the older Sayerets were disbanded. However, because of their great reputation and valued skills, every regular brigade in the IDF has since formed a specialised reconnaissance unit.

Sayeret Golani

One of the most famous units was the Sayeret Golani, which was formed in 1959 from the 1st Golani Infantry Brigade, Special Reconnaissance Platoon (also known as the Flying Leopards Unit). In combat they have proven to be a great asset as their fighting capabilities extend far beyond that of a normal dedicated reconnaissance unit. They have seen action in Israel, Lebanon, Beirut, Syria and even Uganda as part of the Entebbe operation.

Sayeret Golani fought its first action in January 1960 at Tewfiq, in the Golan Heights, against Syrian mortar positions. Similar actions followed which enhanced the unit's

reputation to an almost legendary status. In the 1967 war, the unit fought alongside the Golani Brigade when they successfully assaulted the feared Syrian redoubt at Tel Fahar in the Golan Heights.

During the War of Attrition, Sayeret Golani fought against PLO guerillas in the Lebanese 'Fatahland' and Gaza Strip in what was a long and frustrating operation. However, their most spectacular action took place during the latter stages of the 1973 Yom Kippur War, when they fought their way up the slopes of Mount Hermon to retake a strategic listening post that had fallen into the hands of the elite Syrian 82nd Paratroop Regiment. During the vicious nine-hour battle that ensued, 55 Golani soldiers were killed and a further 79 wounded before the Syrians eventually surrendered the position, making it a very costly victory. Among those killed was Sayeret leader Captain Vinnick (posthumously advanced to the rank of Major), who was mortally wounded during the initial phase of the attack, yet continued to direct his men right up until he was removed from the battlefield by medics.

Sayeret Golani also played a major part during the Israeli invasion of Lebanon in June 1982, where they captured Beaufort Castle (located on top of a gorge) in a daring night assault, which cost them their leader.

Yet despite many impressive victories, Sayeret Golani is still engaged in ongoing operations against Hizbollah in South Lebanon and the PLO in the Gaza Strip. In 2002, the unit found itself under intense pressure to stop Palestinian suicide bombers from entering Israel and carrying out attacks against Israeli citizens. In response Sayeret Golani, along with many other elements of the IDF, entered Palestinian territory and mounted a series of operations to flush out the terrorists. Although certain aspects of the operation were successful, the terrorist attacks still continued.

Sayeret Golani are very selective about their members and employ a gruelling selection process to weed out unsuitable candidates. After completion of the Gibush (selection phase), successful candidates move on to an intensive training course that lasts for almost 20 months. Skills covered include parachuting, escape and evasion, weapons familiarisation (including enemy weapons), demolitions, survival, intelligence gathering and, of course, long-range reconnaissance. In addition, Sayeret Golani also has its own urban warfare training centre, which is known as Hell Town. Those who pass training receive the badge of Sayeret, a small pin with a flying tiger as an emblem.

Sayeret Matkal (GHQ Recon)

Formed in the late 1960s as a special commando force within the IDF's GHQ Intelligence Corps, the Sayeret Matkal or Unit 269 (General Staff Reconnaissance) is a highly secretive force that has carried out many daring and often spectacular military operations since its formation, the most famous being the Entebbe rescue in 1976.

Although much of its history is unknown, some of its operations are public knowledge, such as the rescue mission performed in 1972 at Lod Airport following the hijacking of a Belgian Sabena airliner, where four Black September terrorists were killed and all of the passengers were rescued unharmed.

Barely a month later, Unit 269 carried out a daring commando operation in Lebanon and kidnapped five high-level Syrian intelligence officers, the idea being to trade them for three Israeli pilots who were being held captive. In April 1973, following the murder of Israeli athletes during the Munich Olympic Games, the unit carried out a retaliation attack in Beirut against a significant number of high-ranking PLO officials in which many were killed or seriously wounded.

Although only a small unit, Sayeret Matkal operates on the A-team principle as used by the British SAS and US Delta Force. Officially the unit is under the command of the Intelligence Branch, however its commander answers to the Chief of Staff directly.

Potential candidates for Sayeret Matkal are hand-picked from the IDF, as well as reservists and regular conscripts. Former members include several major generals, two chiefs of staff and two prime ministers.

Sayeret Tzanhanim

Sayeret Tzanhanim is a highly trained commando force that is similar in capability to the US Army's Ranger Force. The unit is capable of mounting both airborne and ground insertion operations, and has conducted numerous long-range patrols within Lebanon since the Israeli invasion in 1982.

During the Gibush phase of training, which lasts for three days and rigorously tests the mental and physical stamina of potential recruits, only about 24 out of 100 candidates will pass. Once through selection, recruits face the gruelling Masaa Kumta or Beret March, an exercise that requires a 90km (50 miles approximately) forced march with full kit over rough terrain.

Although Sayeret Tzanhanim has participated in many operations since its inception, its most famous mission was the raid on the airport at Entebbe in Uganda, in which it supported Sayeret Matkal in the rescue of 103 Jewish and Israeli hostages. During the operation, Sayeret Tzanhanim was responsible for securing the airport against possible attack from the Ugandan Army and

Many terrorist or dissident groups attract women to their cause, who are trained just as fastidiously as any man – and hence are of equal threat to the special forces.

for placing beacons on the airport's runways as there were no lights to guide the C-130s.

During Operation Law and Order, Sayeret Tzanhanin terminated a Shi'ite Hizbollah terrorist cell that was operating from the town of Maidun in a bloody action that featured point-blank use of RPGs, .50 calibre machine guns and light anti-tank weapon (LAW) rockets. During the battle over 50 terrorists were killed, as well as two Sayeret Tzanhanim officers and one NCO, along with dozens wounded.

Unit 5707

Based at Palmahim Air Force Base, Unit 5707 is a highly effective army unit that specialises in both pre-bombardment intelligence and post-bombardment bomb damage assessments. The unit was formed in 1996 following air operations in Lebanon where it was proving difficult to bomb terrorists after they had fired their ground-to-ground rockets at Israeli targets and then gone into hiding in highly populated areas where retaliation carpet bombing was impossible.

The role of Unit 5707 is to covertly infiltrate populated areas and gather intelligence on where terrorists are hiding. Once a target has been positively identified, the unit waits until there are no civilians about and then calls in a precision air strike.

The unit uses state-of-the-art advanced infra-red and low light level imaging systems to provide real time Bomb Damage Assessments (BDAS) to aircrew and operational command centres. On occasion, the presence of Unit 5707 personnel on the ground has meant terrorists fleeing safe houses in vehicles can be targeted by both ground and air units. Also, if a tactical situation warrants it, Unit 5707 can be tasked with searching building wreckage and the bodies of dead terrorists for useful intelligence.

Unit 5707 consists of four teams, each manned by eight soldiers armed with either M16 assault rifles with M203 grenade launchers or Colt M4 assault rifles.

The unit is probably unique in its operational capabilities and operates primarily in Lebanon.

Shaldag

Unit 5101 – or Shaldag – is primarily tasked with targeting enemy fixed facilities, such as buildings, communications towers, bunkers and ammunition dumps, for Israeli ground attack aircraft and helicopter gunships. In addition to fixed ground targets, Shaldag can also attack moving targets such as boats and vehicles.

For precision air strikes, Shaldag uses high energy laser designators that paint potential targets with a beam that can be tracked by aircraft-launched, laser-guided bombs or Hellfire missiles fired from the AH-64 Apache helicopter.

Due to the unit's excellent infiltration skills, it is often used for roles such as long-range reconnaissance, counter-terrorism and hostage rescue. Shaldag is based at Palmahaim Air Base and consists of some 40 soldiers divided into five teams, each manned by eight operators.

Shaldag is considered an elite unit and as such all of its members have to undergo a rigorous selection and training programme comparable to that of Sayeret Matkal and Sayeret Tzanhanim. Shaldag's training course lasts for almost 20 months and consists of long marches, navigation, communications, weapons handling and tactical forward air control.

The unit proved its worth during the 1996 Lebanon operation when it located mobile rocket launchers that had been firing on Israeli settlements located near the border. Once the targets were identified, air strikes were called in and the launchers were destroyed.

Weapons used by Shaldag include the M16 assault rifle with M203 40mm grenade launcher, Colt M4 assault rifle, Mauser SR 82 sniper rifle, Glock 17 pistol and SIG-Sauer P228 pistol.

Parachute Reconnaissance (Sayeret)

Israel's first cadre of budding paratroopers were trained in Czechoslovakia in 1948, with the first IDF parachute unit forming in 1949. In 1955 the first Parachute Reconnaissance Sayeret was created following the formation of the first (202nd) Parachute Brigade.

Most of the unit's initial volunteers were from the disbanded Unit 101 and 890th Parachute Battalion. The Parachute Reconnaissance unit lost no time in gaining its operational spurs as it soon found itself involved in a number of anti-terrorist operations that gave the new soldiers combat experience. During the 1956 Sinai Campaign, the unit fought as a separate force in the fierce battle for the Mitla Pass.

Following the formation of the 35th Parachute Brigade in 1964, the Recon unit became an elite within an elite. In 1967 the Brigade fought in a series of battles around Rafa Junction, with the Recon Sayeret leading from the front. However, it was the War of Attrition which brought the Sayeret into prominence following a number of daring commando raids deep within Egypt (in some cases these raids extended almost 300km – 200 miles – into enemy territory).

During the Yom Kippur War, the Sayeret fought alongside the brigade in the Sinai against the Egyptian A-Saiqa. These actions often took place on both sides of the Suez Canal and were very costly in human terms. In 1976 the unit took part in the raid on Entebbe along with a number of other Sayerets.

During the 1982 war in Lebanon, the Para Recon Sayeret used boats to infiltrate enemy territory via the Awali River, where they encountered stiff resistance from the PLO while moving towards Beirut. Like many of Israel's special units, the Parachute Recon Sayeret is engaged in almost constant operations against both PLO and Hizbollah guerillas.

Weapons used by the Sayeret include the Galil assault rifle, IMI Tavor CTAR 21 assault rifle, IMI Tavor VTAR assault rifle, M16 assault rifle, Colt M4 assault rifle, AK-47 assault rifle, Colt-Commando assault rifle, mini Uzi sub-machine gun, M249 SAW light machine gun, FN MAG medium machine gun, Browning M2 .50 heavy machine gun, M203 40mm grenade launcher and Gill/Spike anti-tank missile system.

Caesarea

Israel's Caesarea is a special operations hit squad tasked with the elimination of commanders, controllers and financiers of Israel's enemies abroad. Although disbanded some years ago, after a failed assassination attempt on Hamas leader Khaled Masha'al, the unit was reactivated again in September 2002, following a serious upsurge in violence against Israeli citizens and members of its armed forces by Palestinian terrorists belonging to the terrorist groups Islamic Jihad and Hamas.

Despite almost two years of perpetual violence in which hundreds of Israelis were either killed or injured by suicide bombers, the cycle of death continued, leaving the Israeli government and its security advisors with no choice but to take drastic action against the terrorists and their supporters.

Caesarea is currently headed up by former army commando and agent Meir Dagan who operates under the command and control of the Israeli intelligence service, Mossad.

According to Mossad, Islamic extremists living abroad will become as vulnerable to attack as those killed by the IDF in the West Bank and Gaza, and with Mossad's reputation that is likely to be the case.

Caesarea comprises some 30 highly trained fighters from within the Israeli security services. The squad is generally made up of former commandos who are fluent in at least one foreign language and have the ability to blend into new environments without attracting attention. For security reasons their faces are never shown, even to other Mossad agents, and many of them live as 'Sleepers' in foreign countries. For many Caesarea agents serving out their tour of duty, years can pass by without any mission, but once activated their reactions are immediate and precise.

As the selection criteria for joining Mossad is extremely demanding, with only one applicant in every 1,000 receiving an employment offer, it comes as little surprise that, within this already specialised group, only one candidate in 100 will make a Caesarea operative. Once deployed on operations and regardless of the numbers involved, only the best Caesarea agent within the hit squad will be allowed to carry out the hit.

Although much of Caesarea's operational history is highly classified, they are known to have killed the Palestinian terrorists responsible for the murder of 11 Israeli athletes during the 1972 Munich Olympics, with further operations sanctioned in Lebanon, Syria and Iraq.

The Caesarea mission statement is very simple: whatever they can't kill, they close down.

Italy

GIS

The Gruppo d'Intervento Speziale (GIS) was formed in 1978 and is one of the world's most active counter-terrorist units. Consisting of only 100 highly trained operators who are drawn from the Carabinieri, the GIS is constantly engaged in operations against the Sicilian Mafia, the Red Brigade and other criminal organisations.

Becoming an operator within the GIS is hard, with almost 40 per cent of candidates failing the entry test alone. These tests involve exhaustive security checks, medical tests, psychiatric tests and intensive questioning by senior GIS officers. Those who pass then move on to a two-week selection process, followed by a ten-month course that includes high-speed driving (on Ferrari's test track), combat shooting and CQB.

Although most operations take place out of the public eye, in May 1997 the GIS carried out an assault on the 100m (325ft) belltower in St Mark's Square, Venice in front of millions of TV viewers following its occupation by ten Italian separatists. GIS operators using helicopters and ground forces eventually removed the terrorists by force.

Weapons used by the GIS include: the HK MP-5, Beretta SC70/90 5.56 assault rifle, HK PSG-1 sniper rifle, Mauser SP86 7.62 sniper rifle,

Italian GIS operators show off their range of weaponry.

Barret M82 .50 long-range sniper rifle, Franchi SPAS 12 and 15 12-gauge combat shotgun, .357 magnum revolver and Beretta 92 SB pistol.

Folgore Parachute Brigade

Based in Pisa, the Folgore Parachute Brigade is a permanent part of the Italian field army. It is composed of a parachute infantry regiment (two battalions), an artillery battalion, a Carabinieri battalion, an aviation flight, an engineer company, a signal company plus an administration support unit, all of which are air-portable.

The airborne Carabinieri has a long history dating back to the First World War (it was disbanded in 1942 but reformed in 1951). In 1975 the unit was named the Tuscania 1st Airborne Carabinieri Battalion and then became part of the Folgore Airborne Brigade. Although an airborne unit, most operations have been conducted against the Mafia using a fleet of armoured personnel carriers – highly unusual for paratroopers, but very necessary under the circumstances. The unit is also trained in anti-terrorist and anti-guerrilla warfare and has participated in UN peacekeeping missions.

Weapons used by the Folgore Parachute Brigade include the Beretta SCP 90 assault rifle, Beretta AR70/90 light machine gun, Beretta 92F pistol and M2 .50 heavy machine gun.

An Italian Marine provides security, while the remainder of the team safely boards a local cargo dhow via fast-rope to conduct a search of the vessel.

Special Assault Team

Japan

The Special Assault Team (SAT) is Japan's counter-terrorist unit and was formed in April 1996, following a number of terrorist attacks by the Japanese Red Army. The most well-known attack was, however, perpetrated by the Japanese Aum Shiri Kyo religious sect who carried out a deadly Sarin gas attack on the Tokyo subway in 1995, which killed 12 and wounded over 5,500. Fearing further attacks on their cities, the Japanese government decided to act swiftly and set up a SAT platoon within each of their seven prefectures (comparable to a state or province).

In total, the SAT has ten platoons, each consisting of 20 operators, giving it an operational force of 200 personnel. The SAT is actually part of the Japanese National Police and not the military, as they are forbidden to have such a force. Although little is known of them, or their capabilities outside Japan, they are considered to be well trained and equipped and have cross-trained with the French GIGN. Their biggest operation was in 2002, when Japan and South Korea co-hosted the Football World Cup. During this event they were tasked with protecting the various football teams and their VIP visitors, as there were great fears for the footballers' safety following the events of 11 September 2001.

Japanese Ground Self Defense Force Rangers practise their roping drills from a UH-1 Huey helicopter.

Jordan

SOU 17 is Jordan's primary counter-terrorist unit and is part of the Special Forces Brigade which was formed in 1971. The Hashemite Kingdom of Jordan boasts one of the best trained and motivated armies in the Middle East, and its special forces are the best of the best within the Royal Jordanian Army.

The Jordanian special forces can trace their history back to 1963, when a company-sized force was recruited from loyal Bedouin tribesmen who volunteered to undergo parachute training and form an elite unit. This unit was of battalion strength (about 700 men) and came under the authority of the Royal Jordanian Special Operations Command.

The SOU fought a series of actions against Palestinian guerillas at Wachdat and Amman during the Black September crisis in 1970, and proved to be formidable fighters. In the early 1970s the newly formed Special Forces Brigade also found themselves involved in clashes with the Palestinian guerrillas and foiled a number of their attacks.

In recent years Jordan has formed a closer relationship with Israel, which in turn has caused anger and unrest amongst some of its citizens, especially those who sympathise with the Palestinian cause. This unrest has led to a massive increase in counter-terrorist operations throughout Jordan by both SOU 17 and other units of the Special Forces Brigade.

SOU 17 operators are highly professional and cross-train with numerous other counter-terrorist forces such as the British SAS, French GIGN, Egypt's Task Force 777 and the US 1st SOF. Training includes sniping, demolition, heliborne assaults and CQB.

Weapons and equipment used by SOU 17 include the HK MP-5, M16 A2 assault rifle and M203 grenade launcher, Colt M4 Carbine, Browning HP pistol and M60 machine gun.

Through training in close quarters battle (CQB) or unarmed combat techniques, SF operators can turn their hands and feet into deadly weapons.

Lebanon

Lebanon has a number of special forces units within its armed forces, most of which are airborne trained and well equipped for modern warfare. Their primary unit is the Israeli-trained 101st Parachute Company, which is responsible for counter-insurgency operations and internal security. Following the 1989 Taif Agreement, in which Lebanon received substantial military training and equipment from the US, UK and Israel, the country has gone from civil war to relative stability in a very short period of time.

Israel has worked very closely with some of the Lebanese special forces as they share a common enemy, the PLO. One of these units, the Red Berets, has seen action against Hizbollah guerrillas in the Syrian controlled Beka'a Valley in 1997, and against Islamic terrorists in the Dinnieh hills where they performed well.

Lebanon's special forces history dates back to the 1920s, when the French formed the Troupes Speciales du Levant in Syria and Lebanon. In the early 1950s, the first commando battalion was formed, but eventually disintegrated during the civil war because of internal sectarian issues.

Once these problems had been resolved the Israelis stepped in and helped form the 101st Parachute Company. Selection and training standards for the 101st are comparable to those of the Israeli paratroopers who train them.

Weapons used by the 101st Parachute Company include the AK-47 assault rifle, AK-74 assault rifle, M16 assault rifle, Colt commando assault rifle, HK MP-5, Browning HP pistol and M60 medium machine gun.

Lebanon is keen to keep terrorism out of the country, having suffered a decade of violence during the 1980s – hence the tough training for its special forces personnel.

Republican Guard

Libya

The Republican Guard is Libya's main special forces unit and was set up with the help of Russian Spetsnatz instructors. Libya does not have a counter-terrorist capability as such, since terrorist groups such as the IRA and the PLO have used the country as an overseas training base and view Libya as a friend and not an enemy.

However, things may change in light of Libya's admission that its agents carried out the bombing of Pan-Am Flight 103 over Lockerbie in Scotland, which killed hundreds of innocent people. Libya has now offered compensation to the victims' families as an act of goodwill.

However, the West feels that this gesture is being used as a means to lever them (the West) into lifting all UN-imposed economic sanctions which have crippled the country If the sanctions are lifted however, there will be conditions, one of which would be the total cessation of links to known terrorist organisations around the world. Should Libya totally comply with these conditions, there is a strong likelihood that its former terrorist friends may turn on the country, leading to the possibility of terrorist attacks against Libyan nationals or interests.

Should this happen, Libya has a considerable force of some 19 para/commando battalions at its disposal, plus the Republican Guard, which operates at Brigade strength.

Although little is known of the Republican Guard in the West, it can be assumed that its training includes counter-insurgency, sabotage, VIP protection, hostage rescue and Russian-style deep penetration attacks using massive force.

Libya is desperate to lose its pariah status, and has recently purchased a significant quantity of weapons and equipment from the West in exchange for its oil. The West also has its own agenda for Libya, viewing its territory as a good strategic location for a US Forward Operations Base (FOB). To illustrate this point, only recently the British Prime Minister, Tony Blair, visited the country and was protected by both Libyan bodyguards and members of the British SAS.

Weapons used by the Republican Guard include the AK-74 assault rifle, AK-47 assault rifle, RPK light machine gun, Type 74 medium machine gun and RPG-7 man-portable anti-tank rocket launcher (which can also be used against low flying helicopters).

Force F – 'Zorros'

Mexico

Based north of Mexico City is the counter-terrorist unit, Force F, or 'Zorros'. Although Force F is a police unit, it models itself heavily on military-style units and is equipped accordingly. The unit comprises some 350 well-trained commandos who are all experts in a specific discipline such as weapons handling, CQB, hostage rescue, sniping, bomb disposal or communications.

Typical missions include hostage rescue, bomb disposal, counter-terrorism and anti-narcotics.

Weapons used by Force F include the HK MP-5, M16A2 assault rifle, CAR-15 assault rifle, Smith and Wesson 12-gauge shotgun and Beretta 9mm pistols.

The unit also has its own fleet of armoured vehicles and helicopters.

Royal Guard

Morocco

The Royal Guard was formed in response to a requirement for a highly trained unit capable of rapid deployment. To meet this need the Royal Guard consists of one infantry battalion that is mechanised and two cavalry squadrons that are capable of reconnaissance and light strike roles.

Most aspects of the Moroccan armed forces have a French influence as many of its soldiers served in the French Army up until 1956, including their special forces. At present, Morocco has two paratroop brigades and six commando battalions in service,

along with a number of specialised support units.

During the Yom Kippur War, a force of Moroccan para commandos under Syrian command fought against the Israelis on the slopes of Mount Hermon in the Golan Heights.

In 1976, elements of the Moroccan special forces fought Mauritian forces in Western Sahara and the Polisario around Bir Enzaran. In addition to these actions, Moroccan commando units also deployed to Zaire in 1977 for a large-scale operation.

The Netherlands

BBE

The Bijzondere Bijstands Eenheid (BBE – Close Combat Unit) is Holland's main counter-terrorist unit. The BBE is highly unusual in that it is an ad hoc unit, formed only when needed for terrorist-related incidents. The unit is made up of around 100 volunteers, who are drawn from the elite Royal Dutch Marines and make up a force of three platoons, which are then subdivided into five-man teams, with each platoon containing specialists in EOD, sniping, communications and combat medicine. Potential candidates wishing to join the BBE have to undergo 48 weeks of intensive training before they are accepted into this small but highly professional unit.

In addition to the Marines, the BBE has a group of psychologists available who specialise in hostage situations and are available at short notice. The BBE has seen action on a number of occasions, the first being in October 1977 when the unit regained control of Scheverngen prison following a

A BBE **operator practising point and shoot firing techniques.**

revolt by interned Palestinian terrorists. Even though the terrorists were armed, the BBE only used stun grenades and hand-to-hand combat, preferring to capture rather than kill.

The most famous BBE operation, however, was on 11 June 1977, when a group of South Moluccan terrorists seized over 200 hostages and held them captive aboard a train and in a school house. Under cover of a spectacular diversion, which involved two F-104 Starfighters buzzing the train at low altitude and at supersonic speed (resulting in the terrorists being disoriented by the sonic boom), a simultaneous assault took place on both the train and the school house. During the assault on the train, which involved members of the British SAS in support, the BBE killed six terrorists and, unfortunately, two hostages, before they were able to free the remaining hostages.

In the early 1990s, members of the BBE were deployed to the Adriatic as boarding parties ready to search ships attempting to break the Serbian arms embargo; however, they were never used.

Weapons used by the BBE include the HK MP-5, HK-G3 assault rifle, Steyr SSG, SIG-Sauer P-226 pistol and Colt .357 magnum revolver.

Korps Commandotroepen (KCT)

The Netherlands, like many countries in Europe, lives under the constant threat of terrorism, but unlike most of its neighbours it has a very capable and highly trained deterrent, the KCT.

KCT comprises three commando companies (104, 105 and 108) and is a dedicated special forces company tasked with the planning and execution of special operations during times of crisis. One unusual aspect of the KCT is the fact that all three companies have their own counter-terrorism teams as part of their ORBAT, along with other specialists who are experts in all aspects of infiltration.

A Dutch Marine applies face paint in preparation for a beach landing.

This system works extremely well as it gives the Dutch Government and its armed forces a greater flexibility in the planning and conducting of both proactive and reactive missions against terrorist cells operating in Holland and indeed overseas.

The KCT is well placed to quickly respond to a crisis and works very closely with the 11th Air Mobile Brigade, as well as other units within the Dutch Armed Forces. The skill levels within each team are very high with each team consisting of two demolition experts, two snipers, two communication specialists and two medics.

Training requirements for the KCT are extremely demanding, with each

Above: A Dutch Marine tackles his parachute down after jumping from a C-17 aircraft as part of a joint air assault exercise with US Marines and other foreign forces to enhance proficiency in air delivery operations.

Right: Making radio contact during a live firing exercise.

potential recruit having to go through 12 months of commando training if they are already serving soldiers and 14 months for those who volunteer from civilian life. This training is split into preparatory training (depending on experience, this is either four or 12 weeks), 14 weeks of basic commando training and 26 weeks of advanced commando training. Those who make it as far as phase two receive the coveted green beret and go on to complete the final 26-week phase, which involves operational training and the requisite skills that go with it such as free-fall parachuting, combat driving, sniping, demolitions, medical and communications.

New Zealand

Based at Whenuapai, and consisting of only five Troops (120 men) and an HQ, is New Zealand's small but highly effective 1st Special Air Service Squadron. The NZSAS was first formed in 1954 to operate alongside the British SAS during the 'Malayan Emergency', however problems with selection and training delayed this deployment until 1957. After serving with distinction in Malaya the unit disbanded. It then reformed, but at Troop strength only.

Kiwis get everywhere, so it's no surprise to find them serving both within and alongside British forces. One New Zealander was even a member of the infamous 'Bravo Two-Zero' SAS patrol in the first Gulf War in 1991.

After the Malayan deployment the NZSAS tried to increase its numbers, but was unsuccessful as the Defence department preferred them to remain a small but well trained unit. They did, however, allow them to undergo parachute training in Australia prior to New Zealand forming its own training school near Auckland.

In 1962, New Zealand sent a small detachment of around 35 men to Korat in Thailand to work alongside US forces who were training the Thai Rangers in anti-guerrilla warfare. Then in 1963 the Squadron changed its name to the 1st SAS Rangers Squadron (SRS) in commemoration of two ranger formations that fought in the Maori Wars.

The next deployment for the unit was in Brunei in 1965, where they fought alongside the British SAS against Indonesian insurgents, an experience that would prove invaluable as the unit soon found itself fighting in Vietnam in support of the Australian SAS Squadron that was deployed there. From their first deployment to Vietnam in November 1968 to their withdrawal in February 1971, each Troop from the Squadron served out a one-year tour before being rotated, which ensured maximum operational efficiency. The SRS fought with great distinction in Vietnam and gained enormous respect from their enemies, the North Vietnamese Army (NVA).

In 1978, the designation of the unit was changed yet again, from the 1st SAS Rangers Squadron to the 1st SAS Squadron, which was at that time based in Papakura. In 1991, the Australian and New Zealand SAS linked up again to form the ANZAC element of the Allied Coalition Force which fought against Iraq during the Gulf War. Following the terrible events of 11 September 2001, elements of the 1st SAS Squadron were deployed to Afghanistan in support of the Australian and British SAS who were engaged in a series of operations against the Al-Qaeda and

New Zealand is just one of the countries in the multinational Combined Task Force One Five Zero (CTF-150), which boards suspect shipping in the war on terrorism. Here, a fast-rope is used to load the boarding team quickly into an RHIB (Rigid Hull Inflatable Boat).

Taliban forces. The Kiwis (the nickname for New Zealanders) were highly praised in the US for their hard work in Afghanistan; however, the New Zealand government was heavily criticised for failing to give them enough funding for manpower and equipment during this long and difficult operation.

New Zealand is very secretive about its SAS Squadron and refuses to discuss any aspects of its training or operational capabilities. However, they are believed to be capable of the following missions: counter-terrorism, long-range reconnaissance, counter-insurgency, sabotage, hostage rescue and hit-and-run operations.

Selection and training requirements for the NZSAS are every bit as tough and demanding as their Australian and British

counterparts, however there are very few vacancies available each year for new recruits. Because of this shortage of places, many of the better candidates either join the British SAS directly (if eligible) or apply for an exchange posting.

Apart from training opportunities with the British and Australian SAS, the 1st SAS Squadron also cross-trains with a number of Asian countries such as Indonesia, Thailand and Singapore.

Weapons and equipment used by the 1st SAS Squadron include: the M16A2 assault rifle with M203 grenade launcher, M249 Minimi SAW, HK MP-5, PSG-1 sniper rifle, FN 7.62mm SLR and Remington M870 shotgun. The 1st SAS Squadron wear uniforms and combats very similar to the British SAS Regiment, including the famous sand-coloured beret.

Norway

The 7th Jaeger Company is part of Norway's Finnmark Regiment and plays a key role in the country's defence strategy. As a small country Norway recognises that its military capabilities are limited and that its best means of survival rests in fighting a guerrilla-type war rather than a conventional one.

The role of the 7th Jaegers is to stay behind enemy lines and cause disruption to their forces and operations by means of sabotage and harassment. Their main area of operation is likely to be in the north of Norway which is covered in snow for almost eight months of the year and is heavily forested, making it ideal for the camouflage and concealment of men and equipment.

The 7th Jaeger Company is divided into four platoons (Tropps) – a command/mortar platoon and three rifle platoons, each containing three eight-man teams. These teams are highly mobile and use cross-country skis and white Yamaha snowmobiles to carry weapons and equipment over rough terrain.

The 7th Jaegers are experts in arctic warfare and are able to survive and fight in conditions that would restrict any other force. Members of the unit are highly trained in the use of small arms, sabotage techniques, communications, survival, combat medicine, reconnaissance and hit-and-run operations.

They have to be able to operate independently for up to two weeks without resupply and should a resupply be necessary, the 7th Jaegers can call in Bell 412 helicopters from the Royal Norwegian Air Force.

Weapons used include the HK-G3 assault rifle, HK MP-5 and Vapensmia A/S NM-149 sniper rifle. Heavy weapons include the Carl Gustav 84mm anti-tank weapon, 40mm grenade launcher, RO 81mm mortar, Eryx anti-tank missile system and the Stinger MANPADS. Air support is available from RNAF F-16s.

Although most of the 7th Jaegers' training is carried out in Norway with other Norwegian units, they are known to work very closely with the British Royal Marines, who are experts in Arctic warfare.

After 9/11, Norway despatched its special forces to Afghanistan, where they served with great distinction. During Operation Anaconda, for instance, they provided a cut-off force in the mountain regions that surrounded the main area of operations to prevent any terrorists from escaping the American-led ambush.

Norway's role in this operation cannot be underestimated and their ability to deploy highly qualified personnel in such difficult and demanding conditions is admirable, as such troops are always in short supply.

Norwegian operators on patrol. Although a small force, it is highly capable in the art of maritime warfare.

Pakistan

Pakistan's Special Services Group – SSG (A) – consists of three battalions and an independent counter-terrorist company. The primary role of the SSG is to support conventional units in mounting commando operations behind enemy lines and to assist the intelligence services in counter-insurgency type missions. Other alleged roles include training guerrilla forces for operations in India and Afghanistan, something that Pakistan vehemently denies.

At present, Pakistan is supposedly committed to supporting US forces operating on the Afghan border, as Al-Qaeda is still highly active in this part of the world. In early 2004, Pakistani special forces had a number of notable successes against known terrorists who had taken to hiding in the mountains.

However, the fact still remains that some elements of the military in Pakistan are sympathetic to the terrorists' cause and have even tipped them off about US special forces, just prior to any offensive action being taken against them. It is an uneasy relationship for all concerned.

The SSG (A) is also unusual in that its missions are tasked by Pakistan's three intelligence bodies: Military Intelligence (MI), the Directorate of Inter-Services Intelligence (ISI) and the Intelligence Bureau (IB) rather than the Army.

Weapons used by the SSG (A) include the HK MP-5, Remington 870 shotgun and Glock 17 pistol. In addition to their weapons, all SSG operators are proficient in unarmed combat and various martial arts.

A Royal Anglian GPMG team in an Observation Post somewhere on the Afghan–Pakistan border. SF intelligence is key to their survival, as Pakistan often allows UK forces within its borders for such information-gathering missions.

Special Forces Regiment (Airborne)

Philippines

The Special Forces Regiment (Airborne) is the Philippines' primary special forces unit and is tasked with performing unconventional warfare, counter-insurgency and counter-terrorist operations. The SFR can trace its history back to 1962 when a unit called the Special Forces Group (Airborne) was formed following the withdrawal of US military support in 1962.

The unit had the role of home defence and counter-insurgency and grew rapidly until it was decided that the size of the unit was just too big for its intended operational role. It was then renamed the Home Defence Forces Group (Airborne) as this title was a better reflection of its capabilities. As the unit continued to develop its range of core skills, such as scuba diving and HALO parachute infiltration, it suffered a severe setback when it lost almost 70 per cent of its entire force to a peacekeeping mission in Vietnam, reducing its strength down to that of a company.

In 1973, the unit started to expand again until it reached an operational strength of five combat companies and one HQ company and reverted back to its original name, the Special Forces Group (Airborne). On 16 November 1989, the unit changed its name again this time to the Special Forces Regiment (Airborne) and became subordinate to the Special Operations Command.

The SFR's operational role is to develop, organise, train, equip and command and control indigenous paramilitary forces; to provide mobile training teams (MTT); to organise, train and advise cadres of conventional forces tasked to administer paramilitary forces; to conduct denial operations to prevent enemy access, influence and control over a particular area of strategic value; to perform psychological operations (PSYOPS), civil action operations and humanitarian assistance; to provide strike operations by SF or jointly with indigenous troops; to provide forward air control for air missions; to undertake sabotage, subversion and abduction of selected personnel; and search-and-recovery operations.

Although the SFR has never been involved in a large-scale conventional war with another country, its forces have been involved in numerous contacts with guerrilla insurgents and pirate marauders who rob and kidnap foreign tourists.

Since 11 September 2001 the SFR, along with US special forces, has been involved in extensive combat operations against both local guerrilla forces and Al-Qaeda terrorists who fled Afghanistan.

Weapons used by the Special Forces Regiment include the M16A2 assault rifle, Colt Commando assault rifle, HK MP-5, Remington 870 shotgun, Ultimax light machine gun, M249 SAW light machine gun, M60 medium machine gun, M203 40mm grenade launcher, 81mm mortar and M2 .50 heavy machine gun.

In recent years, the Philippines has been a hive of terrorist activity. However, due to the efforts of the US and Filipino governments, this has largely been kept in check.

Poland

Poland's Grupa Reagowania Operacyjino Mobilnego (GROM) counter-terrorist unit was only formed in 1991 and has already gained an excellent reputation within the world's special forces communities. GROM operators are recruited from other Polish special forces units such as the Army's 1st Commando Regiment and the Navy's 7th Lujcka Naval Assault Brigade.

Much of GROM's success is down to its commander, Colonel Slawomir Petelicki, a man who is greatly admired and respected for his dedication and high standards.

GROM is very security conscious, although its combat force is believed to number some 250 operatives plus support personnel. As well as standard military training, GROM operatives must speak at least two langauges and have good medical skills. In fact almost 75 per cent of GROM's personnel are either paramedic or nurse qualified and as such provide excellent support for the unit's doctors. GROM also has female operatives who carry out intelligence gathering and surveillance, both in Poland and overseas.

Generally GROM operates in four-man assault teams in the same manner as the British SAS, with specialised support teams available for tasks such as EOD. These teams are often run by former operators who have

GROM **operators prepare to assault a house in an urban training facility.**

been either injured or are too old for operational service but want to continue serving with the unit.

All members of GROM must have high standards in weapons handling as all training is carried out using live ammunition. Training is made as realistic as possible to ensure sharp reactions and often involves mock assaults on ships, aircraft and buildings.

In 1994, GROM was selected to participate in Operation Restore Democracy, the American-led invasion of Haiti. Prior to this operation, 55 members of the unit were sent to Puerto Rico to train with members of the US 3rd Special Forces Group. While there, they were briefed in Haitian politics and social systems to help them understand the need for the operation. On arrival in Haiti, GROM operators were tasked with providing security for several VIPs, including UN General Secretary Butros Butros Ghali and US Secretary of Defense William Perry. While in Haiti they

A GROM **operator gets down and dirty – the best place to be, as you are a smaller target.**

A GROM team gets into a defensive position in the port of Umm Qasr at the height of Operation Iraqi Freedom.

took part in a hostage rescue operation, which involved storming a building, putting out a blaze and rescuing a young boy who had been taken hostage by a group of heavily armed gunmen. The boy was freed without any bloodshed and as a result GROM received enormous praise for its actions, earning Commander Colonel Petelicki the US Army Commendation Medal – the first time in American history that a foreign unit has been commended in this way.

Further operations in which GROM have participated include protecting Pope John Paul II during his visit to Poland in 1995, as well as a tour in Bosnia in 1998, during which they apprehended a suspected Bosnian war criminal.

US and Polish SF operators advance across an Iraqi field during Operation Iraqi Freedom.

During Operation Iraqi Freedom, GROM operatives played a key role in supporting the Allied forces' efforts both covertly and overtly. They worked primarily with the US Navy SEALS, British SBS and the Australian diving teams in and around the Iraqi deep-water port of Umm Qasr, on the Al-Faw peninsula. Operations carried out included search and control missions, the boarding and searching of Iraqi vessels, anti-sniper missions, EOD, force protection missions, overt water patrols, covert water patrols, tactical reconnaissance and urban CQB missions.

Weapons used include the HK MP-5, Tantal 5.45mm assault rifle, HK PSG-1 and Mauser 86 7.62 sniper rifles. Personal sidearm selection is at the individual operator's discretion.

Portugal

Portuguese Army Long Range Recon Patrol (LRRP) Detachment

The Portuguese Army LRRP Detachment was formed in 1996, following a major reorganisation and modernisation of the Portugese Military. The LRRP is the Portugese component of the Allied Command Europe (ACE) Mobile Force (Land) or Allied Mobile Force (AMF) as it is more commonly known. AMF is a brigade-sized unit, tasked with rapidly deploying to any military or humanitarian crisis in Europe within 72 hours.

Although the LRRP Detachment has only 48 members, it is well trained and equipped and has the ability to perform missions similar to those carried out by the British SAS or US Delta Force. The LRRP Detachment is held in high regard within AMF (L) and has participated in a number of its deployments. Typical missions include LRRP, locating enemy command and control centres, raids against high-value targets such as radar sites, POW rescue operations, aircrew recovery and targeting and destroying enemy air defence systems.

The LRRP Detachment can be inserted behind enemy lines by helicopter, parachute, vehicle, boat or foot and can operate independently for up to ten days. The LRRP Detachment is made up of a special operations platoon, communications section, medical section and a transportation section. The unit's special operations platoon comprises a six-man command section and four five-man patrols. The communications section uses state-of-the-art equipment and provides a secure link between the operational teams and HQ. Although small, the transportation section provides all vehicles needed, including moving the unit's equipment and supplies.

Most of the LRRP Detachment training takes place in Portugal, however the unit has recently deployed to Norway for Arctic Warfare training.

Weapons and equipment used include the HK-G3, HK MP-5, Uzi SMG and Israeli Galil assault rifle. The LRRP Detachment vehicle pool consists of six trucks and two all-terrain vehicles (ATVs).

GOE

The Portugese Grupo de Operacoes Especiais (GOE) was formed in December 1979, following a desire in Europe to create a counter-terrorist capability after the 1972 Munich Olympics. GOE has close ties with the British SAS and has set up its force of 150 operators in a structure that is similar to that of the SAS.

Training for GOE involves a brutal eight-month training course. Subjects covered include tubular assault (aircraft, trains and buses), house clearing, maritime operations and VIP protection.

GOE has only been involved in one operation which ended when a group of terrorists holding hostages in the Turkish Embassy in Lisbon blew themselves up along with two hostages before GOE could intervene.

Weapons and equipment used include HK MP-5, HK 502 12 gauge shotgun, HK PSG-1 7.62mm and Galil 7.62mm sniper rifles, and Browning, SIG and Glock pistols. Vehicles include modified Range Rovers and Mercedes Benz cars, fitted with platforms and hoists to make aircraft and building assaults safer and faster.

Portuguese special forces personnel have extensive experience in bush warfare – and are experts in the art of reconnaissance.

Russia

Alpha/Beta Group

Alpha and Beta Group were formed in 1974 as a part of the 7th (Surveillance) Directorate of the KGB, following an upsurge in terrorist activities both within the Soviet Union and its satellite countries. Essentially, Alpha Group is responsible for all anti-terrorist operations within Russia and its borders, while Beta Group, which models itself on Delta Force and has more or less the same role, operates abroad.

Both Alpha and Beta Group recruit their operators from specially selected Spetsnaz volunteers (*see page 155*). Candidates for both groups are subjected to a lengthy selection process, as well as nine months' basic infantry training. Additional training includes language skills, unarmed combat, reconnaissance, high-speed driving, intelligence gathering techniques, sniping, tracking, heliborne insertion and extraction techniques, as well as airborne skills (both line and HALO).

Although most of Alpha and Beta Groups' operations are classified, it is common knowledge that Alpha Group has been involved in numerous operations within Russia against organised criminal gangs and Chechen terrorists, while Beta Group has seen extensive action both in Afghanistan and Chechnya.

At the time of writing, Alpha's most infamous operation was the Moscow Theatre siege. An ill-fated rescue mission was mounted, following the storming of the theatre by Chechen terrorists – an act which netted them hundreds of innocent civilians enjoying a night out. In response, Alpha pumped the theatre full of gas, to knock everyone out. However, many inhaled lethal doses of the gas and others, namely the terrorists, not enough. The end result was massive casualties, many fatal.

In their defence, this was an extremely difficult situation for any special forces operator to handle. Many of the hostages and

A Russian special forces soldier receiving training on a man portable anti-armour weapon.

Russian Alpha operators at the height of the Moscow Theatre siege in October 2002. Despite their relative success in this operation, they were never deployed during the Beslan school incident in September 2004.

terrorists were wired up to explosive devices and under those circumstances they did well to rescue anyone alive.

Interestingly, no Russian special forces were involved in the Beslan hostage situation in 2004, despite press reports to the contrary. Indeed, the outcome may have been better for the children and their parents involved in this tragedy if they had.

Spetsnaz (Special Purpose Forces)

At the height of the Cold War, the mere mention of the word Spetsnaz would send shivers down the spines of Western soldiers, as they were the unknown and unseen enemy and had a fearsome reputation. The word Spetsnaz is taken from the Russian words *spetsialnoye naznacheniye* (special purpose). There are other names such as *reydoviki* (raid) that describes diversionary, sabotage and reconnaissance troops, but Spetsnaz is the most commonly used designation for describing Russian special forces.

Spetsnaz operate under the command and control of the Soviet General Staffs Main Intelligence Directorate (GRU – *Glavnoe Razvedyvatelnoye Upravleniye*) and has no Western equivalent. The main purpose of Spetsnaz is to carry out what the Russians term Special Reconnaissance (*spetsialnaya razvedka*), which is defined as 'reconnaissance carried out to subvert the political, economic and military potential and morale of a probable or actual enemy'. The primary missions of Special Reconnaissance are: acquiring intelligence on major economic and military installations, and either destroying them or putting them out of action; organising sabotage and acts of subversion; carrying out punitive operations against rebels; conducting propaganda; and forming and training insurgent detachments. Special Reconnaissance is conducted by the forces of covert intelligence and special purpose troops.

In more general terms, the main missions of Spetsnaz are sabotage and reconnaissance. However, they are known to have carried out insurgent training in Africa and Cuba in a manner that dates back to Soviet ideologies of the Second World War. During the Cold War their main purpose was described as Diversionary Reconnaissance (*diversiya razvedka*), which meant carrying out sabotage operations against vital Western installations, such as cruise missile sites and bridges in advance of the main attack force. Other missions envisaged at the time included laying mines on likely tank routes, killing NATO pilots in their accommodation blocks, marking suitable insertion sites for paratroopers and transport helicopters, and assassinating senior NATO commanders. Although these practices were never used in anger against Europe, many Spetsnaz tactics, techniques and procedures were tested for real during the Soviet invasion of Afghanistan in 1979, as Spetsnaz units spearheaded the main invasion force and were highly successful.

Spetsnaz units are trained to infiltrate enemy territory by many methods both overt and covert, and can operate up to 1,000km (600 miles) behind enemy lines without support. Although their primary role is to locate targets for other forces, such as paratroopers, strategic bombers and armoured units, they can if necessary launch attacks themselves. Typical targets include mobile missile sites, cruise missile bases, integrated air defence systems, radar sites, command and control facilities, airfields, ports and lines of communication.

The basic Spetsnaz unit consists of eight to ten soldiers who are commanded by an officer. Within each team there is a specialist in communications, reconnaissance, sniping and explosives, but every member of the team has a degree of cross-training, as this ensures a mission can continue even if a specialist is lost.

Modern Russian forces are structured in

operational fronts, and each contains a brigade of Spetsnaz. Each Spetsnaz brigade consists of three to five battalions, a signal company, a support unit and an HQ company, which equates to a wartime strength of some 1,300 men capable of deploying 100 operational teams.

In addition to the brigade units, most Russian armies also have a Spetsnaz presence of several companies, which gives them a force of 115 men or 15 operational teams.

Each company is organised in a similar manner to that of a brigade and contains three Spetsnaz platoons, a communications platoon and a support unit. Apart from the Brigade and Army Spetsnaz there are a numbers of other units that operate directly under the command of the GRU and Naval Spetsnaz brigade, giving a peacetime strength of some 15,000 personnel.

Known Spetsnaz units include:
- Razvedchiki – consists of one battalion divided into two companies (one for airborne and one for LRRP operations)
- Reydoviki – consists of a brigade-sized formation that operates in battalion or company-sized reconnaissance units

A Russian marine secures a beach-head during a training exercise. Note his basic equipment compared to that of a Western soldier.

• Vysotniki – consists of a brigade-sized formation that operates in small 11-man units, performing SAS-type missions

Spetsnaz selection and training requirements are extremely demanding with potential Reydoviki conscripts needing to be physically fit, intelligent and politically reliable before they will even be considered as Spetsnaz candidates. Once approved for the induction phase, conscripts have to sign a loyalty oath in which they acknowledge their awareness of the death penalty for anyone who betrays the Spetsnaz. Following on from induction, some of the brighter conscripts will be selected for NCO training at the NCO school. Those who pass the six-month long course graduate as NCOs, while those who fail revert back to the rank of private soldier.

In addition to their basic military training, all conscripts receive specialised instruction in hand-to-hand combat, silent killing techniques, parachuting, infiltration techniques, sabotage, demolition, foreign languages, survival, rappelling, sniping, reconnaissance, map reading, foreign weapons, foreign vehicle operation and foreign tactics, techniques and procedures.

During the training phase conscripts face obstacle courses and long, gruelling marches, many of which are conducted in full chemical warfare protective clothing, including gas masks.

Most of the physical training is extremely harsh, with conscripts often being denied rations so that they have to forage for food themselves. More specialised training includes mountain climbing and skiing, often in locations abroad.

Once through specialised training, the conscripts face a series of battlefield exercises which test their skills to the limit. These exercises take place in realistic environments such as mock cruise missile bases, NATO airfields and communications facilities, and involve the use of explosives and live rounds.

Since most Spetsnaz missions take place behind enemy lines, soldiers tend to be lightly armed and only carry a small selection of weaponry. A soldier will carry either an AK-74 or AN-94 assault rifle, a silenced 9mm pistol, ammunition, a knife and up to ten grenades.

In addition to personal weaponry, each team carries an SVD sniper rifle, RPG-16 grenade launcher, under-rifle grenade launcher, SA-14 MANPADS, plastic explosives, anti-personnel mines and an R-350M burst transmission radio, which has a range of some 1,000km (600 miles).

Spetsnaz units can only be successful if they have good intelligence. For this reason they report directly to the GRU and to some degree the second directorate of the front staff who is responsible for intelligence matters. Within this group there are separate departments that process agent intelligence, signals intelligence and Spetsnaz intelligence, which is normally gathered via sleeper agents within.

Although much has changed in the Russian military since the end of the Cold War, including how Spetsnaz units operate in Europe, bear in mind that despite Russia's parlous financial state, its Spetsnaz units still receive generous funding and are now training and re-equipping to operate more like the British SAS and US Delta Force.

Spetsnaz training now includes tubular work, counter-terrorism, urban warfare training (based on lessons learned in Chechnya) and mobility warfare (vehicle-based).

Airborne Assault Troops (VDV)

In terms of size and capability there is no force in the West that compares to the VDV. They are in a league of their own. Their operational role is to provide Russia with a quick response unit that is both self-contained and self-deployable in times of crisis. Although impressive in size and number by Western standards, the VDV by traditional Soviet military standards is deemed small as each division only contains some 6,000 lightly armed troops plus their armoured support vehicles. They are, however, a strategically valuable force as they have special training in airborne assault tactics and have the mobility to deploy anywhere in the world at short notice by long-range transport aircraft.

They also have a significant parachute assault capability, which dispenses with the need for an airbase as they can be inserted anywhere within airlift range in a matter of hours. However, the VDV lacks the self-sustaining combat and logistical support of regular ground forces and therefore has to be resupplied and reinforced within days of deployment.

Russian operators take a smoke break following an intense firefight in Chechnya. Note the Mexican bandit-style ammunition bandoliers they are wearing.

In the mid-1990s the Airborne Troops comprised five airborne divisions and eight air assault brigades (the former USSR had seven divisions), all of which were based in European Russia: one division in the Northern Military District, two in the Moscow Military District, and one each in the North Caucasus (this division participated in the Chechen conflict) and Volga Military Districts. The eight airborne assault brigades have a reduced combat capability compared to the divisions, as they lack artillery and armour assets, which greatly limits their heavy firepower and speed of advance. Once deployed by parachute or helicopter (their preferred method of deployment), the airborne assault brigades have to rely on speed and aggression to overcome their adversaries as reinforcements are likely to be days away.

In 1991, the Airborne Troops were designated as a separate service with direct responsibility to the Ministry of Defence via Airborne Troop HQ instead of through ground forces command and control. The rationale behind this reorganisation was that the airborne troops could not respond quickly enough under the control of a ground forces command structure. However, it later emerged that this decision came about mainly as a response to internal politics rather than any military requirement. The Russian leadership did not want airborne forces under the control of the General Staff or indeed the ground forces.

In 1992, Moscow carried out a review of its military capabilities and discovered to its horror that Russia had little or no military reserves and could only deploy to potential trouble spots with limited forces. This situation was unacceptable to the president of Russia, Boris Yeltsin, and he ordered the creation of a new Mobile Force that would be similar in capability to the Airborne Assault Troops but would have the quality and quantity of the American mobile forces. This dream force, however, never materialised and instead of creating a new force, the Airborne Troops were reorganised yet again, the net result being a reduction, rather than an enhancement, in performance.

Russia, however, still needed an Instant Deployment Force (capable of deploying in three to five days) and a Rapid Deployment Force (capable of deploying in 30 days) of some 100,000 to 150,000 men to rival NATO's rapid deployment forces such as the Allied Rapid Reaction Corps (ARRC). In 1996, a concept Mobile Force was created which on paper comprised some 100,000 men (of which 60,000 were Airborne Troops) plus motor rifle formations, naval infantry, transport aircraft and logistical support. To make this concept a reality, four of the eight independent airborne brigades and two of the five airborne divisions were placed under the command of their respective district commanders, while the three remaining divisions became part of the strategic reserve.

In late 1996, two of the airborne divisions were disbanded, which brought the total strength of the VDV down from 64,300 to 48,500 personnel, and although still an impressive figure by Western standards, the new Russian force was a shadow of the once mighty

Russia's Airborne Assault Troops (VDV)

The current ORBAT for the VDV is as follows:

- The 106th Guards parachute division holding the order of the Red Banner and the order of Kutuzov of the 2nd degree

- The 76th Guards parachute Red Banner division of Chernigov

- The 98th Guards Svirsk parachute division holding

the order of the Red Banner and the order of Kutuzov of the 2nd degree

- The 7th Guards parachute division

- The 104th Guards parachute division

- Military Schools

- The 242nd centre of training for Parachute Troops

Airborne training is an important element of VDV training.

airborne forces of the former Soviet Union.

By Russian military standards the VDV are considered an elite force, as each member of the unit is individually selected from volunteer recruits cadres. Selection criteria is based upon intelligence, loyalty and physical fitness, with candidates having to go through a series of psychological and physical tests before being accepted for airborne training.

Once accepted for parachute training, candidates are subjected to a daily routine of long and arduous physical training work-outs that are designed to build up stamina and general fitness. Discipline is harsh within the airborne forces – and it needs to be – since their operational role is extremely demanding; they are, after all, Russia's shock troops.

Every VDV soldier is trained to a high standard in personal weapons handling, with great emphasis placed on marksmanship and ammunition usage. This is a key issue during operations behind enemy lines as resupply is likely to take several days. In addition to their weapons training, VDV soldiers are also trained in hand-to-hand combat, which is an indispensable skill for

airborne forces to possess, as they might have to fend off assailants within seconds of landing on the ground.

To help build confidence and dispel the natural fear of parachuting, each soldier packs his own 'chute after completing just three jumps, the theory being that it focuses the soldier's mind. Training jumps are carried out by day and night from fixed-wing aircraft in highly realistic combat conditions, and include the use of live rounds and explosives.

The VDV have seen action in many places including Hungary, Czechoslovakia, Afghanistan, Chechnya and almost in Kosovo after a Mexican stand-off developed between them and Western forces protecting the airfield at Pristina. Thankfully, this incident ended peacefully after intense political negotiations between Russia and NATO.

Weapons used by the VDV include light tanks, APCs (mainly BMD-3s), self-propelled artillery, anti-tank and anti-aircraft artillery, MANPADS, mortars, light machine guns, medium machine guns and heavy machine guns.

Saudi Arabia

The Saudi Special Forces Brigade is made up of two airborne and airmobile battalions, which are grouped together with three parachute-trained special forces companies and a Royal Guards Regiment with three battalions. It is a complicated setup that brings about much confusion when this Brigade operates because each individual unit is under the command of a different Ministry.

The Special Forces Brigade receives considerable support from US forces in respect of specialised training and advice on special forces tactics, techniques and procedures as Saudi Arabia has little experience in operating outside its own territory.

Known operations that have involved Saudi forces include the invasion of Kuwait in 1961, when a company-strength battle group supported British Royal Marine Commandos against Iraqi forces. The other key operation occurred during the 1973 Arab-Israeli War when Saudi Special Forces operated alongside Syrian forces in the Golan Heights.

During the Gulf War in 1991, the Special Forces Brigade helped Allied Coalition forces defend key installations from possible ground attack. They are also believed to have been involved in the expulsion of Iraqi forces from Kuwait City, although this has always been denied.

In recent years, the Saudis have been fighting a bitter internal security battle against elements of Al-Qaeda, who target westerners living in the Kingdom. In 2004, Saudi Special Forces mounted a spectacular rescue operation after a number of people were taken hostage by Islamic terrorists. It would seem that such attacks are on the increase and will only be thwarted by better co-operation between other oil producing states in the region.

The Special Forces Brigade is well trained and equipped for modern warfare and is keen to play its part in protecting Saudi Arabia from any possible terrorist or conventional threat.

Weapons used by the Brigade include the HK-MP5 SMG, M16A2 assault rifle with M203 grenade launcher, M249 Minimi SAW and Remington M870 shotgun.

A USAF KC-135 tanker refuels a US Navy F/A-18C 'Hornet' in the skies over Saudi Arabia. Such exercises are key to Saudi Arabian security, where there is currently much Al-Qaeda activity in the country.

South Africa

The Special Forces Brigade was formed in 1996 and is an amalgamation of the South African 'Recce' units who served with distinction in Angola during the late 1970s and early 1980s. A specialist unit was formed in Durban in 1972 called 1 Reconnaissance Commando (Recces). The need for such a unit had long been recognised within the South African Defence Force (SADF) as the airborne forces were engaging more in conventional warfare, rather than special forces-type operations.

Set up along the same lines as the British SAS, 1 Reconnaissance Commando was tasked with mounting LRRPs deep behind enemy lines, as well as hit-and-run operations. This proved to be a capable and useful unit and quickly led to the formation of additional Recce Commandos (RC), such as 4 Recce.

In 1981, the Special Forces became an independent organisation that was answerable only to the SADF. In 1991, the HQ element of the special forces was disbanded and a Directorate of Reconnaissance formed in its place. Just as the Special Forces were adapting to their new setup, there was yet another name change; this time they were called 45 Parachute Brigade. This meant that all RC units now had to add the prefix '45' to their unit number, so that 1 Reconnaissance Commando became 451 RC.

In 1996, the Recces were subjected to another name change and became known as the Special Forces Brigade, a name they hold to this day. In terms of operational experience, there are few units around the world who can match the Recces and their formidable reputation. The Recces played a major part in 1989 in defeating the SWAPO (South West African People's Organisation) terrorist group who wanted Namibia to be separated from South Africa. The SWAPO guerrillas were well trained and were a formidable enemy. When on patrol behind their lines, the Recces painted their faces black to pass themselves off as guerrilla fighters.

In 1979, SWAPO guerrillas mounted a major attack against South African forces, but it was repulsed by the Recces and other conventional forces. In 1982, the Recces took part in Operation Mebos, a deep penetration raid within Angola that destroyed the SWAPO's HQ and much of its terrorist infrastructure. In 1994, the Recces entered Angola on horseback and cut off most of the SWAPO's supply lines, which helped bring about their defeat.

Like many special forces around the world, the Recces find themselves under constant pressure to carry out missions that are technically out of their operational remit. Their key operational role is strategic intelligence gathering, although they have performed tactical intelligence-gathering missions on numerous occasions, especially in Angola. Although a highly trained and well armed force, they are too valuable to be risked in direct combat missions and now operate more in a covert observation role.

The SADF never discusses any operational or tactical aspects of the Special Forces Brigade. However, it is known that the Recces have good experience in inserting small teams of men behind enemy lines by various means including helicopters, parachuting, horseback, small vehicles, boats and by foot.

Recce teams can vary in size, but the average size of an LRRP team would be six soldiers, with each man having a specialist combat skill. A patrol might include a tracker, sniper, medic, navigator, signaller and explosives expert.

South African operators have worked alongside those of the UK for many decades – and it's not uncommon to hear a British accent among their ranks.

South Korea

Based at Songham City, south-east of Seoul, is South Korea's prime counter-terrorist unit, the 707th Special Missions Battalion. The unit was formed in 1972 following the murder of Israeli athletes at the Munich Olympic Games. It has an operational strength of some 250 personnel. The unit is organised into six companies, four of which act as support, while the other two carry out counter-terrorist operations.

Each of the counter-terrorist companies is made up of four 14-man teams, which have additional specialists such as explosives experts and combat medics as back-up.

South Korea lives in fear of invasion constantly, so it is imperative that airborne operations are practised until they are second nature, as this is the fastest method of reinforcement from the outside.

The 707th SMB also has a team of female operatives for use in surveillance and undercover operations, as they can can be highly effective in male-dominated Korean society where women are not generally seen as a threat in crisis situations, such as aircraft hijackings. Women can move close to aircraft or board them without causing any alarm.

South Korea's biggest threat comes from its neighbour North Korea, which continues to mount clandestine operations deep within her territory. These incursions are used as a means of destabilising and intimidating the South Korean Government and the 707th SMB has been involved in several firefights with them.

The 707th SMB has also mounted operations in North Korea against key intelligence-gathering centres and sensitive military installations to prevent further attacks on South Korea. During the 1986 Asian Games, 1988 Seoul Olympic Games and the 2002 Football World Cup, the 707th SMB was tasked with protecting VIPs and key facilities.

Training requirements are stringent, with only qualified special forces personnel from other units allowed to apply. Selection and training lasts for a year and includes six months' basic infantry training and six months' special warfare training, such as parachuting, martial arts, rappelling, mountain warfare, CQB and demolition techniques.

Once qualified, new members can look forward to harsh physical training work-outs, such as swimming in freezing water without any protective clothing, as well as long runs with heavy backpacks.

The 707th SMB have one of the finest training facilities in the world, with a mock-up of a Boeing 747 airliner, multiple shooting ranges and a CQB range. The unit works closely with other Korean special forces, as well as police counter-terrorist units such as the Korean National Police Agency's SWAT team. The 707th SMB also has links with similar units around the world.

Weapons and uniform of the 707th Special Missions Battalion

The 707th SMB is extremely well funded and has access to a wide variety of foreign and locally produced weapons such as the HK MP-5, HK PSG-1 7.62mm sniper rifle, RAI .50 calibre long-range sniper rifle, Daewoo K1 and K2 assault rifles, Benelli Super-90 shotgun, Colt .45 pistol and Daewoo 9mm pistol. It also uses heavy weapons such as the M60E3 and K3 7.62 belt-fed machine gun, M203 40mm grenade launcher and the British Javelin SAM system.

All ROK special forces must reach black-belt standard in Tae Kwon-Do or a comparable martial art. Uniform consists of a black beret with a silver SF badge and standard ROK camouflage combat suits.

Spain

The Spanish Legion

The Spanish Legion (Tercio de Extranjeros – Regiment of Foreigners) is part of Spain's Rapid Reaction Force and consists of 7,000 men who are deployed as follows:
- 1st Tercio Gran Capitan (HQ Mellila) – 1st, 2nd and 3rd Banderas
- 2nd Tercio Duque de Alba (HQ Ceuta) – 4th, 5th and 6th Banderas
- 3rd Tercio Don Juan de Austria (HQ Fuerteventura, Canary Islands) – 7th and 8th Banderas and 1st light Cavalry Group
- 4th Tercio Alejandro de Farnesio (HQ Ronda in Malaga) – 9th and 10th Banderas, Banderas de Operaciones Especiales (BOEL); this SF battalion has capabilities in mountaineering, LRRP, parachuting and amphibious operations

The Spanish Legion was formed in 1920 to suppress dissidents in the protectorate of Morocco, as the Spanish conscript army at the time was struggling to keep control. The Spanish were great admirers of the French Foreign Legion and decided to form an equivalent unit, but with key differences. The French Foreign Legion consists mainly of foreigners, while the Spanish Legion is almost 90 per cent Spanish.

During the Spanish Civil War, General Franco's Nationalist forces had 18 Legion battalions available who acted as a spearhead force. After the war ended, the Legion was reduced down in size to six battalions and posted back to Morocco to continue operations against local insurgents. These operations continued until Spain granted most of Morocco its independence, apart from two enclaves in northern Morocco – Ceuta and Mellila, where Legion units are still based.

Like their French counterparts, training is harsh and at times brutal, with new recruits pushed to their physical limits. The initial training phase lasts for only three months, which for a modern day soldier is totally inadequate and is currently under review.

Spanish operators carry out a boarding exercise in readiness for performing it for real against drug smugglers off the Canary Islands in 2005.

Discipline within the Legion is strict, with frequent beatings for those who fail to adhere to the Legion's code of conduct. The Legion is an all-volunteer force, with recruits signing up for an initial three years of service, which can be extended if required. However, getting out of the Legion, legally, is almost impossible.

Although the Spanish Legion consists of four Regiments (Tercios), which each contain four Battalions (Banderas), only one has a

Practice in rigid inflatable boats (RIBS) makes perfect. Note the wide variety of weapons carried by these Spanish operators.

Special Operations role. That is the Bandera de Operaciones Especiales de la Legion (BOEL), which consists of some 500 men and is a battalion within the 4th Tercio de Alejandro Farnesio (the 4th Alexander Farnesio Regiment), which is based in Ronda.

The BOEL unit is trained in scuba, sabotage and demolition, arctic and mountain warfare, LRRP, parachute and HALO techniques and counter-terrorism.

Weapons used by the Spanish Legion include the CETME assault rifle, Ameli light machine gun and SB 40 LAG automatic grenade launcher.

The Spanish Airborne Brigade

This Brigade consists of three parachute battalions (Roger de Flor, Roger de Lauria and Ortiz de Zarate), an artillery, engineer and support battalion, as well as a highly skilled pathfinder company. The SAB is part of Spain's commitment to the Allied Rapid Reaction Corps (ARRC) and is known as the Fuerzo de Accion Rapide (FAR) – Rapid Action Force.

Spain's first parachute battalion, the 1st Airborne Bandera, was part of the Spanish Air Force until handed over to the army. It was an excellent unit, highly capable in special forces work and free-fall infiltration, and saw action in the Spanish Sahara in 1956 and in Morocco in 1958.

Weapons used include the CETME LC assault rifle, Colt-Commando assault rifle, CETME Ameli light machine gun, 40mm grenade launcher, 60mm mortar and 81mm mortar.

In 2002, when signalled to stop, the North Korean cargo vessel *So San* attempted to evade capture. Spanish special forces troops conducted a hostile boarding by helicopter and small boat. The boarding team later found 15 disassembled Scud missiles concealed by bags of cement, bound for Yemen.

SSG – Special Protection Group

Sweden

Sweden's SSG, or Forsvarsmaktens Sarskilda Skvdds Grupp as it is known in Sweden, was formed in the early 1990s as a special forces unit capable of SAS- or Delta-type operations.

Although Sweden pursues a stated policy of neutrality, its government is well aware of the threat of terrorism and has taken preventative action to ensure the safety of Swedish citizens both in Sweden and abroad. The SSG recruits primarily from Sweden's elite Ranger unit, as well as other specialised units within the Swedish military and paramilitary forces.

Sweden is very secretive about its military capabilities and has released little information about the SSG and its true operational roles. Former and current members of the unit are prevented from speaking about its size, organisation and training; they have to sign a legal document that forbids them from revealing any information about the SSG.

The name Special Protection Group implies defensive, rather than offensive operations, so it can be assumed that the unit will protect vital installations, high ranking military officials and Swedish citizens.

Apart from the Ranger training which most SSG candidates will have undertaken, new members of the unit receive training in static- line parachuting, HALO and HAHO parachuting, explosives handling, unarmed combat, sniping, VIP protection, combat diving and small boat operations.

All SSG members are trained to the same skill level before they are assigned to their respective unit. Once assigned to their unit, each new member is required to specialise in a skill such as combat diving, sniping, HAHO/HALO operations, EOD, combat medicine or communications.

SSG members also train with other special forces such as the British SAS and US Delta Force, and undertake specialist training courses both within both the UK and the US.

Weapons used by the SSG include the AK5 assault rifle, HK-MP5, PSG-90 sniper rifle and SIG P226 pistol.

A Swedish soldier, working with Multinational Brigade South, checks out a piece of kit used by the US Marines at a small base camp in Prizren, Kosovo, during Operation Dynamic Response.

Switzerland

FSK-17 is Switzerland's main special forces unit and is part of the Swiss Air Force rather than the Swiss Army. Formed in the early 1970s and originally known as the Fallschirm-Grenadiers (Parachute Grenadiers) of the Swiss Air Force, the unit changed its name in 1980 to the Fernspah-Grenadiers and was given the role of LRRP.

Despite the large title, the unit is generally known in Switzerland as FSK-17 and comprises some 100 personnel of various ranks, who are divided between three platoons, but operate in four-man teams.

Members of FSK-17 are highly trained in military skills such as intelligence gathering, demolitions, CQB, survival skills and parachuting, both static-line and freefall. In fact, FSK-17 has pioneered its own 'Tactical Diamond' insertion technique.

Weapons used by FSK-17 include the HK-MP5, Sig-P228 pistol and various knives and grenades.

Swiss operators practise watermanship skills during a training exercise.

14th Special Forces Division

Syria

The Syrian Armed Forces probably have the best trained and equipped army in the Arab world, with a legendary special forces capability. Within Syria the special forces are known as the Al-Wahdat al-Khassa (Special Units) and operate under the umbrella of the 14th Special Forces Division. This is based in Lebanon with its four special forces regiments: the 35th, 46th, 54th and 55th, which are all located in the Beirut area. There is also the 44th Special Forces Regiment near Shikka, the 53rd south of Haibi near Tripoli, and the 41st and 804th east of Juniya. Each regiment consists of three para-trained companies, which are supported by an anti-tank company, an 82mm-mortar company and a machine-gun platoon.

In addition to the 14th Special Forces Division, Syria also has an airborne rapid deployment brigade and the Saraya al Difa (Syria Defence Companies), which is a small paratroop battalion. Since their formation in 1958, the Syrian Special Forces have fought in numerous actions against Israel, the most famous being the assault on the Israeli Defence Force monitoring station on top of Mount Hermon in the Golan Heights during the Yom Kippur War. Elements of the 14th SFD also fought against the PLO in Lebanon and

Syrian special forces have a fearsome reputation in the Middle East – as Israel knows to its cost.

performed extremely well considering the difficult urban conditions in which they had to operate.

Since 2003, Syria's special forces have been on a high state of alert due to fears of an American backlash on account of Syria's support for insurgents operating in Iraq. The us has also made it clear that Syria is one of a growing number of countries that is on its hit list – unless, of course, the country changes its attitude towards terrorism.

Selection and training standards within the Syrian special forces are extremely high, with only the best and most reliable soldiers from its armed forces put forward for consideration as possible commandos. These forces bear comparison with the finest worldwide.

Weapons used by the 14th Special Forces Group include the AK-74 assault rifle, AK-47 assault rifle, M23/25, SSG69 sniper rifle and RPG-7.

1st Special Forces Group

Taiwan

Taiwan's special forces were initially formed after the end of the Second World War with us help and eventually resulted in the formation of the 1st Special Forces Group in 1958.

Since then, a number of other units have been formed including:
• The 1st Peace Preservation Police Corps Special Weapons and Tactics Unit (SWAT)
• The 100-strong Military Police Special Service Company

• The 100-strong Airborne and Special Warfare Command Special Operations Unit (trains with both Delta Force and the us Rangers)
• The 100-strong Chinese Marine Corps Special Operations Unit (responsible for maritime security)

All these units operate under the direct command and control of Security Task Force HQ, which is answerable to the prime minister of Taiwan.

Turkey

With almost a million personnel at its disposal, Turkey has one of the largest armed forces in the world, making it a key member of NATO. It also has a large number of special forces able to deploy at very short notice for overseas operations.

Turkey's special forces organisation consists of three airborne brigades, each containing 5,000 men, and one counter-terrorist battalion of some 150 operators.

Because of its NATO membership, much of Turkey's special forces equipment and training is based on Western standards, such as those of the British SAS and US Delta Force. Turkey's special forces history dates back to 1949 when US forces began supplying and training the Turkish Army. This eventually lead to the formation of the 1st Airborne Platoon of the Guards Regiment, which was followed in 1958 by a 2nd Airborne Platoon and in 1963 by a 3rd platoon.

All of these units saw extensive action in 1974 during the Turkish invasion of Cyprus, which quickly led to the formation of two further brigades. After further reorganisation within the Turkish armed forces, the brigades' responsibilities were split again between one airborne, one para-commando and one para-marine, with each one having its own support company and, in the case of the airborne brigade, its own artillery company.

At present, Turkey's special forces are working more and more with other European special forces because they are all facing the growing threat of Islamic terrorism. In the case of Turkey, a supporter of the US-led war on terrorism, it has been a recent victim of terrorist outrages and it has no intention of letting the situation continue.

Other threats come from the Kurds, who are again voicing their anger over promises as to their future wealth and destiny, made by the US at the start of Operation Iraqi Freedom. These issues will not be quickly resolved, and so Turkey's special forces will be on alert for the foreseeable future at least.

US **Marines transport Turkish soldiers in their Zodiacs as part of multinational ship-to-shore familiarisation training during a** NATO **exercise.**

United Kingdom

AIR CAVALRY

16 Air Assault Brigade

The UK's 16 Air Assault Brigade (AAB) was formed in 2000 and is a lethal combination of air assault infantry and attack helicopters. Its awesome capabilities bring a new meaning to the term manoeuvre warfare. It has both the means and method of rapidly inserting a large, well-equipped force deep behind enemy lines at very short notice by day or night and in all weather.

Although originally conceived as a hard-hitting mobile tank-killing force (when it was 24 Airmobile), its capabilities have grown to encompass many other missions such as hostage rescue, seizure of strategic assets, infiltration and extraction of Allied forces, counter-penetration, flank protection, raids on key targets, humanitarian aid and civil aid.

The unique capabilities of 16 AAB allow it to attack from any direction; concentrate, disperse or redeploy rapidly; delay a larger force without becoming decisively engaged; provide responsive reserve and reaction forces; react rapidly to tactical opportunities; place forces at natural choke points; provide surveillance and target acquisition; react to rear threats; bypass enemy positions; facilitate surprise and deception; and rapidly reinforce committed areas.

The Brigade has an operational strength of some 10,000 personnel and comprises:
- An HQ and Signals squadron – HQ is responsible for direction and co-ordination of air assault operations, while the parachute-deployable 216 Signal Squadron's responsibility is to establish and maintain communications between all elements of 16 AAB.
- Pathfinder Platoon – responsible for reconnaissance, marking of helicopter landing zones and parachute drop zones.
- 3rd, 4th and 9th Army Air Corps Regiments – responsible for reconnaissance (using Gazelles), anti-tank operations (Lynx and

A Landrover from 16 Air Assault Brigade practises 'Eagle patrol' tactics with a Lynx helicopter prior to Operation Telic.

Apache) and light utility support (using Lynx). At present 16 AAB is scaled for 48 Apache Longbow attack helicopters (with each regiment operating two squadrons of eight helicopters).
- Air Assault Infantry Battalions – three battalions are assigned to 16 AAB, of which two are always from the Parachute Regiment. Within each battalion there are five companies: three rifle, one support and one HQ. Fire-power levels are extremely impressive. Each battalion has 80 GPMGs, 14 .50 calibre Browning heavy machine guns, nine 81mm mortars and 16 MILAN anti-tank missile systems.
- 7th Para, RHA (Royal Horse Artillery) – directly supports 16 AAB with three batteries (each with six guns) of 105mm light guns.
- 21st Defence Battery, RA (Royal Artillery) – provides air defence for the Brigade (with Javelin and Starstreak MANPADS).
- 9th Parachute Squadron, RE (Royal Engineers) – provides engineering support.
- Household Cavalry Regiment (HCR) – provides medium reconnaissance as and when required with three troops of four Scimitar armoured reconnaissance vehicles.

- 47 Air Despatch Regiment – responsible for managing and packing equipment into aircraft.
- The Parachute Regiment provides two of the three infantry battalions assigned to 16 AAB.
- RAF Support Helicopter Force – provides 18 Chinooks and 18 Pumas for mobility (the RAF also provides 16 AAB with C-130 Hercules transport aircraft as and when required).

In 2003, 16 AAB deployed to Iraq as part of Operation Telic and was heavily involved in intensive high tempo actions to secure oil fields in the south of Iraq; there were fears that Iraqi militants would blow them up as part of a strategy to hinder allied forces.

The mission was extremely successful and led to calls for the Brigade to be deployed elsewhere in Iraq. These requests were largely ignored by the British Government as they were keen to avoid mission creep. The 16 AAB did, however, make an exception in the case of operations centred around Basra, following an increase in attacks by Fedayeen insurgents.

Other operations during this period included: mounting 'Eagle patrols' to deny the enemy movement and attack opportunities; mounting sweep-and-clear missions to hunt down ringleaders and supporters of Saddam's regime; and house-to-house weapons searches, conducted primarily at night.

Following major combat operations in Iraq, 16 AAB returned to the UK, where it is now currently working up its capabilities in anticipation of future military operations.

47 Squadron (Special Forces Flight) RAF

Primarily based at RAF Lyneham, Wiltshire, 47 Squadron RAF is tasked with providing the UK's special forces with a dedicated long-range transport capability. The squadron operates a small fleet of specially modified C-130

Hercules transport aircraft that are equipped with terrain-following-radar (TFR) systems that enable aircraft to fly at very low levels and in all weathers.

The aircraft are also well equipped with a comprehensive defensive aid suite that consists of anti-missile flares, chaff and electronic sensors capable of detecting incoming SAMS.

Aircrews assigned to 47 Squadron are screened for their ability to fly at low level for prolonged periods of time. This can cause severe disorientation for pilots who do not have an aptitude for this type of flying. For those who make the grade, working with the SAS and SBS can be very rewarding, as there are numerous opportunites to travel and develop new skills.

There is also a downside; it is high risk. In recent years, 47 Squadron has lost three aircraft: one in Scotland, while practising low-level special forces insertion techniques; one in Kosovo, after it clipped a building, causing its load to shift during the landing phase; and one in Iraq – the exact circumstances of the loss are as yet undetermined, but insurgent action is believed to be responsible. This loss was particularly hard felt, coming on the same day (30 January 2005) as Iraq's first free elections since the fall of Saddam Hussein.

At the time of the loss, the aircraft was flying a short mission from Baghdad airport to a remote US military base near the town of Balad, just 65km (40 miles) away. Shortly after the crash, the Iraqi insurgent group, the 1920 Revolution Brigade, claimed responsibility and even released a cobbled collection of video images purporting to be the actual incident. These were quickly dismissed as bogus except for one segment which was probably the genuine crash scene. Although UK and US special forces were rapidly deployed to the crash area, they found no survivors amongst the ten passengers and crew who had been on the aircraft.

Techniques regularly practised by 47 Squadron include ghost insertion (a technique whereby aircraft fly so close together that they appear on radar as one image) and jet-assisted take-off (JATO).

Looking ahead, 47 Squadron is likely to expand its range of platforms, with the A400M seen as a serious replacement for the Hercules. Also, the RAF would like to operate a

An RAF Hercules practises low-level flying – a key requirement for 47 Squadron.

British operators would like to have the capabilities of the armed MC-X Merlin (top) and that of the Osprey (below). However, so far they remain desired items rather than ordered ones.

gunship, such as the AC-130, but these are extremely expensive platforms. British SAS and SBS have made use of the US-built AC-130 in the past, particularly in Afghanistan and Iraq, and are clearly sold on its awesome firepower.

Another demand likely to manifest itself on 47 Squadron includes providing heavy lift for the newly formed Ranger Regiment, as this will be the UK's primary airborne expeditionary force and will need a capability comparable to the SAS and SBS. One other concept currently under consideration is that of a light armoured strike force, something similar to the US Stryker brigade.

No.7 Squadron Special Forces Flight, RAF

Known as the 22 SAS taxi service, No.7 Squadron's Special Forces Flight is responsible for the covert insertion and extraction of the UK's special forces. No.7 SFF operates a small fleet of heavily modified Chinook HC.2s that feature air-to-air refuelling probes, state-of-

the-art navigation systems, missile jamming devices, long-range fuel tanks, mini-guns and M60 machine guns. Although many of their operations are secret, they are known to have operated in the Gulf, Bosnia, Kosovo, Sierra Leone, Afghanistan and, of course, in Iraq as part of Operation Telic.

Selection and training standards for No.7 SFF are extremely demanding as much of the Squadron's flying is carried out at low level and at night using third generation NVGs.

At the time of writing, No.7 SFF were going through a highly frustrating period. Their new mount, the much vaunted and more capable HC.3 Chinook, is grounded until further notice, apart from Visual Flight Rule (VFR) conditions. This excludes it for SF-based operations, which are generally conducted in darkness.

This catastrophe stems from a multitude of problems centred around the aircraft's highly complex electronic systems. Basically, the software is incompatible. So bad is the problem that serious consideration is being given to scrapping them, as it would be cheaper than fixing them. Consequently the current nickname for this variant of the Chinook is the 'Flying Turkey'.

However, on the plus side, No.7 SFF is due to expand its operational portfolio with new platforms that have yet to be decided. At present, the likely choices are the NH 90 and the EH 101, both of which are highly capable aircraft. Looking much further ahead, it is likely that No.7 SFF will acquire a tilt-rotor platform for long-range mission profiles, possibly the US Osprey or a European equivalent. Such capability, though, is a long way off. It is also no secret that the UK desires a combat capability similar to the US 160th SOAR, albeit on a smaller scale.

Parachute Regiment

Based at Colchester, the Parachute Regiment is an integral part of the UK's 16 Air Assault Brigade and provides most of its infantry component. The Regiment is currently made up of three battalions: 1, 2 and 3, two of which are always assigned to the Brigade's air assault infantry. However, one battalion is due to be disbanded in 2005 and re-roled as a Ranger-style special forces support force.

In comparison to other countries with a long history of parachute-based operations, such as Russia, Germany and Italy, Britain was slow to realise the potential of airborne forces and only formed a capability in 1940. However, once a unit was formed, volunteers from the existing commando forces soon came forward, leading to the formation of the 2nd Airborne Brigade.

The first action fought by the paras was in Tunisia (although they were not airdropped), where they earned the nickname of *Die Roten Teufel* (The Red Devils) from the Germans, a name they still have. By 1943, the Brigade had considerably grown in size and capability and now had its own gliderborne force. Following a change of name to the 1st Airborne Division, the paras were dropped into Sicily wearing their Pegasus airborne insignia and red berets. This was to be a precursor for the ambitious but ill-fated Operation Market Garden, where the paras fought a valiant action at Arnhem in Holland in September 1944.

As these events were taking place, a new formation known as the 6th Airborne

Division was preparing for the D-Day invasion of Normandy. After the war ended the paras found themselves involved in numerous conflicts and internal security operations in Palestine, Malaya, Suez, Aden, Borneo and Northern Ireland, culminating in the Falklands War in 1982.

In 1999, the paras led the way into Kosovo for NATO and also participated in a spectacular hostage rescue operation in Sierra Leone. On their return to the UK, they were permanently assigned to the newly formed 16 Air Assault Brigade in which they are a key component of its unique capabilities. Following the events of 9/11, a small force was sent to Afghanistan as part of an international peacekeeping force, but did not involve 16 AAB.

In 2003, the paras were deployed to Iraq as part of Operation Telic, where they seized valuable oil fields to prevent their destruction. Other notable missions included mounting 'Eagle patrols' and sweep-and-clear operations, which severely hampered the movement of insurgents who were terrorising the local Shi'ia population.

All officers and men of the Parachute Regiment are volunteers and have to attend

British paras prepare for a jump during the Second World War, synchronising their watches before take-off.

A para shows off the business end of an SA-80 A2 assault rifle, complete with 4× magnification sight.

a rigorous two-day pre-selection course before attempting the paras' feared recruit training course.

The course lasts for some 23 weeks, with the first eight concentrating on basic military training covering drill, weapons handling and fieldcraft. The recruits then spend some time on leadership training, rock-climbing, canoeing and abseiling; and then it's the big one – 'P Company' (Pre-Parachute Selection Company). This part of the course is the most physically demanding and is comparable to the Royal Marines Commando course.

For the 35 per cent who pass P Company, a basic parachuting course awaits them, which is their final hurdle before being presented with their 'Parachute Wings'.

Weapons used by the Parachute Regiment include the SA-80 A2 assault rifle, M16A2 assault rifle with M203 40mm grenade launcher, SA-80 A2 LSW, M249 Minimi light machine gun, GPMG medium, M2 .50 heavy machine gun, 81mm mortar, LAW 80 anti-tank missile, Milan anti-tank missile and Starstreak MANPADS.

Pathfinder Platoon

Based in Colchester is Britain's elite 16 Air Assault Brigade and its reconnaissance force, the Pathfinder Platoon. By any normal military criteria this unit would be deemed special forces, but in Britain it is only classed as an elite specialist unit. However, for the members of the Pathfinder Platoon this poses no problem. They view themselves as being

expert only in the art of covert reconnaissance, and not as a fighting force.

They are members of the Parachute Regiment, a unit that has a fearsome fighting reputation around the world; they are an elite within an elite. Their excellent skills make them obvious candidates for the SAS and many view the Pathfinders as a stepping stone between the Parachute Regiment and the SAS.

Originally formed during the Second World War, the Pathfinder unit had the unenviable role of jumping ahead of the main force of paratroopers and securing a Drop Zone (DZ) for them. In September 1944, Pathfinders of the 21st Independent Company parachuted into Arnheim to find and secure a DZ for Operation Market Garden. Although their part of the operation was a complete success, the unit was disbanded after the end of the war.

In 1981, 2 Para recognised the need for a pathfinder platoon and set about creating a modern equivalent that would have more or less the same role as the original Pathfinders of the Second World War. Despite it being only platoon strength (16 men), the new unit was known in 2 Para as 'C Company', and effectively became the eyes and ears of the Regiment.

In 1982, 2 Para's Pathfinder Platoon was split up and reformed into two platoons, Recce Platoon and Patrol Platoon. The title of platoon was somewhat ironic because the unit was now operating at company strength.

In 1985, the Pathfinder Platoon became part of 5 Airborne Brigade and took on additional operational roles which involved covert reconnaissance and sabotage. Again, the title platoon was retained even though the unit was at company strength.

In 1999, the Pathfinders played an important role in Kosovo, where they were tasked with identifying safe and secure landing zones (LZs) for helicopters bringing in British spearhead forces prior to the arrival of the main allied invasion force.

In September 2000, the Pathfinders deployed to Sierra Leone and participated in a spectacular hostage rescue operation that involved 2 Para, the SAS and elements of the SBS. The rescue operation was sanctioned after a group of British peacekeeping soldiers were taken hostage by a group of rebels, known locally as the 'West Side Boys'. Although aspects of this operation still remain highly classified, the role of the Pathfinders was significant as they identified suitable helicopter assault points for a Para and then provided fire support as they fast-roped on to the LZ (*see pages 40–7*).

This was, in fact, the Pathfinders second combat action in Sierra Leone, as they were involved in a skirmish with rebels while on a peacekeeping mission in 1999. They were also deployed with 2 Para to Kabul in Afghanistan in 2002 for a short peacekeeping operation and to Iraq in 2003 as part of Operation Telic.

The Pathfinders Platoon acts as 16 AAB's advance force. Its operational roles include covert reconnaissance, the location and marking of DZs, tactical LZs and helicopter LZs for subsequent air assault operations. After the main force has landed, the platoon takes on the role of tactical intelligence gathering and works very closely with the Brigade's HQ.

Pathfinder Platoon equipment

Equipment used includes state-of-the-art GPS and NVG systems, portable satellite communications, Land Rover 110 SOVs, Land Rover 90s, quad bikes and Argocat ATVs. The Pathfinders make extensive use of the Land Rovers for LRRPs and greatly value their ability to carry a large variety of weapons such as the GPMG, Mk-19 40mm automatic grenade launcher and Browning .50 heavy machine gun. Other weapons include the M16A2 with M203 grenade launcher, M249 Minimi, 7.62 GPMG, Browning HP, Colt Commando and SA-80 A2.

For HALO operations the Pathfinders use the GQ360 Ram Air parachute as it gives them a greater amount of control. It features an automatic chute deployment device, which opens the chute at a preset altitude using the Hitefinder opening instrument. The standard height for HALO jumps to start is 7,500m (25,000ft) with the parachute set to deploy at around 750m (2,500ft). These heights offer the aircraft protection from radar detection and also give the soldier a chance to deploy his reserve 'chute in the event of a failure. For HAHO missions the soldier needs to jump with oxygen as his jump-and-chute deployment height is 9,000m (30,000ft). This height allows the soldier to glide for almost 90 minutes before hitting the ground. In good wind conditions a soldier can glide for a considerable distance, reducing the chances of radar detection for both him and the insertion aircraft.

Pathfinders wear standard British Army combat uniforms, but tend to wear either Para or SAS smocks depending on personal preference. They also wear the famous Para Red Beret with its distinctive cap badge.

The selection of Pathfinder candidates is similar to that of the SAS, with only the best passing through the rigorous assessment phase. New recruits to the Pathfinders have to be placed on a year's probation before they are officially accepted into the unit's ranks. Any soldier not already parachute qualified must attend the basic parachute training course at RAF Brize Norton. Once qualified, soldiers undergo HALO training, with some going on to complete the more advanced HAHO course.

The soldiers are then assigned to either Air or Mountain Platoon, where they will be posted to one of the five four-man platoons. The essential difference between the two platoons is that all Air Platoon troops are both HALO and HAHO trained, while Mountain Platoon is only trained in HALO and specialises in arctic warfare.

Being a para can be demanding, but serving as a Pathfinder is something else, as there is a constant demand on each soldier to both maintain and aquire new skills. Soldiers learn survival and escape and evasion (E&E) techniques until they become second nature. This is vital because most of their time is spent operating behind enemy lines. Although their primary mission is to operate covertly, if compromised they are trained to defend themselves in a truly devastating manner. Each four-man team carries two M249 Minimis, two M16A2s fitted with M203 grenade launchers and copious amounts of hand grenades.

Soldiers serving in the Pathfinders are expected to complete at least three years' service, with the option of a further extension, while officers only serve for two years. The thinking behind these short-service postings is so both the officers and soldiers have a chance to share their knowledge and experience with other units and regiments.

The Pathfinders have links with foreign units including the Jordanian Special Forces, US Army Rangers, US 82nd Airborne Pathfinders and the 2nd REP, French Foreign Legion.

Royal Marines

The Royal Marines are an integral part of the Royal Navy and were formed in 1942 as a commando force. Their current ORBAT comprises some 500 officers and 5,500 men, all highly trained and well equipped for the rigours of both land and sea warfare. By UK standards they are only deemed an elite force,

Royal Marines on patrol in Iraq – dirty and at times dangerous work.

but by other countries' standards they are special forces.

The US, in particular, holds them in high esteem, as they have a very close working relationship with the US Marine Corps. The Royal Marines are always ready and willing to deploy at a moment's notice, as they are both a spearhead and expeditionary warfare force.

The bulk of their manpower is grouped into lightly armed battalion-sized units known as commandos, of which there are currently three, and together they form 3 Commando Brigade. The Brigade is a key component of the UK's Joint Rapid Deployment Force (JRDF) and played a major role in fighting the Al-Qaeda terrorist network in Afghanistan before participating in Operation Telic.

Looking further ahead, the Royal Marines plan to form a fourth Commando, which will controversially be manned by Commando-trained soldiers drawn from a regular army battalion, rather than directly recruited candidates. There is already a precedent for this, however; the Royal Marines artillery component – 29 Regiment, Royal Artillery – is made up of regular soldiers who are Commando qualified.

Another controversial idea being discussed at the time of writing is the desire by some in the British government to see the Royal Marines removed from the ORBAT of the Royal Navy and passed over to the British Army. However, it will be a brave government that ever tries to change the current relationship between the Marines and the Royal Navy.

Royal Marines equipment

Weapons used by the Royal Marines:
SA-80A2 assault rifle, SA-80A2 LSW, 5.56 Minimi SAW, 7.62 GPMG, Colt M4 assault rifle, Diemaco 7 assault rifle, M16A2 assault rifle, M203 grenade launcher and the HK MP-5 sub-machine gun. The Royal Marines Amphibious Force deployed on Operation Telic comprised of

some 4,000 personnel drawn from the following units:
• 40 Commando Royal Marines
• 42 Commando Royal Marines
• 45 Commando Royal Marines
• 29 Regiment, Royal Artillery (equipped with 105mm light guns)
• 539 Assault Squadron, RM
• 59 Commando Squadron, RE
• plus elements of the SBS (Special Boat Service)

Brigade Recce Force (BRF)

The Brigade Recce Force is the reconnaissance arm of the UK's elite amphibious force, the Royal Marines. The BRF is tasked with covert intelligence gathering deep behind enemy lines (deep being described as anything beyond 50km [30 miles] or more).

The unit was born out of the highly regarded Royal Marines Mountain and Arctic Warfare Cadre and compare in many ways with the Parachute Regiment's Pathfinder Platoon.

Although primarily tasked with covert reconnaissance and intelligence gathering, the unit also has a secondary role of providing an arctic and alpine warfare capability, both covert and overt, and works closely with the

Royal Marines man a GPMG during Operation Telic. Although an old weapon, the GPMG is still highly effective.

Royal Marines Commando Brigade Patrol Troops.

During Operation Telic, the BRF led the way for the Royal Marines as they assaulted the Al-Faw peninsula, operating similarly to the Royal Marines special forces, the SBS.

Weapons used include the SA-80A2 assault rifle, SA-80A2 LSW, M16A2 assault rifle with M203 grenade launcher, Colt M4 assault rifle, Diemaco 7 assault rifle, HK MP-5 sub-machine gun, M249 Minimi SAW and the GPMG.

Strategic Reconnaissance Regiment (SRR)

Formed in April 2005, the Strategic Reconnaissance Regiment is the UK's latest weapon in the fight against global terrorism. Essentially, it will be the forward intelligence arm of the SAS and SBS, providing a capability reminiscent of that performed by the legendary Long Range Desert Group (LRDG) during the Second World War, in the barren and desolate deserts of North Africa, but far better trained and equipped.

The SRR will initially be based in Credenhill, Hereford, along with the SAS, and will come under the ORBAT of UK special forces. The Regiment will primarily recruit internally, from within the UK armed forces where possible, but is also likely to recruit from

outside, especially within the secret services community, namely MI5 and MI6.

In essence, the SRR will be a bigger and more capable version of 14 Int – a highly capable covert intelligence gathering unit within the British Army – that has much in common with the US Army's Gray Fox intelligence gathering cell. Gray Fox provides intelligence for Delta Force, amongst others, whereas 14 Int supplies the SAS. Its most famous exploits and successes have been in Northern Ireland, at the height of the IRA terror campaign, and it is easy to understand why the UK now requires such a force for its fight against Al-Qaeda, especially following the London suicide-bombing attacks of 7 July 2005.

Equipment is likely to be sensors rather than firepower. A good benchmark for personal armaments is that of the elite Pathfinder Platoon: light enough to carry, but heavy enough to punch your way out of trouble.

Other kit very much in vogue and likely to be operated by the SRR is the UAV. It provides an eye in the sky and little risk to the operator who is using it hundreds of miles away from where it is overflying. However, as good as all this equipment is, it is the person behind it that counts and we must never lose sight of that.

SAS (Special Air Service)

The SAS is the most feared and respected special forces unit in the world with numerous imitators but few equals. Based at Credenhill, Hereford, 22 Special Air Service Regiment (SAS) has a reputation that is legendary, and certainly lives up to its motto 'Who Dares Wins'.

Before 5 May 1980, few people around the world knew anything about the SAS. However, when men wearing black overalls, respirators and body armour, armed with HK MP-5s, Browning HP pistols and stun grenades stormed the Iranian Embassy in London and killed five terrorists who had been holding a number of people hostage, everything changed. The entire operation had been witnessed by millions of people on live TV.

Unfortunately, the old saying 'any publicity is good publicity' does not apply to special forces. They like to work in the shadows and this exposure gave the SAS an image of being invincible, creating a perception of a unit that was large in size and manned by supermen.

The reality is somewhat different as the SAS comprises only one regular (22 SAS) and two part-time TA (21 SAS Artists Rifles and 23 SAS) regiments who are supported by 264 Signal squadron (a regular unit attached to 22 SAS) and 63 Signal squadron (a TA unit that supports both 21 and 23 SAS).

The SAS has some 700 highly trained operators within its ranks who are divided between four 'Sabre' (Fighting) squadrons. Each squadron consists of four 16-man troops who normally deploy on operations as four-man teams or eight-man patrols, depending on tactical requirements.

In addition to the Sabre squadrons, the SAS also has the support of an HQ squadron, Operations Research Wing, a Planning and Intelligence Unit, a Training Wing and various attached personnel such as medics, drivers, cooks, EOD specialists and engineers. Control of the three SAS regiments and their support units is undertaken by the Director of Special Forces.

The SAS can trace its history back to 1941, when under the command of its creator, Col David Stirling, a unit was formed called L Detachment, Special Air Service Brigade. However, despite its grand title the unit was little more than a handful of unconventional soldiers, who were thrown together to form a new unit as part of a massive deception plan to fool the Germans. As a means of sowing further confusion, the name Special Air Service Brigade was created for a bogus formation of parachute and glider units who were supposedly deployed in the Middle East as part of an invasion force.

In Col Stirling's words, the SAS was formed to 'firstly, raid in depth behind enemy lines, attacking HQ nerve centres, landing grounds, supply lines and so on; and secondly, to mount sustained strategic activity from secret bases within hostile territory and, if the opportunity exists, recruit, train, arm and co-ordinate local guerrilla elements'.

Within the British Army there was intense suspicion of the SAS and its capabilities. Even when the SAS was successful, it was never enough for its critics who despised the idea of small unconventional units that seemed to be totally autonomous.

The SAS, however, did have friends in high places who were so pleased with their performance in North Africa and the Mediterranean that they agreed to form a new force for operations in north-west Europe.

By 1944, the SAS had become a Brigade and consisted of two British regiments (1 and 2 SAS), two French regiments (3 and 4 SAS), one Belgian squadron (5 SAS) and a number of signal squadrons.

After the war ended the SAS was disbanded along with other elite units that had served their country well throughout the war. The SAS, however, did not go quietly and fought a campaign within the British MoD to be reformed. In part it was successful. It was allowed to reform in 1950 as the TA Artists Rifles, a part-time unit that was to eventually

The silent and deadly submarine is perfect for covert SAS insertion/extraction missions, as few countries have the capability to detect them.

become the 21st SAS Regiment (Artists Rifles) Volunteers.

Not content with just being a TA unit, the SAS saw an opportunity during the Malayan Emergency in 1952 to form a regular SAS unit. The highly successful Malayan Scouts, who were created in Malaya, were looking for a new name that would be more representative of their role. Once agreed, the unit became the Malayan Scouts (SAS), later to be renamed the 22nd SAS Regiment. The SAS was back in business.

Since reforming in Malaya, the SAS has participated in more wars and conflicts than any other special forces unit in the world and is the most combat experienced. The following pages chronicle *known* SAS operations.

SAS Equipment

Weapons used by the SAS include:
- HK MP-5 SMG (entire range), HK MP-7 SMG, HK-53 SMG, Ingram Model-10 SMG, UZI SMG, M16A2 assault rifle with 40mm M203 grenade launcher, Diemaco 7 assault rifle, Colt M4 carbine, Colt Commando assault rifle, HK-G3 assault rifle, HK-G8 assault rifle, HK-G41 assault rifle, FN 7.62 SLR (although no longer in use with the British Army, the SAS still use it on certain types of operations), Steyr AUG assault rifle, SA-80A2 assault rifle (used by TA SAS only), SA-80A2 LSW (used by TA SAS only), M249 Minimi light machine gun, Ameli light machine gun, HK-13E light machine gun, Ultimax 100 light machine gun, 7.62mm GPMG, Browning M2 .50 heavy machine gun, Accuracy International PM sniper rifle, Tikka M55 sniper rifle, SSG 3000 sniper rifle, Barret .50 long-range sniper rifle, Franchi SPAS 12 combat shotgun, Franchi SPAS 15 combat shotgun, Remington 870 combat shotgun, Browning HP pistol, Glock 18 pistol, SIG 226 and 228 pistols.

Heavy weapons include:
- LAW 80 anti-tank rocket launcher, M72 anti-tank rocket launcher, Milan anti-tank missile, 81mm Mortar, Javelin MANPADS, FIM-92 A Singer MANPADS, MK 19 40mm automatic grenade launcher, SB 40 LAG automatic grenade launcher and 20mm AMW (anti-material weapon).

Vehicles used include:
- Land Rover 90 ('Dinkies'), Land Rover 110, Land Rover SOV (special operations vehicle), Light Strike Vehicle (LSV), Argocat mini-ATV (all-terrain vehicle), Harley-Davidson track bike, Quad ATV, Unimog utility truck, DAF utility truck, Pinzgauer lightweight utility truck, Ranger Rover and unmarked vehices. The SAS are well-known for their armed vehicles and often use some of the following vehicle-mounted weapons: Browning M2, GPMG, M249 Minimi, 25mm cannon, Milan, TOW, MK-19 40mm grenade launcher, 0.5in GAU-19 three barrel machine gun, 51mm and 81mm mortars.

In addition to their large fleet of ground vehicles, the SAS also operates a fleet of small boats such as the Rigid Raider, Klepper canoe, Gemini, Zodiac and submersible Recovery Craft SRC.

The SAS also has their own fleet of Agusta A-109A light utility helicopters (two of which were captured from the Argentinian forces during the Falklands War in 1982), which are flown by pilots of 8 Flight AAC (Army Air Corps). These helicopters are painted in civilian colours and are used for discreetly transporting counter-terrorist operators within the UK.

SAS troopers generally wear standard British Army DPM combats while training, along with their famous sand-coloured beret and winged dagger badge. While on operations, they can wear anything they like and are given complete freedom in their choice of weaponry. Troopers will wear clothing that is comfortable and practical for the conditions in which they are operating. If feasible, they will dress the same as the local population and blend in with them as best as they can. This particular tactic worked extremely well in Afghanistan, where they used SAS Gurkhas for reconnaissance missions, as their clothing and features were similar to the local Afghanis. However, for counter-terrorist operations the troopers wear black nomex clothing as it allows them to be more easily seen by their colleagues while operating in smoke or dust-filled rooms. In addition they also wear Avon S10 respirators and bullet-proof assault vests with pockets for stun grenades, spare magazines and a knife. SAS CT operators also attach spare magazines to their wrists known as wrist rockets for quick reloads.

Date: 1958–59
Location: Oman

Two SAS Squadrons are deployed to Oman to put down a rebellion on the formidable natural fortress of Jebel Akhdar.

Date: 1963–66
Location: Borneo

The SAS finds itself back in the jungle fighting Indonesian forces and rebel guerrillas who are opposed to the formation of the Federation of Malaysia.

Date: 1964–67
Location: Aden

SAS operations are mounted in the Radfan area against tribesmen and guerrillas; these were known as 'Keeni-Meeni' operations.

Date: 1969–94
Location: Northern Ireland

The SAS is sent to Northern Ireland to support the British Army and the Royal Ulster Constabulary (RUC) by mounting intelligence-gathering and anti-terrorist operations against the IRA and its supporters. Numerous operations were mounted during this period that resulted in both SAS and IRA fatalities. The most successful operation of this campaign was the ambush of IRA terrorists at Loughall, which resulted in the complete annihilation of the IRA's East Tyrone Brigade.

Date: 1970–76
Location: Oman

The SAS is sent to Oman to defeat Communist guerrillas attempting to overthrow the government of Oman. This particular operation featured a highly successful 'Hearts and Minds' campaign persuading other Omanis not to join in the insurgency.

Date: 1980
Location: London

The SAS carried out one of its most spectacular operations under the gaze of the world's media, and brought them instant worldwide recognition. Operation Nimrod was launched to either kill or capture terrorists who were holding hostages in the Iranian Embassy in London. The operation is now viewed as a text-book example of how to execute a hostage rescue mission.

Date: 1981
Location: Gambia

The SAS helps to restore President Jawara to power in Gambia after a coup.

Date: 1982
Location: Falkland Islands

The SAS are deployed to the Falkland Islands to carry out intelligence and raiding operations against Argentinian forces that were occupying the island illegally. Although there were many significant missions undertaken, the key operations during this conflict were the retaking of Grytviken, South Georgia, and the Pebble Island raid. The SAS was highly successful during this war, but regrettably lost 18 men in a non-combat-related helicopter crash.

Date: 1989
Location: Colombia

22 SAS is deployed to Colombia to take part in the anti-cocaine war after the British government received a request for military assistance. This included training the Colombian forces and missions against the drug barons.

Date: 1990–91
Location: The Gulf

The SAS is deployed to the Gulf in support of the UN-led campaign to remove Iraqi forces from Kuwait. The Regiment found itself operating primarily in Iraq on missions against the Iraqi's Scud missiles and their support infrastructure. They were highly successful and operated in ways similar to the original SAS in North Africa.

Date: 1994–95
Location: Bosnia

SAS teams are deployed to Bosnia in small numbers to gain intelligence on the Serbian forces and to provide target designation for RAF strike aircraft.

continued
SAS **Operations 1958–2003**

Date: 1997
Location: Peru

A six-man SAS team is sent to Lima, Peru, along with operators from the US Delta Force, following the takeover of the Japanese Ambassador's residence in January 1997.

Date: 1998
Location: The Gulf

In February 1998, the SAS deployed a squadron to the Gulf when Saddam Hussein threatened to start another war. They were tasked with reconnaissance missions and the rescue of downed pilots.

Date: 1998
Location: Albania

In March 1998, a four-man team was deployed to Albania to rescue a British aid worker named Robert Welch. The team located him and secured his rescue by driving to the coast using Land Rovers. Upon arrival they were met by two helicopters; one provided a security force at the RV point, while the other extracted the rescue team and their vehicles.

Date: 1999
Location: Kosovo

Following the invasion of Kosovo by Serbian forces, the SAS was deployed to assist in finding targets for NATO aircraft and to rescue downed aircrew. They also provided support to the Kosovo Liberation Army (KLA) and helped in the apprehension of Serbian war criminals.

Date: 2000
Location: Sierra Leone

The SAS were initially called in to provide an overt presence in Sierra Leone in support of a UN peacekeeping effort. However, a number of British soldiers were captured and held hostage by the WSB. In response the SAS launched a spectacular rescue operation in conjunction with 1 Para and secured the release of the hostages for the tragic loss of one soldier.

Date: 2001
Location: Afghanistan

Following the terrorist attack on the US on 11 September 2001, the SAS was deployed to Afghanistan in support of UK operations against terrorism. The SAS carried out recce and targeting missions for US forces against Taliban and Al-Qaeda soldiers and their equipment. They also provided support to the Northern Alliance.

Date: 2003
Location: Iraq

The SAS found itself back in Iraq. Essentially, their role was to: prevent Iraqi surface-to-surface missile attacks; engage the enemy on all fronts; carry out covert reconnaissance; cut Iraqi lines of communication; and designate targets for Coalition aircraft. Operators were deployed throughout Iraq, with squadrons mainly in the south and western regions, while smaller elements of the Regiment – such as the highly secretive Increment – operated in north-eastern Iraq.

Date: 2004
Location: Iraq

SAS units carry out intensive counter-insurgency operations throughout Iraq, following a major upsurge in terrorist attacks and kidnappings.

Date: 2005
Location: Afghanistan

Following an increase in Al-Qaeda and Taliban activity, SAS units are deployed along the Pakistan border area as part of Allied sweep-and-clear missions designed to flush out insurgents.

Date: 2005
Location: UK

SAS CT units deploy around Gleneagles, Scotland, as part of a security operation to protect the participants of the G8 summit. In addition, other elements of the SAS commence covert activity around London following the 7/7 suicide bombings.

SBS (Special Boat Service)

Based in Poole in Dorset, the SBS is the naval equivalent of the SAS and is a highly effective combat unit, both on land and sea. In recent years, the SBS has found itself operating alongside the SAS both in Afghanistan and Iraq, as they simply do not have the manpower to sustain long-term special forces operations alone. This shift in operational doctrine is down to the fact that the SBS now comes under a general UK special forces umbrella and is tasked with supporting the SAS during times of conflict.

This has not gone down well with the SBS, as they see their unit's identity becoming a maritime-roled squadron within the SAS ORBAT. This process has already slowly started. The SAS made the SBS change its name in the late 1990s from Special Boat Squadron to Special Boat Service, a title it previously held during the Second World War.

A further issue relates to maritime operations, because the SAS already has its own boat troop. At one time the general rule between the two forces was that the SAS handled all maritime operations above the surface, while the SBS took care of everything underwater, such as sabotage, equipment recovery and underwater demolitions. This area of responsibilty has now blurred, with both units carrying out maritime operations as and when required.

Part of the reason behind these changes is that the SAS is under strength at present and cannot meet all its operational requirements. This is understandable as the SAS and SBS have been involved in numerous conflicts in recent years, including the Falklands, the Gulf, Bosnia, East Timor, Albania, Kosovo, Sierra Leone, Afghanistan, Somalia and Iraq.

The SBS tends to operate in the shadows far more than the SAS and is very secretive about its exact roles. The unit's operational strength is approximately 120 regular operators plus a small part-time reserve unit that is highly professional and extremely well trained. Although the SBS is considerably smaller than the SAS, many operations and missions credited to the SAS have in fact been carried out by the SBS.

During the Gulf War in 1991, SBS units were inserted behind enemy lines to destroy some of Iraq's underground communications systems which were essential for supplying targeting data to the mobile Scud launchers. In 1999, both the SBS and SAS fought side by side in Sierra Leone against the WSB after they had taken a small group of British soldiers hostage. During the subsequent rescue mission over 80 rebels were killed for the loss of one SAS trooper, with all hostages released unharmed.

However, the biggest deployment for the SBS has been in Afghanistan as part of

Royal Marines carry out a search exercise prior to Operation Telic. They are armed with SA-80A2 assault rifles rather than HK MP-5s, which are usually the weapon of choice.

SAS troopers pose for a staged photo during Operation Desert Storm in 1991. They are armed with an M16A2/M203 combination – a lethal mixture.

Operation Enduring Freedom following the events of 9/11. First deployed to Bagram Airbase in Northern Afghanistan, the SBS were acting in support of US forces who were hunting Al-Qaeda/Taliban (AQT) forces known to be operating in the area. Following a number of military actions by both UK and US forces, who were acting in support of the Northern Alliance, the AQT forces surrendered and were taken to a fortress just outside Mazar-e-Sharif. A few days later the AQT prisoners overpowered their guards and a fierce battle took place before order could be restored by UK and US special forces.

During the insurrection hundreds of lives were lost, including a number of US personnel who were within the fortress. It was later revealed by the US DoD that, at the height of the revolt, six SBS troopers had stormed the fortress and charged a force of some 200 AQT soldiers who were trying to kill US forces trapped within the compound. Despite being totally outnumbered they drove the AQT away and rescued the Americans. On hearing the news, President George W. Bush awarded the SBS troopers the Congressional Medal of Honor.

As SBS operations continued in Afghanistan, Britain's MI6 intelligence service identified a valley where it was believed Osama bin Laden, the Al-Qaeda leader, was in hiding. In response, two SBS Squadrons containing 60 troopers were deployed to the valley. As they awaited further instructions, orders came through from the British government that they were to withdraw from the valley and let US forces carry out the operation instead. As the SBS withdrew, there was a delay in the US deployment which was to have devastating consequences. Between the British withdrawal and the US forces' arrival, Osama bin Laden slipped out of the valley unnoticed and made his way to Pakistan where border security was slack. Unaware that

bin Laden had gone, America launched Operation Anaconda, but it ran straight into trouble almost from the beginning.

By mistake, US Forces landed in the middle of the valley instead of the outside and all hell broke loose. As they tried to fight their way out of the valley, they sustained heavy casualties: 11 killed, 88 wounded; two Chinooks shot down, plus a number of other helicopters so badly damaged that they were sent back to the US for repair. Although the Americans inflicted hundreds of casualties on the AQT forces, their forces were not trained or prepared for such warfare. Following an urgent request for assistance from the US government, Britain deployed over 1,800 Royal Marines to the area along with a force of SBS personnel. For several weeks the force carried out intensive search operations in the valley, but there was no reported contact with any AQT forces.

In 2003, the SBS deployed to Iraq as part of Operation Telic where they performed superbly. Missions carried out included covert reconnaissance on the Al-Faw Peninsula prior to the allied invasion, and target designation against both fielded and urban forces. In this role, they identified a building in the city of Basra that contained some 200 Ba'ath party members and duly targeted both the building and its occupants.

The SBS has an enviable reputation amongst other special forces around the world, and will fight hard to maintain its independence and identity.

Weapons used include the Diemaco 7, M16A2 with M203 grenade launcher, Colt M4, Colt Commando, M249 Minimi, SA80A2, HK MP-5 (all versions), HK-G3, STEYR AUG, Remington M870, Barret 50 and Browning HP.

The Ranger Regiment
Special Forces Support Force
Announced in December 2004, the Ranger Regiment is the UK's latest special forces unit, designed to provide direct support both to the SAS and SBS during high intensity operations.

Essentially, the British Rangers are modelled on the US 75th Ranger Regiment, who support Delta Force. The key difference is size: the US Rangers have three battalions, whereas the British have only one, primarily consisting of ex-paratroopers drawn from the recently disbanded 1st Battalion Parachute Regiment.

The British have in effect already had this capability in everything but name, albeit in an ad hoc form, rather than a permanent arrangement. This was ably demonstrated during the Operation Barras hostage rescue mission in Sierra Leone in 2000, performed by elements of the SAS, SBS, RAF, Royal Navy and the 'Red Devils' (the Parachute Regiment).

In setting up this new Ranger-style Regiment, the rationale behind using a former Parachute Regiment battalion is quite simple. The troopers are already trained and equipped for such mission tasking as special forces operations generally dictate. Of course, the fact that membership of the Parachute Regiment is already seen as a good stepping stone towards a special forces career can only be a major bonus, both to the Paras and the special forces operators themselves.

The British Rangers' job will be to close with the enemy either overtly or covertly. The Rangers will provide at least Squadron-strength assets for small-scale operations, but will be equally capable of mounting large scale company-strength attacks, should the need arise.

In many ways, they will be just like the

Rangers of the 17th century – pioneering and daring, but with lots more combat firepower.

The Ranger Regiment will consist of around 600 operational personnel, of which at least 500 will be deemed combat capable. The other elements of the Regiment will be used for direct support, providing medical, logistical and communications capability, with a small HQ for tactical liason duties.

For mobility, the Rangers will have their own tactical assets, comprising:
• Rigid raiders for littoral and inshore water-based missions, and
• Light strike vehicles, for deep penetration recce and fighting patrols, plus an airborne assault capability, based around medium-sized tactical helicopters such as the NH 90 (rumoured to have been ordered by the British under an SF enhancement programme).

Weaponry will consist of SA80A2 assault rifles with UGL (underslung grenade launcher), SA80A2 LSW, Colt M4 assault rifles, Diemaco assault rifles with M203 grenade launchers, Minimi light machine guns, GPMGs, .50 calibre heavy machine guns, .50 Barrat sniper rifles, 7.62 AI sniper rifles, 81mm mortars, Starstreak MANPADS plus Javelin ATMs.

Typical mission profiles will be based around the eight-man section formation, split into two four-man squads.

Each squad will be armed as follows:
• 1 operator armed with an SA80A2 LSW (designed for long-range precision fire-support)
• 1 operator armed with an SA80A2 assault rifle fitted with a UGL
• 1 operator armed with a Minimi light machine gun
• 1 operator armed with an SA80A2 assault rifle.

Other weaponry will be drawn as tactically required.

At the time of writing, there was much heated debate within the UK MoD and the British Army as to the final title of the Special Forces Support Unit/Group. Many argue the point that Ranger Regiment sounds too American. There are also those who want the name Ranger Regiment, even though it is without precedent within the British Army. But regardless of what title is finally bestowed on this new force, the UK now has a much needed special forces support capability.

Track bikes are excellent for recce-type missions as they rarely get bogged down in rough terrain and are a favourite mode of transport within the SAS.

United States of America

CIA's Special Operations Group (SOG)
SOG is the agency's secret army and was formed in the late 1990s to combat the rise in global terrorism. The CIA is no stranger to paramilitary operations, having been involved in numerous covert activities over the years.

Because of past failures and scandals, the CIA was forced to adopt a low profile for many years, but the events of 11 September 2001 brought it back into the covert paramilitary business with a new-found purpose – to protect America and its interests both at home and overseas.

The architect of the modern SOG is former CIA director George Tenet, who first began rebuilding the unit upon his appointment in 1999. Originally, the plan was to slowly build up a new and enhanced operational capability before declaring the force ready and available, but the 9/11 attacks threw that plan out the window.

With the US facing its worst domestic crisis since Pearl Harbor, the decision was taken to deploy the SOG into Afghanistan as soon as possible. The rationale was that it gave the US an unofficial covert presence on the ground prior to the official predicted military response.

In essence, SOG operators are not soldiers but spies, trained to fight in an unconventional manner – very much in the vein of a guerrilla force, making them perfect for encouraging insurrection and revolt amongst a disaffected population. In the dim and distant past, traditional CIA officers tended to garner intelligence via embassy cocktail circuits or by bribing foreign officials. Nowadays, the methods are far more sophisticated in one way, yet more crude and brutal in others. They include the use of unmanned aircraft, such as the Predator UAV – a platform that is capable of photographing a footprint 20km (12 miles) away, while on the ground they have operators who carry out missions either alone or in small teams. Assassinations, coups, kidnappings and encouraging insurrection are all in a day's work, with action and varied work guaranteed.

SOG is the new hard edge of the CIA and is perfect for targeting unconventional forces such as Al-Qaeda and the Fedayeen Saddam. Basically, SOG takes the war to the level of the terrorist, employing combatants who are willing, adaptable and at times ruthless – fear is the key to the demise of a terrorist group.

The use of such operatives, however, is not without its critics in America. The US military is also not too impressed with the idea of an unconventional guerrilla-type force waging war by its side, especially as it virtually has carte blanche to do what it likes with little apparent accountability. The view of the US special forces is that they can perform any mission of which SOG is capable. SOG, however, believes that only they are capable of infiltrating enemy territory without arousing attention. This argument has merit, as members of SOG and Gray Fox spent months operating clandestinely within Baghdad without being compromised.

US **operators train with the Osprey – a unique platform for long-range missions and ideal for the CIA.**

It was an old Mil helicopter similar to this one that brought the CIA's SOG into Afghanistan after 9/11.

Interestingly, SOG had men operating on the ground in Afghanistan within 15 days of 9/11, while US military forces took until 7 October before they commenced official retaliatory operations under the banner of Operation Enduring Freedom.

Shortly after the collapse of the Taliban regime, SOG was in action again, this time in Yemen. Having received a tip-off that one of bin Laden's lieutenants, Mohammed Atef, was at large in the country and planning other attacks, SOG went to work.

Using a Predator UAV, SOG modified it to carry Hellfire missiles. In an operation that was the first of its kind, not to mention highly controversial, they attacked Mohammed Atef and his entourage, killing all in the process.

Not content with its success, SOG set about devising further operations involving UAVs. The location this time was Iraq. In anticipation of the upcoming war, SOG quietly slipped into the Kurdish-held enclaves in the northern part of the country and began recruiting a guerrilla force. The Kurds already had the Peshmerga, a tough and resilient group who were feared by the Iraqis – and perfect for SOG's plans.

During Operation Iraqi Freedom, SOG guided US forces through hostile areas, set up safe houses for downed pilots and special forces, mapped areas for potential targets and helped encourage insurrection among the Kurds in the north and Shi'ites in the south.

Concerned at the rise in its popularity, the US Defense Secretary Donald Rumsfeld set about creating his own version of the CIA's SOG. Known as Gray Fox or the Army's Intelligence Support Activity (ISA), the unit is essentially a death squad and a re-creation of the Vietnam War's Operation Phoenix assassination programme (*see page 188*).

Within the Washington corridors of power, there is something of a power struggle taking place between the CIA leadership and Donald Rumsfeld. Rumsfeld is deeply worried about SOG's rapid rise in power and mission capability. If not checked politically, SOG may start wars that his military forces may have to finish, hence the formation of Gray Fox.

If someone wants to join SOG, this is what they will have to do. Firstly, they will be sent to the 'Farm' or, to give it its official designation, the Camp Peary training centre, located on 9,000 heavily wooded acres near Williamsburg, Virginia.

This establishment is surrounded by barbed-wire topped fences and motion detectors, so once a trainee has been recruited there is no escape. During the year-long training stint, recruits are taught such as infiltrating hostile countries, communicating in codes, retrieving messages from dead drops and recruiting foreign agents to spy for the US. In addition to stealing secrets for the Americans, trainees are taught how to blow up bridges, bring down aircraft and the art of assassination. However, they will probably spend most of their time using the laptops that are supplied to all Camp Peary trainees for sending back reports from afar.

Other skills taught at Camp Peary include sharpshooting with various kinds of weapons and setting up LZs in remote areas of the world. The agency makes extensive use of all types of aircraft and helicopters. For some there will be training at Fort Bragg, the home of Delta Force, and for others, field deployments with various members of the special forces.

Since 9/11 the focus of SOG is counter-terrorism. Over recent years, the group has seen more than its fair share of action, having carried out some of the CIA's most dangerous assignments. In the main foyer of the agency's headquarters is a wall that commemorates all those who have fallen in the service of the CIA since it was founded in 1947. Almost half of the 79 stars chiselled into the wall belong to paramilitary officers, the latest being Johnny (Mike) Spann, who was killed at the fortress revolt near Mazar-e-Sherif in Afghanistan.

Despite the unconventional methods and practices of the SOG, they are a vital tool in America's arsenal in the war against terrorism and have a tenacious determination to get the job done that few can match.

Delta Force

Based at Fort Bragg in North Carolina, is America's leading counter-terrorist unit, Delta Force, which was formed on 19 November 1977. The idea was the brainchild of Col Charles A Beckwith (known as Charging Charlie), who was both founder and CO of Delta from its inception. The inspiration to create a highly trained special forces unit came about after Col Beckwith returned to the US after serving in the British SAS (Special Air Service Regiment) on an exchange posting in the early 1960s.

Col Beckwith was fascinated by the SAS and its methods of fighting in an unconventional manner, deep behind enemy lines for months on end with little or no support. He also greatly admired the multiple skills that each SAS trooper possessed, which enabled small four-man teams to operate with a greater effectiveness than a larger conventional force.

Col Beckwith was so impressed with the SAS that he decided to form his own US version. It would be virtually identical in terms of training and methods of operation, but would have local differences such as choice of weaponry, uniforms and operational accountability. Getting Delta Force off the ground was no easy task as there were many military and political hurdles to overcome before such a force could be formed. However, after much pleading and lobbying to the Pentagon and Congress, Col Beckwith's request was granted and the 1st Special Forces Operational Detachment Delta (SFOD-Delta) was born.

Delta Force was set up in great secrecy as an overseas counter-terrorist unit that specialised in hostage rescue. However, it soon became clear that Delta could perform other missions such as long-range covert reconnaissance, and snatch-and-grab missions.

Delta's selection and training programmes were initially based on the tried and tested methods used by the SAS. However, as Delta developed they refined the training programmes to better reflect US thinking on CQB operations, which placed a much greater emphasis on the use of firepower.

Delta's first operational deployment took place in April 1980, after the American Embassy in Tehran was attacked on 4 November 1979 by supporters of the Ayatollah Khomeini, who took 66 US hostages in a bid to force the US to hand over the pro-Western deposed Shah of Iran.

Once all political avenues had been totally exhausted, US President Jimmy Carter gave Delta Force the go-ahead to enter Iran covertly and mount a rescue operation that was code-named Eagle Claw. It was an extremely ambitious plan that required Delta to fly into a remote desert area by C-130, where they were to RV with eight Sea Stallion helicopters that were to be used in the actual rescue attempt. However, before the operation had even begun there were problems. Two helicopters were lost on their way to the RV point, while another developed mechanical problems on the ground. In addition, some operators had been forced to stop a bus containing civilians as it attempted to drive past the parked aircraft on the ground. Another group of men had been forced to open fire on a fuel truck that failed to stop at one of Delta's road blocks. As it was hit, it exploded, lighting up the night sky. It was a nightmare scenario: Delta's rescue plan hinged on the use of at least six working helicopters and there were now only five. There was no choice but to abort Operation Eagle Claw.

As Col Beckwith gave the order to withdraw, there was a catastrophic explosion as one of the hovering helicopters hit a C-130 that was about to take off. Despite valiant efforts by the surviving aircrew and Delta to save those trapped in the burning wreckage, eight US servicemen died and five were seriously injured.

Even though Eagle Claw ended in failure, there was no blame apportioned to Delta as many of the contributing factors that caused the operation to fail were down to sheer bad luck and mechanical failure. During the

The moment disaster strikes – Operation Eagle Claw is captured in this painting by Ronald Wong. (AVPRO)

Delta Force weapons and equipment

Colt M4 assault rifle, M16A2 assault rifle, Mini 14 assault rifle, Steyr AUG assault rifle, HK-G3 assault rifle, SOPMOD (Special Operations Peculiar Modification) M4A1 assault rifle, CAR 15 assault rifle, Stoner SR-25 self loading rifle and Colt Model 733 assault rifle

Walther MP-K SMG, HK MP-5SD SMG, MAC 10 SMG and UZI SMG

M249 SAW light machine gun, HK-13E light machine gun, M60 medium machine gun, M240B medium machine gun and Browning M2 .50 heavy machine gun

Remington 870 combat shotgun and Mossberg Cruiser 500 combat shotgun, HK-PSG sniper rifle, M40A1 sniper rifle, M24 sniper rifle and Barret M82A1 .50 heavy sniper rifle

Support weapons include M203 40mm grenade launcher, M79 'Blooper' 40mm grenade launcher, 81mm Mortar, Carl Gustav 84mm recoilless rifle, 66mm LAW and Mk 19 40mm automatic grenade launcher, Stinger MANPADS and the M136 AT-4 anti-tank rocket. Beretta 92F handgun and SIG-Sauer P-228 handgun

Specialist weapon sights include Aimpoint Comp M close quarter battle sight, M68 Aimpoint, M28 Aimpoint sight, AN/PEQ2 Infrared Target Pointer/Illuminator/Aiming laser (IPITAL) dual beam aiming device

Uniforms worn by Delta Force include standard US Army combat fatigues, Lizard suits, Ghillie sniper suits and black Nomex overalls which are worn during counter-terrorist operations

Operators make extensive use of body armour and night vision devices such as the AN/PVS-7 NVGs and for additional protection they wear Bolle T800 ballistic goggles while operating in open areas. During counter-terrorist operations, Delta operators wear British Avon S10 respirators, body armour, anti-laser goggles and Nomex clothing.

Delta also operates an extensive fleet of vehicles that includes the Land Rover Defender 110 SOV (special operations vehicle), Humvee, Quad ATV (all-terrain vehicle), Harley-Davidson Track Bike and LSV (light strike vehicle). Weapons mounted on vehicles include Mk 19 40mm automatic grenade launchers, M60 medium machine guns, M240B medium machine gun, General Electric 7.62 mini gun, 20mm cannon and Browning M2 .50 heavy machine gun

Other specialist equipment includes Zodiac boats, submersibles, high speed patrol boats and rigid raiders. Delta also uses heavily modified parachutes for its HALO/HAHO operations

The most common means of transport is the helicopter. Types used include the MH-47 D/E Chinook, MH-60 K/L Blackhawk, MH-6 Little Bird, which are operated by the US Army's 160th SOAR. For long-range missions, Delta uses the MH-53J, which is operated by the USAF's Special Operations Group (SOG). However, plans are well advanced to develop exploitation tactics for the Osprey Tilt-Rotor aircraft, which is a hybrid design that encompasses the best qualities of both an aircraft and helicopter.

official Congress enquiry that took place to examine all of the issues surrounding Eagle Claw, no mention or reference was made about Delta. Even to this day, it does not officially exist.

After Eagle Claw, Delta intensified its training and was deployed to Panama in 1989 as part of Operation Just Cause. During this operation Delta was highly successful in a number of key operations, such as the capture of General Manuel Noriega and the rescue of US citizen Kurt Muse, who was held captive by the Panamanian Defence Force (PDF) in Carcel Modelo prison in Panama City.

Although many of Delta's operations remain secret they are known to have participated in a considerable number of missions in South America against Colombian drug cartels who are known to fund organised crime in the US.

During the Gulf War in 1991, Delta played a key part in hunting down Iraq's mobile Scud missile launchers, which were causing considerable problems for the Allied Coalition force. Delta worked alongside the British SAS, mounting constant fighting patrols in the areas where Scud launchers were most frequently known to operate, and within weeks they had forced the Iraqis to move out of this area.

In 1999, Delta deployed a small number of detachments to Bosnia and Kosovo for operations against Serbian war criminals. But the biggest man-hunt so far has been in Afghanistan, hunting down the world's most wanted terrorist, Osama bin Laden and his Al-Qaeda group.

In 2003, Delta found itself back in Iraq, only this time the war for them was far more complicated. They had to contend with conventional Iraqi forces fighting as terrorists. Other operations carried out during this conflict included searching underground bunkers for Saddam Hussein and mounting search operations in and around the nothern Iraqi border near Syria.

Delta is organised along the same lines as the British SAS and consists of three operating squadrons – A, B and C – which are subdivided into smaller units known as troops. Each Delta troop specialises in a particular skill such as mountaineering, HALO, scuba or land mobility.

For greater operational efficiency, each troop can be divided into smaller four-man

Delta Force operational history

1979 Worked alongside the FBI as part of an anti-terrorist team that was set up in anticipation of a possible terrorist attack during the Pan American Games in Puerto Rico

1980 Deployed to Iran to rescue US hostages held by Iranian fundamentalists in Tehran. However, shortly after a decision to abort the mission, a helicopter collided with a transport aircraft on the ground which left eight US servicemen dead

1983 Participated in Operation Urgent Fury in Grenada and carried out a helicopter assaut on Richmond Hill Prison where a number of local government officials were being held hostage

1984 Sent to the Middle East after two Americans were killed during the hijacking of a Kuwaiti Airways airliner

1985 Deployed to Cyprus in response to another hijacking, only this time it was an American aircraft owned by the airline TWA

1987 Deployed to Greece following a report that Vietnamese agents were going to kill US Army Col James Rowe

1989 Participated in Operation Just Cause in Panama, where they successfully rescued a US citizen who was held hostage in Panama City. They also helped in the capture of Gen Manuel Noriega

1991 Took part in Operation Desert Storm during the Gulf War where they provided protection for senior US officers and helped locate and destroy Iraq's mobile Scud launchers

1993 Deployed to Mogadishu in Somalia as part of Task Force Ranger where they mounted numerous operations against Somali warlords. One ended in a major battle that left 18 Americans dead and 70 badly injured. The Somalis, however, lost over 500 men

1995 Deployed to Bosnia as part of an international effort to find Serbian war criminals

1997 Sent to Lima in Peru along with six members of the British SAS following the takeover of the Japanese Ambassador's residence

1999 Deployed to Kosovo in support of US Forces operating against the Federal Republic of Yugoslavia

2001 Following the events of 9/11, Delta was deployed to Afghanistan in search of AQT forces, in particular their leader, Osama bin Laden

2002 Deployed to Kuwait in anticipation of hostilities against Iraq, but quickly withdrawn and redeployed to Pakistan for counter-terrorist operations against Al-Qaeda

2003 Participated in Operation Iraqi Freedom, initially in and around the deserts of western Iraq. However, after the eventual fall of Saddam, Delta finds itself involved in a vicious counter-insurgency war that pushes its personnel and skills as never before

2004 Deployed to Afghanistan as part of an intensive allied sweep-and-clear mission near the Pakistan border area

2005 Elements of Delta protected President Bush at the G8 summit in Gleneagles, Scotland

units that either operate alone or join up to form a section.

Delta also has its own support squadron which handles selection and training, logistics, finance, technical and medical issues. The technical unit provides Delta with highly sensitive equipment such as human tracking devices and eavesdropping sensors, which are used during hostage rescue operations.

Delta operators enjoy some of the best training facilities in world, with access to an Olympic-sized swimming pool, dive tank, three-storey climbing wall, as well as numerous shooting ranges. Most of Delta's recruits come from the elite Ranger and Airborne battalions. However, some candidates also come from conventional Army units.

Gray Fox

Of all the units operating in Iraq at the present time, there are none that have generated as much debate as the US Army's Gray Fox unit. This is because Gray Fox is essentially a death squad, set up for the purpose of carrying out high-value player assassinations, in the same manner as those carried out under Operation Phoenix.

The unit was set up prior to Operation Iraqi Freedom by Donald Rumsfeld, after he became seriously alarmed at the rapid growth and influence of the CIA's SOG (*see pages 184–5*).

Gray Fox is effectively run by the US Army's Intelligence Support Activity (ISA) and serves as an intelligence capability for Task Force 20, as well as Task Force 11, which is concerned with the ongoing war against terrorism.

Gray Fox is well armed and equipped for its operational role and has access to virtually every type of modern weapon available, including those of the former Iraqi Army.

Although the unit is capable of operating anywhere within Iraq, it tends to focus its efforts around central and northern Iraq, as these are proving to be fertile areas for insurrection and revolt.

Gray Fox has generally been very successful in its operations against former Regime members, including Saddam's sons Uday and Qusay, who were killed as a result of an intelligence tip-off. Of course, their greatest claim is the capture of Saddam Hussein himself.

Green Berets

The main role of the Green Berets is to conduct unconventional warfare, foreign internal defence, special reconnaissance and direct-action missions in support of US national policy objectives within the designated areas of responsibility.

Green Beret Weapons and Equipment

Colt M4 assault rifle, M16A2 assault rifle, Mini 14 assault rifle, SOPMOD (Special Operations Peculiar Modification) M4A1 assault rifle, CAR 15 assault rifle, Stoner SR-25 self-loading rifle and Colt Model 733 assault rifle. Walther MP-K SMG, HK MP-5SD SMG, MAC 10 SMG, and UZI SMG

M249 SAW light machine gun, HK-13E light machine gun, M60 medium machine gun, M240B medium machine gun and Browning M2 .50 heavy machine gun

Remington 870 combat shotgun and Mossberg Cruiser 500 combat shotgun, HK-PSG sniper rifle, M40A1 sniper rifle, M24 sniper rifle and Barret M82A1 .50 heavy sniper rifle

Support weapons include: M203 40mm grenade launcher, 81mm mortar, 66mm LAW, Mk 19 40mm automatic grenade launcher, Stinger MANPADS and M136 AT-4 anti-tank rocket

Personal weapons include the Beretta 92F handgun and the SIG-Sauer P-228 handgun

Specialist weapon sights include the Aimpoint Comp M close quarter battle sight, M68 Aimpoint, M28 Aimpoint sight and the AN/PEQ2 Infrared Target Pointer/Illuminator/Aiming laser (IPITAL) dual beam aiming device

Uniforms worn by the Green Berets include: standard US Army combat fatigues, Lizard suits and jungle tiger suits

Extensive use of body armour and night vision devices such as the AN/PVS-7 NVG, and while operating in urban, dusty or sandy conditions, they wear Bolle T800 ballistic goggles

The Green Berets also operate an extensive fleet of vehicles both commercial and military, such as the Land Rover Defender 110 SOV, Humvee, Quad ATV and the Harley-Davidson Track Bike. Vehicle mounted weapons include; Mk 19 40mm automatic grenade launchers, M60 medium machine guns, M240B medium machine guns, General Electric 7.62 mini guns, 20mm cannons and Browning M2 .50 heavy machine guns

Other specialist equipment includes Zodiac boats, high speed patrol boats, rigid raiders and heavily modified parachutes for HALO/HAHO type operations

The most common means of transport is the helicopter. Types include the MH-47 D/E Chinook, MH-60 K/L Blackhawk, MH-6 Little Bird, operated by the US Army's 160th SOAR, while for long-range missions, the Green Berets use the MH-53J, which is operated by the USAF's Special Operations Group (SOG)

The Green Berets are organised in a formation known as the 12-man Operations Detachment 'A' or an 'A Team'. This unit is the key operating element of the force. Five of these A Teams make up a B Team, which comprises six officers (including the Major commanding the unit) and 18 men. There are 12 A Teams per company, five companies per battalion and three battalions per group. At present, there are seven groups – three regular, two National Guard and two reserve.

All members of the Green Berets are volunteers who must be parachute qualified, either before joining or after. Once accepted, candidates participate in a rigorous training programme that lasts for 60 weeks. Those who qualify undergo further training in advanced skills, including demolitions, signals, engineering, languages, communications and intelligence gathering. All Green Berets must be specialists in at least two skills and can volunteer for advanced parachute courses, such as HALO/HAHO.

The motto of the Green Berets is *De oppresso Liber* (Freedom from Oppression). During Operation Iraqi Freedom, the Green Berets deployed to northern Iraq, their primary mission being to galvanise friendly indigenous forces, such as the Kurdish Peshmerga, into a cohesive fighting unit; to provide a harassment capability against dug-in Iraqi forces, especially those located in and around the northern oil fields; to provide a buffer force between the Iraqis and the Kurds; and to provide a reconnaissance and intelligence-gathering capability for coalition forces in the area.

Fast-roping is a skill in which Green Berets must be accomplished.

Task Force 11 weapons and equipment

Colt M4 assault rifle, M16A2 assault rifle, Mini 14 assault rifle, Steyr AUG assault rifle, HK-G3 assault rifle, SOPMOD M4A1 assault rifle, CAR 15 assault rifle, Stoner SR-25 self loading rifle and Colt Model 733 assault rifle. Walther MP-K SMG, HK MP-5 SMG, MAC 10 SMG and UZI SMG

M249 SAW light machine gun, HK-13E light machine gun, M60 medium machine gun, M240B medium machine gun and Browning M2 .50 heavy machine gun

Remington 870 combat shotgun and Mossberg Cruiser 500 combat shotgun, HK-PSG sniper rifle, M40A1 sniper rifle, M24 sniper rifle and Barret M82A1 .50 heavy sniper rifle

Support weapons include: M203 40mm grenade launcher, 81mm mortar, 66mm LAW and Mk 19 40mm automatic grenade launcher, Stinger MANPADS and the M136 AT-4 anti-tank rocket. Beretta 92F handgun and SIG-Sauer P-228 handgun

Specialist weapon sights include: Aimpoint Comp M close quarter battle sight, M68 Aimpoint, M28 Aimpoint sight, AN/PEQ2, IPITAL dual beam aiming device.

Uniforms worn by Task Force 11 include: standard US Army combat fatigues, Lizard suits, urban combat fatigues, Ghillie sniper suits and black Nomex overalls which are worn during hostage rescue type operations

Task Force 11 Operators also make extensive use of body armour and night vision devices such as the AN/PVS-7 NVGs, and for additional protection they wear Bolle T800 ballistic goggles while operating in open areas. During counter-terrorist operations, TF-11 operators wear British Avon S10 respirators, body armour, anti-lazer goggles and Nomex clothing

TF-11 also operates an extensive fleet of vehicles that include the Land Rover Defender 110 SOV, Humvee, Quad ATV, Harley-Davidson Track Bike and LSV. Weapons mounted on vehicles include Mk 19 40mm automatic grenade launchers, M60 medium machine guns, M240B medium machine gun, General Electric 7.62 mini gun, 20mm cannon and Browning M2 .50 heavy machine gun

Other specialist equipment include Zodiac boats, submersibles, high speed patrol boats and rigid raiders. TF-11 also uses heavily modified parachutes for its HALO/HAHO parachute operations

Although the most common means of transport for Task Force 11 is the helicopter, they will use literally anything, including horses – as they ably demonstrated in Afghanistan. Helicopter types used include the MH-47 D/E Chinook, MH-60 K/L Blackhawk and MH-6 Little Bird, which are operated by the US Army's 160th Special Operations Aviation Regiment. For long range missions, TF-11 uses the MH-53J which is operated by the USAF's Special Operations Group (SOG). Task Force 11 is extremely well funded, and can buy any weapon or piece of equipment it wants without going through laborious purchasing procedures. For its size, Task Force 11 is the best armed and equipped unit in the world

Task Force 11

Task Force 11 is a super elite unit, comprising several hundred Navy SEALS, Army Delta Force soldiers and their respective support units from the Joint Special Operations Command in north Carolina. The unit was formed in late 2001, following the events of 9/11.

In response, US president, George W. Bush vowed to hunt down all terrorists who threatened the US and its way of life, and launched Operation Enduring Freedom, a rolling campaign of military action to fight worldwide terrorism for decades to come.

Task Force 11 has the primary mission of hunting down senior members of the Al-Qaeda network and will continue to do so until they are taken out. Although most of the unit's operations are highly classified, they are known to have participated in Operation Anaconda in March 2002. This 16-day counter-terrorist mission involved more than 1,200 US personnel, including 200 special forces who were deployed by the 101st Airborne Division (Air Assault) into the high mountain ranges of eastern Afghanistan in what was to be a dangerous and very difficult operation. Although the operation was successful, inflicting hundreds of casualties on the AQT forces and driving them en masse from Afghanistan into Pakistan, it was also costly as eight Americans were killed and 73 wounded.

After Anaconda ended, numerous follow-up operations were mounted in Afghanistan by Task Force 11, mainly around villages and cave complexes, but some involved pursuits over the border into Pakistan. Task Force 11 generally operates in small four-man teams, but these can be increased in size if tactically viable. As the President said at the beginning of Operation Enduring Freedom: 'This will be a war that's going to go in various phases, some of which will be visible, some will not.'

In September 2002, Task Force 11 played a key part in two significant operations: one in Afghanistan, the other in Pakistan. On 5 September 2002, a team of US special forces, acting as bodyguards for Afghan President Hamid Karzai, foiled an assassination attempt after his motorcade was attacked by a lone gunman wearing the uniform of the new Afghan Army. During the short firefight, the gunman was killed along with one of the president's Afghan bodyguards. A US special forces operator wearing civilian clothing was slightly wounded as he attempted to protect the president.

The second incident took place in Pakistan on 14 September 2002 and involved other agencies such as the American CIA and the Pakistani intelligence service, the Inter-Services Intelligence agency (ISI). It occurred due to a careless satellite telephone call made by one of the world's most wanted terrorists, Ramzi Binalshibh, the mastermind behind the 9/11 attacks. US intelligence agencies and Task Force 11 were able to trace the call to an apartment in Karachi and immediately launched an operation to apprehend him. For political reasons the arrest was made by members of the Pakistani security services. However, US special forces were on hand in the background, ready to assist if called upon.

As these operations were taking place, members of Task Force 11 were training and preparing for operations against Iraq, following Saddam Hussein's refusal to comply with UN demands to hand over information to Western weapons inspectors.

Although Task Force 11 was set up as a vehicle for carrying out specific missions during Enduring Freedom, its success during this campaign has warranted an increase in both its operational responsibilities and military capabilities, leading to calls for it to be turned into a permanent counter-terrorist 'super force'.

Task Force 11 operational history

2002 Deployed to the Philippines, Pakistan, Yemen, Saudi Arabia and Afghanistan as part of Operation Enduring Freedom

2003 Deployed to Iraq as part of Operations Iraqi Freedom and Enduring Freedom following Saddam Hussein's failure to comply with UN Resolution 1441. Also during this period, elements of Task Force 11 were deployed to South Korea following a rise in tensions between the US and North Korea

2004 Deployed again to South Korea, following revelations that North Korea now possessed nuclear weapons – status unknown. Elements were also deployed to Pakistan and Iraq as part of ongoing counter-insurgency operations

2005 Engaged in sweep-and-clear missions around the Pakistan/Afghanistan border, with the loss of one Chinook to ground fire and many SF personnel – among them eight US Navy SEALS.

Task Force 20

Task Force 20 was formed as a mission-specific unit tasked with operating covertly against Iraqi forces, both conventional and unconventional. Now it has the role of supporting conventional forces in post-war Iraq, its mission being to find and destroy insurgents and their leaders, and to find, capture or kill any remaining senior members of the Ba'ath Party still at large.

The name Task Force 20 reflects the date on which official hostilities commenced with Iraq under the banner of Operation Iraqi Freedom – 20 March 2003. The impetus for setting up such a force stems from the success of Task Force 11 (*see page 190*). Indeed, some elements of this force were involved in combat operations in Iraq.

Task Force 20 is primarily composed of operators drawn from Delta Force, who act as both the cutting edge and the core of the unit. Elements of the highly secretive Gray Fox unit provide its intelligence capability. Other units available to assist Task Force 20 include the US Navy SEAL teams, the USAF's SOG and the US Army's 160th SOAR.

Since being deployed to Iraq, Task Force 20 has gained a reputation for being hard-hitting and controversial. This stems from several operations mounted in Baghdad, where the unit has appeared to have shot first and asked questions later. One such incident occurred on 27 July 2003, when a car full of Westerners in civilian clothing, driving an expensive customised 4×4 vehicle, pulled up outside the Al Sa'ah restaurant in the wealthy Mansur district of Baghdad. They began observing the locals coming and going from the vicinity of Prince Rabiah Muhammed al-Habib's house, some two blocks away. After a while, the men got out of the vehicle and slowly moved towards the house. As they did so, a small convoy of US Army Humvees began sealing off nearby roads, effectively acting as both a cut-off group and a perimeter security force. On a pre-arranged signal, there was a loud explosion from the Prince's house, followed by a flurry of activity from the nearby streets as men wearing gas masks, body armour and black T-shirts covered in brightly coloured identification vests stormed the house. Their mission: to arrest Saddam's son, Ali.

As the operation progressed, crowds began

Task Force 20 weapons and equipment

Colt M4 assault rifle, M16A2 assault rifle, Mini 14 assault rifle,
   SOPMOD (Special Operations Peculiar Modification) M4A1
   assault rifle, CAR 15 assault rifle, Stoner SR-25 self loading rifle
   and Colt Model 733 assault rifle, Walther MP-K SMG, HK MP-5SD
   SMG and MAC 10 SMG
M249 SAW light machine gun, HK-13E light machine gun, M60
   medium machine gun, M240B medium machine gun and
   Browning M2 .50 heavy machine gun
Remington 870 combat shotgun and Mossberg Cruiser 500
   combat shotgun, HK-PSG sniper rifle, M40A1 sniper rifle, M24
   sniper rifle and Barret M82A1 .50 heavy sniper rifle
Support weapons include M203 40mm Grenade launcher, 81mm
   mortar, 66mm LAW and Mk 19 40mm automatic grenade
   launcher and the Stinger MANPADS
Personal weapons include the Beretta 92F handgun and the
   SIG-Sauer P-228 handgun
Specialist weapon sights include Aimpoint Comp M close quarter
   battle sight, M68 Aimpoint, M28 Aimpoint sight, AN/PEQ2
   Infrared Target Pointer/Illuminator/Aiming laser (IPITAL) dual
   beam aiming device
Uniforms when worn by Task Force 20 include standard US Army
   combat fatigues, Lizard suits, urban combat fatigues, Ghillie
   sniper suits and black Nomex overalls which are worn during
   hostage rescue type operations. Most operators choose to wear
   civilian clothing when operating covertly in Iraq as it makes it
   easier for them to blend in
Task Force 20 operators also make extensive use of body armour
   and night vision devices such as AN/PVS-7 NVGs. In dusty and
   sandy conditions they wear personal eye protection such as
   the Bolle T800 ballistic goggle; in counter-terrorist operations
   they wear British Avon S10 respirators, close protection kevlar
   body armour, anti-laser goggles and Nomex clothing
TF-20 also operates an extensive fleet of vehicles that include the
   Land Rover Defender 110 SOV, Humvee, Quad ATV, Harley-
   Davidson Track Bike and LSV. Weapons mounted on vehicles
   include Mk 19 40mm automatic grenade launchers, M60
   medium machine guns, M240B medium machine guns,
   General Electric 7.62 mini guns, 20mm cannons and Browning
   M2 .50 heavy machine guns
Other specialist equipment includes Zodiac boats, submersibles,
   high speed patrol boats and rigid raiders. TF-20 also uses
   heavily modified parachutes for its HALO/HAHO operations
Although the most common means of transport is the helicopter,
   they will use anything, including horses. In Iraq, they tend to
   use commercial 4×4 vehicles as they generate far less attention.
   Helicopters used include the MH-47 D/E Chinook, MH-60 K/L
   Blackhawk MH-6 Little Bird, operated by the US Army's 160th
   SOAR. For long-range missions, TF-20 uses the MH-53J, which is
   operated by the USAF's SOG.

to gather out of idle curiousity. The first casualties of this operation were the unlucky occupants of a Chevrolet Malibu that failed to stop for a perimeter security team that was located near a makeshift Humvee road block. This was quickly followed by another incident, in which a Toyota, driven by a disabled man and carrying both his wife and teenage son, was engaged by US forces after they had taken a wrong turn near another road block, resulting in the driver being killed and his wife and son wounded.

Another victim was claimed on the nearby highway when he slowed down to observe what was going on; his bullet-riddled Mitsubishi bore testament to the price of his curiosity. According to local witnesses, the Americans were firing indiscriminately at anything that moved; none of the casualties was found with any weapons. In all, five innocent Iraqis lost their lives. Saddam's son was not in the target house, nor had he been there for several months before the tragic event.

Fearing a backlash from the Iraqi people, the US military apologised for what had taken place and promised to be more careful next time. It was during this apology that details were released for the first time as to the purpose of Task Force 20 and its mission in Iraq. It confirmed that since the end of Operation Iraqi Freedom, Task Force 20 had been involved in numerous operations to flush out Saddam and his followers – many taking place in myriad underground bunkers and tunnels that criss-crossed Baghdad.

Although the US military is generally tight-lipped about its special forces activities in Iraq, it has been remarkably candid when it comes to Task Force 20. It acknowledged that during the war, the unit had fought in the western desert against conventional Iraqi forces, but had failed to find any weapons of mass destruction during these operations.

Ironically, its most notable success came after the end of Operation Iraqi Freedom, when it was involved in the 22 July raid in Mosul that resulted in the deaths of Saddam's sons Uday and Qusay (*see pages 73–5*).

Task Force 20 is believed to comprise 750 operational personnel drawn from Special Operations Command, but there are no official figures to verify this.

Heavily laden marine Amtracs advance forward during Operation Iraqi Freedom.

United States Marine Corps (USMC)

The USMC comprises some 175,000 active and 40,000 reserve marines organised into four divisions, making it one of the largest forces in the world today.

Since 1775, US Marines – or 'Leathernecks' as they are more commonly known – have been involved in almost all American military activities and have earned an enviable reputation for their fighting prowess. They are a vital part of the US Rapid Deployment Force and have always been considered an elite force.

The USMC divisions (three active and one reserve) are organised, armed and equipped on the same triangular basis as the US Army, namely three infantry regiments each of three battalions (however, USMC units normally have approximately 20 per cent more manpower than their Army equivalents). The Marines are self-supporting and have assets such as fighters, attack helicopters, transport aircraft, assault ships, tanks and artillery.

Within this formidable force are specialists such as:
• Marine force reconnaissance units
• Marine long-range reconnaissance battalions (LRRP)
• Search and target acquisition platoons (normally one per USMC regiment)
• Fleet radio reconnaissance platoons (one Atlantic and one Pacific)
• Air-naval gunfire liaison companies (ANGLICO)
• Fleet anti-terrorism security teams (to provide swift, short-term, professional protection on a worldwide basis as and when needed)

Members of such units must undergo similar training to SOF personnel, so that they can undertake their missions by land, sea and air, including parachuting and scuba diving. Each active marine division maintains a reconnaissance battalion for tactical reconnaissance and a force reconnaissance company. The latter contains four platoons and three direct action platoons. The seven platoons each consist of 16 marines, divided into four-man patrols.

These patrols must be expert in aerial infiltration (HAHO/HALO) and scuba diving. Considered to be the elite of the USMC, they can volunteer only after three to four years in the Corps and after qualifying on a specialised course or being a member of a specialised unit such as the Scout Sniper Platoon (SSP). They must also pass the Army airborne test, which includes running 5km (3 miles) in 18 minutes, swimming 500m (⅓ mile), retrieving a heavy object from the bottom of a swimming pool and completing an obstacle course in under five minutes.

Following an interview they then go on to form part of the Reconnaissance Indoctrination Platoon (RIP) to complete their training. Later they attend the school of Amphibious Reconnaissance and have to pass a three-week diving course, followed by a month of parachuting.

The standards are exceptionally high, with only two or three out of the original 60

US **Marines fast-rope from a** CH-**46E helicopter onto a roof in an urban training facility.**

eventually selected. Following their posting to a unit, they will complete their training, which will include courses at Survival, Escape, Reconnaissance and Evasion (SERE) School, Scout Sniper School (SSS) and Jungle Environment Survival Training (JEST). A chosen few may also be integrated into Delta Force (Army) or Team 6 (Marines).

There are also plans to create a USMC Special Operations Command.

USMC **Units deployed during Operation Iraqi Freedom**

1st Marine Expeditionary Force
1st Marine Division
1st Marine Regiment
3rd Battalion – 1st Marines
1st Battalion – 4th Marines
1st, 3rd Battalions – Light
Armored Recon

5th Marine Regiment
1st Battalion – 5th Marines
2nd, 3rd Battalions – 5th
Marines

7th Marine Regiment
1st, 3rd Battalions – 7th
Marines
3rd Battalion – 4th Marines
3rd Battalion – 11th Marines
1st Tank Battalion

2nd Marine Expeditionary Brigade, 2nd Marine Division
1st, 3rd Battalions – 2nd
Marines
2nd Battalions – 8th Marines
1st Battalion – 10th Marines
2nd Amphibious Assault
Battalion
2nd Recon Battalion
2nd Light Armored Recon
Battalion
2nd, 8th Tank Battalions

15th Marine Expeditionary Unit

24th Marine Expeditionary Unit

26th Marine Expeditionary Unit

75th Ranger Regiment

This is one of the finest light infantry units in the world and is a key component of the US Army's Special Operations Command (USASOC) which in turn is part of the US Special Operations Command (USSOCOM).

Based at Fort Benning in Georgia, the Ranger Regiment comprises 2,300 highly trained and well-motivated soldiers who are divided between three battalions. Within each battalion there are three combat companies, each containing three platoons supported by a weapons platoon.

The mission of the Ranger Regiment is to plan and conduct special operations and light infantry operations in any operational environment. The primary special operations mission of the Regiment is direct action (DA). DA operations conducted by the Rangers may support or be supported by other SOF. They can conduct these missions alone or in conjunction with conventional military operations. Rangers can also operate as special light infantry when conventional light infantry or airborne forces are unsuitable for or unable to perform a specific mission. In fact, modern day Rangers conduct basically the same types of missions their forebears conducted 300 years earlier.

The Ranger Regiment is well supported by the US Army and has top priority over other units when it deploys. Its budget alone is that of an entire infantry division. The Rangers work closely with other US SF units such as Delta Force and the 160th SOAR (*see page 203*).

Rangers can deploy anywhere in the world within a few hours as they always have a company at a high level of operational readiness. They are trained to infiltrate enemy territory by land, sea or air and can operate independently for up to five days. To ensure that maximum firepower and tactical flexibility is maintained at all times, every weapon used must be man-portable.

Although the Rangers can undertake many different types of missions, areas in which they specialise are rescue and evacuation, snatch-and-grab, light strike and tactical recon. They are also experts in urban combat and primarily operate at night. They are well equipped for such operations, as demonstrated in Mogadishu in Somalia.

Training requirements for the Rangers are extremely demanding. Soldiers train for 11 months of the year, with only two blocks of leave to break the rigorous programme.

The Regiment conducts training all over the world in various environments such as jungle, desert, arctic and mountain terrain, so that its soldiers are physically conditioned for different types of climate.

At present the main training focus within the Rangers is on the 'Big Four' –

fundamental skills that each Ranger should possess. These are marksmanship, battle drills, medical training and physical training.

With a fearsome reputation to protect, the Rangers are selective in their choice of soldiers. Technically, within the US Army every soldier is guaranteed a Ranger enlistment option, however the reality is somewhat different. They have to pass the three-week-long Ranger Indoctrination Phase first. The RIP, as it is more commonly known, assesses and prepares soldiers for their eight-month stint with a Ranger battalion before attending Ranger School.

Before attending RIP, soldiers must first pass through basic training and infantry school. Once this training is completed the soldiers attend a three-week parachuting course at the Airborne School at Fort Benning in Georgia. After that they attend RIP at one of the active duty Ranger battalions.

Soldiers that pass the RIP remain with the battalion and work up their skills and physical strength to prepare for Ranger School. This will either make or break them. Ranger School has three phases, all of which are held at different locations within the south-eastern US and all of them tough. The first phase of the course starts at the 4th Ranger Training Brigade (RTB) at Fort Benning, where the soldiers face a series of long marches in realistic combat conditions. Throughout this phase they receive little food or sleep and are driven to the edge of exhaustion, carrying full kit at all times.

Once finished here they move on to the 5th RTB at Dahlonega in Georgia where they undergo mountain training, with the final phase – jungle/swamp training – taking place at the 6th RTB at Eglin Air Force Base.

Throughout this course no rank slides are worn, as all Ranger soldiers are expected to show leadership skills. Once qualified, Rangers can undertake further courses in covert reconnaissance, demolitions, communications, combat medicine, sniping, vehicle operations, watermanship, scuba diving and HALO/HAHO parachute infiltration.

Service with the Rangers is also seen as a career stepping stone between conventional infantry and special forces, as many Rangers go on to serve with Delta Force.

Weapons and equipment of the 75th Ranger Regiment

Colt M4 assault rifle, M16A2 assault rifle, Mini 14 assault rifle, Steyr AUG assault rifle, HK-G3 assault rifle, SOPMOD (Special Operations Peculiar Modification) M4A1 assault rifle, CAR 15 assault rifle, Stoner SR-25 self loading rifle and Colt Model 733 assault rifle, Walther MP-K SMG, HK MP 5SD SMG, MAC 10 SMG and UZI SMG

M249 SAW light machine gun, HK-13E light machine gun, M60 medium machine gun, M240B medium machine gun and Browning M2 .50 heavy machine gun

Remington 870 combat shotgun and Mossberg Cruiser 500 combat shotgun, HK-PSG sniper rifle, M40A1 sniper rifle, M24 sniper rifle and Barret M82A1 .50 heavy sniper rifle

Support weapons include M203 40mm grenade launcher, M79 'Blooper' 40mm grenade launcher, 81mm mortar, Carl Gustav 84mm recoilless rifle, 66mm LAW and Mk 19 40mm automatic grenade launcher, Stinger MANPADS and the M136 AT-4 anti-tank rocket

Beretta 92F handgun and SIG-Sauer P-228 handgun

Specialist weapon sights include Aimpoint Comp M close quarter battle sight, M68 Aimpoint, M28 Aimpoint sight, AN/PEQ2 Infrared Target Pointer/Illuminator/Aiming laser (IPITAL) dual beam aiming device

Uniforms worn by the Rangers include standard US Army combat fatigues, Lizard suits, Ghillie sniper suits

The Rangers make extensive use of body armour and night vision devices such as AN/PVS-7 NVGs; for additional protection they wear Bolle T800 ballistic goggles if operating in open areas

The Rangers also operate an extensive fleet of vehicles that include the Land Rover Defender 110 SOV, Humvee, Quad ATV, Harley-Davidson Track Bike. Vehicle mounted weapons include the Mk 19 40mm automatic grenade launchers, M60 medium machine guns, M240B medium machine gun and Browning M2 .50 heavy machine gun

Other specialist Ranger equipment includes Zodiac boats and rigid raiders. Rangers also use heavily modified parachutes for HALO/HAHO operations

In addition to their vehicles, the Rangers also make extensive use of helicopters such as the MH-47 D/E Chinook, MH-60 K/L Blackhawk and MH-6 Little Bird, operated by 160th SOAR

Rangers practise special purpose insertion extraction (SPIE) techniques from beneath a 160th SOAR Chinook.

History of operations

The Ranger Regiment has a long and proud history that dates back some 300 years and is the oldest regiment in the US Army. The name Ranger dates back to the 17th century when American colonists used the word to describe how far they had travelled in a day over rough terrain, such as 'We ranged eight miles this day.'

This is the Rangers' history.

1754–63: First formed by Major Robert Rogers of Connecticut who fought for the British against the French and native American Indians. His most famous operation was against the Abenaki Indians who were based in St Francis, 65km (40 miles) south of Montreal. Travelling by canoe and by foot, Rogers and his force of 200 Rangers covered 650km (400 miles) in 60 days without alerting the enemy to their presence. On 29 September 1759, the Rangers attacked the Abenaki's camp and killed hundreds of them before withdrawing back to their base. It was a spectacular victory and led to Rogers being commissioned into the 60th Foot (The Royal Americans) where he wrote his famous 19 standing orders for the Rangers, many of which are still valid today.

1774–76: Rangers fight on the side of the British during the American War of Independence.

1861–65: Rangers fight on both the Union and Confederate sides during the American Civil War, and later for America in the Mexican War.

1942: The Ranger title is revived again for the Second World War, with six battalions deployed in Europe and the Far East. The first unit was formed at Carrickfergus, Northern Ireland in 1942 and fought at Dieppe alongside British Commandos. Its finest hour was during the D-Day landings when Ranger Force A from the 2nd Battalion assaulted the well defended concrete fortifications on the Point du Hoc. For two days they fought off the German 914th Infantry Regiment, costing them 135 killed or wounded from a force of 225.

At Dog White Beach in Omaha, soldiers of Ranger Force C, 2nd Ranger Battalion were pinned down by heavy enemy gunfire and were unable to move. Near to the Ranger Force was Brigadier Gen Norman Cota, assistant divisional commander of the 29th Infantry Division, who shouted the famous words 'Rangers lead the way', which motivated them into breaking out of the deadly killing zone. Since then, 'Rangers lead the way' has become the force motto.

At the end of the Second World War the Ranger units were disbanded. However, Ranger training still continued and eventually became a qualification that was highly valued in the same way as a parachuting or diving qualification.

1950: During the Korean War, Ranger Companies were attached to every Army Division that fought there, and carried out missions such as reconnaissance, hit-and-run and sabotage.

1969: After the Korean War ended, all Ranger units were disbanded and their soldiers sent to other Army units with LRRPS (Lurps as they were called). The Lurps carried out more or less the same function as the Rangers and superbly performed during the Vietnam War.

At the height of the Vietnam War, the US Army redesignated the LRRPS as specific companies of the 75th Infantry Regiment (which later became the 75th Ranger Regiment). For example, O Company Rangers were attached to the 82nd Airborne, while L Company Rangers went to the 101st Airborne.

In Vietnam, the Rangers were used primarily for recon and intelligence-gathering missions. However, on several occasions they made attempts to rescue American POWs.

1980: A small team of Rangers was sent to Iran, as part of the ill-fated Delta Force (Eagle

The Ranger Creed

Recognizing that I volunteered as a Ranger, fully knowing the hazards of my chosen profession, I will always endeavor to uphold the prestige, honor and high 'Esprit de Corps' of my Ranger Regiment.

Acknowledging the fact that a Ranger is a more elite soldier who arrives at the cutting edge of battle by land, sea or air, I accept the fact that as a Ranger my country expects me to move further, faster and fight harder than any other soldier.

Never shall I fail my comrades. I will always keep myself mentally alert, physically strong and morally straight, and I will always shoulder more than my share of the task, whatever it may be – one hundred per cent and then some.

Gallantly will I show the world that I am a specially selected and well trained soldier. My courtesy to superior officers, neatness of dress and care of equipment shall set the example for others to follow.

Energetically will I meet the enemies of my country. I shall defeat them on the field of battle for I am better trained and will fight with all my might. Surrender is not a Ranger word. I will never leave a fallen comrade to fall into the hands of the enemy and under no circumstances will I ever embarrass my country.

Readily will I display the intestinal fortitude required to fight on to the Ranger objective and complete the mission. Though I be the lone survivor.

'Rangers lead the way.'

Claw) rescue operation in the American Embassy in Tehran. During the operation, Rangers secured the Desert One RV site from where the rescue mission was to be mounted.

1983: Rangers from the 1-75th and 2-75th were deployed to Grenada for Operation Urgent Fury and were involved in numerous actions.

1989: During Operation Just Cause two battalions of Rangers were parachuted into Rio Hato airfield, west of Panama City, and ordered to seize and hold the airfield.

1991: During Operation Desert Storm, Rangers patrolled behind Iraqi lines in heavily armed vehicles, similar to that of the British SAS, and destroyed a communications centre near the Jordanian border.

1993: While performing snatch-and-grab operations against Somali warlords in Mogadishu, Rangers suddenly found themselves under attack from hundreds of Somali gunmen and a fierce firefight soon ensued that was to become the most intense action fought by US soldiers since Vietnam. Although the action lasted for less than ten hours, it cost the lives of 18 US servicemen and left 70 others wounded, while the Somalis had over 500 killed and over 1,000 wounded. It involved Rangers in urban combat, night fighting, combat rescue, snatch-and-grab, sniping, firefights and evacuation of wounded.

1995: Elements of the Ranger Regiment deploy to the Balkans for operations against the Serbs.

1999: Rangers deploy to Kosovo in support of US Forces engaged in operations against Serbian fielded forces.

2001: Rangers deploy to Afghanistan and neighbouring countries as part of Operation Enduring Freedom and help in the search for Al-Qaeda terrorists and Osama bin Laden.

2003: Deploy to Iraq, as part of Operation Iraqi Freedom. They pull off a spectacular rescue, following the capture of a number of US service personnel, including Pfc Jessica Lynch.

2004: Rangers continue to mount ongoing operations in Iraq as part of a major drive to rid the country of insurgents.

2005: Rangers from Task Forces 20 (TF-20) and 11 (TF-11) carry out counter-insurgency missions in Iraq and Afghanistan as part of the ongoing Operation Enduring Freedom.

MANPADS are a key weapon on today's battlefield, so special forces operators must train on all types available.

US Navy SEALs

The US Navy's SEAL (Sea, Air, Land) teams are the youngest of the US Special Forces, and together with their SEAL Delivery Vehicle Teams (SDV) and the Special Boat Squadrons (SBS), form the three branches of the US Navy's Special Warfare Command (NAVSPECWARCOM).

SEALs specialise mainly in unconventional maritime warfare operations that include lakes, rivers, swamps and of course the sea. In some tactical situations, such as those of Operation Iraqi Freedom, SEALs operate inshore in the same manner as conventional light infantry, but generally they limit themselves to incursions that are no more than 32km (20 miles) inland.

As with their special forces colleagues, their roles and capabilities sometimes cross over with those of other units; for example, SEALs can perform light strike missions such as those undertaken by the US Rangers, while they in turn often use inshore craft for operations that are the same as those performed by the SEALs.

The difference is in scale. According to a SEAL team comander: 'We in the SEALs are the US military's small-unit maritime special operations force. We don't belong in anything that involves multi-platoon operations – we've never been successful at it. We keep our units small and separate from large force operations. We have a niche here to be very good in units often less than eight men. That makes us harder to detect, easier to command and control, and better at the small unique operations we train for.

'A further difference is the environment. We keep one foot in the water. That means if we must do inland operations it is because they are attached to maritime reason. Keeping one foot in the water means that we don't get into areas that properly belong to other operators.'

Since their formation on 1 January 1962, SEALs have seen action in Vietnam, Grenada, Panama, Colombia, Afghanistan and Iraq.

There are some 4,000 personnel in the US Navy Special Operations Forces, of which roughly 2,000 are SEALs. In theory, a full SEAL Team is made up of ten platoons of SEALs. In practice, it is roughly 30 officers and 200 enlisted men. Within the ORBAT, there is a small support staff of non-SEALs – in all about 20 naval personnel. Each platoon is 16-men strong (two officers and 14 men). The platoon divides into two squads (each with one officer and seven men), the squad being the preferred size for operations, while a squad subdivides into two four-man fire teams, each fire team comprising two swim pairs.

SBS and SDV teams

The SBS is known as the 'Brown Water Navy' and is key to the whole US naval special forces set-up. Teams operate a variety of special operations craft, from 52m (170ft) patrol boat coastal (PBC) vessels to rigid inflatable boats (RIBS) such as the 5m (15ft) combat rubber raiding craft (CRRC), which are capable of reaching 20 knots.

The SBS essentially has three roles:
• Coastal patrol and interdiction – this requires

A SEAL is inserted on a beach recce mission, although usually this is carried out at night to increase the survivability of the operators involved.

SEAL mission profiles

The US Navy SEALs operate according to five basic mission profiles:

Direct Action – essentially combat operations, such as raiding, sabotage, hostage rescue and the capture of targets afloat or inshore

Special Reconnaissance – the reconnaissance and surveillance of hostile territory, particularly beach-heads. SEAL teams make beach surveys and, like their predecessors (the UDTs), mark landing approaches and demolish obstacles and fortifications in preparation for an amphibious landing

Foreign Internal Defense – the training of the military and security forces of friendly nations, usually in a non-combat environment

Unconventional Warfare – this is very much one of the reasons for John Kennedy's support for special forces. If required, the SEALs train, equip and lead guerrilla forces behind enemy lines

Counter-terrorist Operations – the SEALs, particularly DEVGRU (Naval Special Warfare Development Group), conduct anti-terrorist operations, both reactive and preventative

An operator inserts a 40mm chalk training round into an M203 grenade launcher as part of his close support weapon cadre.

a reasonably large boat, so the mainstay of such missions is the PBC, which is large enough to carry both a significant weapons package and a sizeable SEAL and Naval Special Warfare force. Due to its size it can operate for extended periods of time without support.

• Close inshore operations – using the 65ft (20m) MK III Swift Patrol Boat, currently the subject of a replacement programme; its successor is the MK IV Patrol Boat. Some of these boats saw action in Iraq, where they supported British, Australian and US forces as they fought their way from the deep-water port of Umm Qasr up to the city of Basra.

• Clandestine operations – SEALs use RIBs; they are small, stealthy and capable of high speeds in excess of 25 knots.

For covert sub-surface insertions, there is the Swimmer Delivery Vehicle (SDV) – a mini-submarine that is capable of inserting small six-man SEAL teams in all weathers; usually reserved for highly classified missions.

At the height of Operation Iraqi Freedom, SEALs were involved both inshore and offshore, while post-war, they have been heavily involved in land-based operations, primarily supporting TF-20.

However, the biggest and most important operation for the SEALs came at the end of Operation Iraqi Freedom, when they embarked on the massive US-led manhunt for Saddam Hussein, as part of the ORBAT of TF-20.

SEAL team weapons

The SEALs have access to a wide variety of weaponry and choice is usually down to personal preference or mission profile. Weapons used include the CAR-15 assault rifle and the M16A2 assault rifle, both of which can mount the M203 40mm grenade launcher, and for extra stopping power the old but reliable 7.62mm M14 is still used. Close range weapons include the entire HK MP-5 family, as well as a customer-specific model, the MP5K-PDW, which was designed specifically for NAVWARCOM use. For ship-boarding, urban and jungle work, the SEALs use 12-gauge shotguns such as the Remington Model 870 and the Franchi Spas, while for Squad fire support they generally operate the 5.56mm SAW and the 7.62mm M-60 machine gun.

Other weapons frequently seen on their vehicles and boats include the M2HB .50 calibre HMG, the MK-19 40mm grenade launcher and the good old M-60 machine gun.

Personal sidearms include the 9mm SIG Sauer P-226, the .45 mm M1911A1, the .357 Smith and Wesson revolver, the 9mm HK P9S and the .45 HK Mk23 Mod O Special Operations Forces Offensive Handgun.

Vehicles used include the Humvee and the LSV (Light Strike Vehicle).

82nd Airborne Division

Based at Fort Bragg, North Carolina, the 82nd is made up of a divisional headquarters, a divisional support command and three Airborne Brigades. Each Brigade consists of three parachute battalions plus an HQ and support element that is equipped with mortars, anti-tank missiles and heavy machine guns.

Entry into the 82nd is either through direct application or by volunteering from another unit. Before entering the Airborne brotherhood, all candidates must first pass a tough selection procedure, followed by a rigorous training programme and parachute course, after which they get their 'Wings' and maroon beret.

The primary role of the 82nd Airborne is to arrive by air, take control of the ground and hold it until relieved by a main force unit. At any given time, one parachute battalion is on an 18-hour standby, with one of its companies on two-hour standby.

Airlift capability for the Division is provided by Boeing C-17 Globemasters, Lockheed C-141 Starlifters and C-130 Hercules of the USAF. During operations each soldier is issued with enough food rations, water and ammunition to last for three days.

Weapons used by the 82nd Airborne Division include the M16A2 assault rifle, Colt M4 assault rifle, M-249 SAW, M60 medium machine gun, M2 .50 calibre heavy machine gun, M203 40mm grenade launcher and 81mm mortar.

The 82nd has seen action in places such as Vietnam, Grenada, Panama, Afghanistan and Iraq.

101st Airborne Division (Air Assault) 'The Screaming Eagles'

Based at Fort Campbell in Kentucky, the 101st Airborne Division (Air Assault) is the world's only air assault division. Although not deemed a special forces unit like their neighbours, the 160th SOAR, the 101st Airborne Division is nevertheless an elite unit by any military standards and has no equals in terms of its sheer size and operational capability.

The 101st Airborne Division (Air Assault) is formed from three brigades plus Division Artillery, Division Support Command, the 101st Aviation Brigade, 159th Aviation Brigade, 101st Corps Support Group and several separate commands. In terms of military personnel, the Division comprises 26,819 men directly within its ranks and 18,166 support troops, making Fort Campbell the 3rd largest military population in the Army and the 7th largest in the US DoD.

The 101st can trace its history back to 15 August 1942. Within days of its activation, the first commander, Maj Gen William C. Lee, promised his new recruits that the 101st had a 'Rendezvous with destiny', and he was right. The 101st Airborne Division led the night drop before the D-Day invasion and when surrounded at Bastogne by the Germans and asked to surrender, Brig Gen Anthony McAuliffe gave the famous answer 'Nuts!'. Despite being out-gunned and out-numbered, the 'Screaming Eagles' bravely fought on until the siege ended.

After the end of the Second World War, the 101st faced an uncertain future as there was little need for such a large airborne force during peace time. However, in 1948 and again in 1950 the unit was temporarily reactivated as a training unit at Camp Breckinridge in Kentucky. Finally in March 1956, the 101st was transferred, minus most of its personnel and equipment, to Fort Campbell in Kentucky, where it was reorganised as a combat division.

In the mid-1960s, the 1st Brigade and its support troops were deployed to Vietnam, with the rest of the division joining them in 1967 to form the world's first airmobile division. Vietnam was the birth place of the air cavalry concept and the 101st was instrumental in its great success, proving that combining helicopters with light infantry in the airborne assault role made for a deadly combination. During their seven years in Vietnam, the 101st participated in 15 campaigns and earned laurels to add to their proud history.

In October 1974, the 101st was re-designated as the 101st Airborne Division (Air Assault), resulting in the 3rd Brigade changing its operational capabilities from that of parachute to air assault. In addition to these changes, and to ensure maximum operational efficiency, the 101st created an Air Assault School that was specifically designed to teach new soldiers about the art of helicopter-based warfare.

In the mid-1970s, the 101st conducted

numerous training and readiness exercises as part of its work-up phase. It also opened an Air Assault School to other US Army units to ensure a better understanding of helicopter assault tactics, techniques and proceedures used by infantry during combat operations. This training proved highly valuable and put the 101st in good stead for forthcoming operations.

On 12 December 1985, tragedy struck the 101st when 248 members of the division were killed in a plane crash near Gander in Newfoundland, while returning to Fort Campbell from a routine tour of duty in the Sinai.

Although a major set-back for the division on a personal level, the 101st still had a job to do. On 17 August 1990, elements of the 101st arrived in Saudi Arabia as part of the Allied Coalition force. Their mission was to support Allied Forces in their operations against Iraq. The first units of the 101st deployed in Saudi Arabia comprised 2,700 troops, 117 helicopters and 487 vehicles which were transported on board 110 USAF C-5 and C-141 transport aircraft, while the remainder of the division was transported by sea to the Saudi port of Ad Daman, a journey that took 46 days.

Once in theatre, the 101st established their base camp at King Faud Airport, which was known to the 101st as 'Camp Eagle II'. After a period of working-up the 101st deployed to a Forward Operating Base (FOB), code-named 'Bastogne'. From there they mounted round-the-clock training operations that involved practising night assaults, urban assaults and street fighting.

On 17 January 1991, the mission to liberate Kuwait – Operation Desert Storm – began, with the 101st Aviation Regiment drawing first blood. The initial attacks were carried out by eight AH-64 Apache helicopters against two Iraqi early-warning radar sites that were key targets for the Coalition forces. Once destroyed, Allied strike aircraft were able to bomb Baghdad with little fear of interception from Iraqi fighters. As these attacks went in, Black Hawk helicopters of 1st Battalion were flying CSAR patrols nearby, just in case any Allied aircraft were shot down.

Throughout the air campaign, the 101st flew hundreds of sorties against Iraqi positions until ordered to stand down in preparation for the ground war. On 24 February, the ground war began with the 101st and the French 6th Light Armored Division advancing on the left flank of the Coalition line towards Baghdad and the Euphrates River Valley. The first stage of the operation involved 300 helicopters lifting the 101st Airborne to their first objective, FOB Cobra, 180km (110 miles) inside Iraq. The arrival of the 101st at Cobra took the Iraqis completely by surprise, and following a short firefight they surrendered. By the end of the day the 101st had consolidated its positions and cut off Highway 8, which was Iraq's key supply route. This helicopter assault was the largest to take place in modern warfare history.

The following day, 3rd Brigade moved north to occupy positions on the southern bank of the Euphrates River. While this operation was taking place, the remaining elements of the 101st maintained its positions at Highway 8 and Cobra, acting as a blocking force in the event of an Iraqi counter-attack.

On 26 February, the 101st began accepting the surrender of Iraqi soldiers en masse; the war was over. Desert Storm had been a remarkable success story for the 101st, completing the largest helicopter assault in history, without a single loss of life.

After the Gulf War ended, the 101st Airborne Division returned home before embarking on a number of peacekeeping and humanitarian missions in places such as Rwanda, Somalia, Haiti and Bosnia.

Following 9/11, the 101st Airborne was deployed to Afghanistan in January 2002 to relieve the 26th Marine Expeditionary Unit. Its mission was to destroy the Al-Qaeda terrorist network and Taliban regime. As the 101st began operations in Afghanistan, it suffered its first casualties when one soldier was killed and several more wounded following a raid on a terrorist cave complex near Gardez.

On 2 March 2002, the US launched Operation Anaconda. Its mission was to find, capture or kill Osama bin Laden and his AQT supporters. The mission in the eastern mountain ranges of Afghanistan was to last for 16 days and involved some 1,000 US troops, including special forces and elements of the 101st Airborne and 10th Mountain Division. Anaconda hit problems right from the start, as the 101st Airborne were given an LZ right in the middle of the AQT positions, instead of in a valley that ran parallel to its defensive position.

As a result of this mistake, the US forces were ambushed and suffered many casualties,

including eight fatalities and 73 wounded. The firefight was of such intensity that every helicopter involved in supporting the ground forces was hit by effective enemy fire, with two Chinook losses and several others so badly damaged that they were unable to be used in Afghanistan again. Despite these setbacks, the 101st fought back and killed hundreds of Al-Qaeda terrorists before withdrawing. Although US forces failed to find Osama bin Laden or any of his lieutenants, the operation was deemed successful as it forced the remaining AQT forces out of Afghanistan and into nearby Pakistan.

In 2003, the 101st was deployed to Kuwait, and later Iraq, for Operation Iraqi Freedom. Here, 101st soldiers carried out many attacks against Republican Guard units defending Baghdad, culminating in the city's fall. This victory was in part achieved through combined operations with the 3rd Infantry Division, which fought its way up through southern Iraq as part of a three-pronged attack. At one stage, a plan was drawn up that involved the 101st mounting a massive air assault on Baghdad, but the regime fell before it could be implemented.

101st Airborne Division (Air Assault) Overview of Fort Campbell, Kentucky Size of Post

At 260 sq km (164 sq miles) – 105,068 acres, the installation is one of the largest in the world. Today, approximately 12,000 acres of the installation have been developed into the cantonment area while the remaining 93,000 plus acres of the reservation are dedicated to training and firing ranges.

Ranges	52
Major Drop Zones	5
Assault Landing Strip	1
A_2C_2 Air Sectors	10
Bayonet Assault Course	1
Rappel Tower	1
Urban Training Facilities	3
Impact Areas	3
Demo Areas	1
Manoeuvre Areas	20
Artillery Firing Points	340

101st Airborne Division (Air Assault) primary weapon systems

Infantry, attack helicopters, support helicopters, field artillery, air defence artillery

Helicopter types used by the 101st Airborne Division (Air Assault) include:

AH-64 Apache Attack helicopter – used for close support, light strike, anti-tank and escort missions

OH-58D Kiowa Warrior – used for armed reconnaissance and scouting missions

UH-60 Black Hawk transport helicopter – used for short-range infiltration/exfiltration missions, plus Medevac

CH-47 Chinook – used for medium range support, infiltration/exfiltration type missions plus heavy lift

US Special Operations Command

Special forces have been a part of US history since the 17th century, when Major Robert Rogers decided that unconventional warfare had a place within the American armed forces and set about forming America's first special forces unit, the Rangers (*see pages 194–7*).

Although individual officers and men have used unconventional tactics for hundreds of years, it only became apparent during the Second World War that there was a need for official recognition of such forces. Although the US had the Office of Strategic Services (OSS), which co-ordinated unconventional warfare during the war, its scope was limited and this eventually led to the formation of the 10th Special Forces Group in the early 1950s.

It was only when America became involved in Vietnam that things started to change significantly for the better. This new attitude partly came about because of President Kennedy's interest in Special Operations Forces (SOF), in particular the Green Berets, after granting them permission to wear the distinctive beret for which they are now famous. After the Vietnam war ended, SOF capability declined within the US Army to such a degree that their future was in doubt. Things came to a head in 1980 following the failure of Operation Eagle Claw, which led to the formation of the joint counter-terrorist task force and the Special Operations Advisory Panel. Following years of soul searching and internal re-education of special forces and their future role within the US Armed Forces, the DoD activated USSOCOM.

USSOCOM consists of some 46,000 Army, Navy and Air Force SOF personnel, both active and reserve. These forces are organised as follows:

- US Army Special Forces, 75th Ranger Regiment, 160th Special Operations Aviation Regiment (SOAR), and psychological and civil affairs units
- US Navy SEAL forces, special boat units and SEAL delivery units
- US Air Force special operations squadrons (fixed and rotary wing), foreign internal defence squadron and combat weather squadron
- Joint Special Operations Command (JSOC)

USSOCOM's function is to provide highly trained, rapidly deployable and regionally-focused SOF personnel in support of global requirements from the national command authorities, the geographic commanders-in-chief (C-in-C) and the US ambassadors and their country teams. In 1999, SOF had units deployed in 152 countries and territories (not including classified missions and special access programmes). On a given day, some 5,000 SOF are deployed in 60 countries. The SOF personnel are shaped by the requirements of their missions and include foreign language capabilities, regional orientation, specialised equipment, training and tactics, flexible force structure and an understanding of the political context of the mission.

US Army Special Operations Command (USASOC)

Activated on 1 December 1989 and commanded by a Lieutenant-General, USASOC is the Army component of USSOCOM and controls:

- Five active and two Army National Guard (ARNG) special forces groups, totalling 15 active and six ARNG battalions
- One active Ranger Regiment (75th) consisting of three battalions
- One active special operations aviation regiment (160th SOAR) with a detachment in Puerto Rico
- Four reserve civil affairs (CA) commands, seven reserve CA brigades, and one active and 24 reserve CA battalions
- One active and two reserve PSYOP (Psychological Operations) groups totalling five active and eight reserve PSYOP battalions
- One active special operations support command composed of one special operations signal battalion (112th), one special operations support battalion (528th) and six special operations theatre support elements
- Two active and two reserve chemical reconnaissance detachments (CRD)
- The John F Kennedy Special Warfare Center and School

The 160th SOAR ('Night Stalkers')

The 160th Special Operations Aviation Regiment (SOAR) motto is: 'Night Stalkers don't quit'.

Following the failure of Operation Eagle Claw in 1980, the US Army decided to form its own dedicated special operations aviation regiment. Known as the 'Night Stalkers', the 160th SOAR supports SOF personnel worldwide and can carry out a wide range of missions, such as armed attack, force insertion and

The US Special Forces Creed

I am an American Special Forces soldier. A professional! I will do all that my nation requires of me. I am a volunteer, knowing well the hazards of my profession. I serve with the memory of those who have gone before me: Roger's Rangers, Francis Marion, Mosby's Rangers, the first Special Service Forces and Ranger Battalions of World War II, the Airborne Ranger Companies of Korea. I pledge to uphold the honor and integrity of all I am in all I do.

I am a professional soldier. I will teach and fight wherever my nation requires. I will strive always, to excel in every art and artifice of war.

I know that I will be called upon to perform tasks in isolation, far from familiar faces and voices, with the help and guidance of my God.

I will keep my mind and body clean, alert and strong, for this is my debt to those who depend on me.

I will not fail those with whom I serve.

I will not bring shame upon myself or the forces.

I will maintain myself, my arms and my equipment in an immaculate state as befits a Special Forces soldier.

I will never surrender though I be the last. If I am taken, I pray that I may have the strength to spy upon my enemy.

My goal is to succeed in any mission – and live to succeed again.

I am a member of my nation's chosen soldiery. God grant that I may not be found wanting, that I will not fail this sacred trust.

extraction, aerial security, electronic warfare, and command and control support.

Pilots serving in the 160th SOAR are among the best in the world and train constantly to keep up their proficiency. Since formation, the 160th has seen action in Grenada, Panama, Iran, the Gulf, Somalia and Afghanistan.

The 160th SOAR operates some of the most sophisticated helicopters in the world, including:

- A/MH-6 Little Bird, used for short-range infiltration/exfiltration, reconnaissance, resupply, liaison duties and light strike
- MH-60 K/L Black Hawk, used for medium-range day and night insertion/extraction missions, resupply, MEDEVAC, rescue and recovery, and short-range CSAR
- MH-47 D/E Chinook, used for medium-to long-range all-weather infiltration/exfiltration missions, refuelling operations, rescue and recovery missions, and resupply missions in hostile areas

John F Kennedy Special Warfare Center and School

This facility is responsible for developing doctrine, running training courses for Army special forces in civil affairs, psychological operations, escape and evasion, survival and resistance to interrogation.

Air Force Special Operations Command (AFSOC)

AFSOC was established on 22 May 1990 and is America's specialised air power, capable of delivering special operations combat power 'anytime, anywhere'. AFSOC comprises 10,000 personnel, of which 22 per cent are based overseas. AFSOC's aircrew are highly trained professionals who operate with calm precision and are amongst the most respected aviators in the world today. The unit is capable of rapid deployment at short notice and operates with some of the best rotary- and fixed-wing aircraft available, giving SOF mobility, forward presence and engagement precision.

AFSOC has the following active Air National Guard (ANG) and Air Force Reserve units assigned to it:

- 16th Special Operations Wing (SOW) operates with eight special operations squadrons – five fixed-wing, one rotary-wing, an aviation foreign internal defence (FID) unit and a fixed-wing training squadron
- 352nd and 353rd Special Operations Groups are based in the UK and Japan, and have a theatre-oriented group that comprises one rotary-wing and two fixed-wing special operations squadrons, plus a special tactics squadron
- 919th AF Reserve SOW with two fixed-wing special operations squadrons
- 193rd SOW with one fixed-wing special operations squadron
- 720th Special Tactics Group
- 18th Flight Test Squadron
- The Air Force Special Operations School

16th Special Operations Wing (SOW)

This is the oldest unit in AFSOC and is

A USAF MH-53J extracts a SF team from a training area in the UK, thanks to a Jacob's ladder.

responsible for deploying specially trained and equipped forces from each service on national security objectives. The SOW focuses on unconventional warfare, including counter-insurgency and psychological operations during low intensity conflicts. It also provides precise, reliable and timely support to SOFs worldwide. The squadron operates a mix of aircraft types.

720th Special Tactics Group
This AFSOC unit has special operations combat controllers and para-rescue men who work jointly in special tactics teams. Their mission includes air traffic control for establishing air assault landing zones, close air support for strike aircraft and gunship missions, eastablishing casualty collection stations and providing trauma care for injured personnel.

Special Operations School
This provides special operations-related education to personnel from all branches of the DoD, governmental agencies and allied nations. Subjects covered include regional affairs and cross-cultural communications, anti-terrorism awareness, revolutionary warfare and psychological operations.

Joint Special Operations Command (JSOC)
Established in 1980, JSOC is a joint HQ designed to study special operations requirements and techniques, ensure interoperability and equipment standardisation, plan and conduct exercises and training and develop joint special operations tactics.

USAF P-Jumpers are among the most respected operators in the world and are highly skilled in many disciplines.

Modern Warfare

Future Operators

Today, special forces are a critical component of a modern army and the demands placed upon them in the future can only increase. However, special forces growth is limited to the number of applicants ready, willing and, more importantly, good enough to become operators. Dropping standards means a drop in capability, which is clearly not an option. Standards need to be maintained to be mission proficient at all times. There are, however, ways to overcome this problem.

Firstly, do special forces trained personnel need to operate behind enemy lines? Conventional soldiers can be better trained to support dedicated special forces operations, which is the rationale behind the formation of the new British Ranger Force. In the US, elements of the Marines are becoming both special operations capable and counter-terrorist trained – a logical choice, as they have plenty of quality personnel available.

Secondly, do special forces really need to do all the jobs currently asked of them? Perhaps not. Other conventional forces could, with good selection and training, re-role for missions such as deep strike and amphibious warfare.

And finally, why not relinquish the internal counter-revolutionary warfare (CRW) role to a specially selected and trained force? There is already a precedent – the German GSG-9 Federal Police unit, which is without doubt superb in this role.

Such questions are important, as already special forces in the UK and US are having difficulty recruiting for their armed forces.

The face of future special forces operator warfare.

The B-2 stealth bomber is only effective if its targeting information is reliable, so special forces operators are key to its successful use in future conflicts.

Future Special Forces

Factors responsible for this recruiting crisis in the armed forces includes the ongoing war in Iraq, which has seen desertion rates rocket within the US military. There is also 'political correctness', which has raised many issues. Another reason is the tour duration factor, a growing problem which is seeing record numbers of military personnel ending up in the divorce courts. These may appear to be mundane issues, but they are real and need to be addressed as a matter of urgency. More recently, there has been another unforeseen development that has caused more depletion within the already thin special forces ranks. This is the increase in the 'guns for hire' concept or Private Operators for Contract, as the personnel prefer to be called.

The idea of hired guns is, of course, nothing new. Many former SF personnel go on to highly paid security jobs after completing their military tenure. But what is new is the current targeting of serving SF personnel by private security companies, willing to pay enormous sums of money for their expertise. So high is the demand for former SF personnel that many of the hirers are willing to buy the operators out of their military contracts, although in some cases this is not always possible. The financial rewards for private operators can be enormous, with many earning high six-figure sums as a matter of routine. There are operators who are earning £10,000 per month for working in Baghdad.

Private security operators now make up the fourth largest armed force in Iraq – and their role is growing all the time. Some aspects of their modus operandi are very admirable, such as in the case of the protection team responsible for the security of America's most senior administrator in Iraq, Paul Bremer. His team was made up of former operators, still in touch with soldiers serving in Iraq. These contacts worked out well for all concerned, as they had the backing of their former colleagues when things got hot.

However, there are those still serving in Iraq who deeply resent the private operators, as the special forces operators do the same job for a third of the money.

Options currently being considered to alleviate this problem include offering SF personnel gap years, flexible contracts and even short-term tenures. However, these options will take some time to implement, if they are implemented at all.

SEALs are – and always will be – key players in US special forces strategies, as they have an enviable record of success.

In future it may be a robot and not a soldier taking point. However, that is some way off and until then, the man at the front is still valuable as well as vulnerable.

On a positive note

Current special forces operational doctrine focuses on covert reconnaissance, both tactical and strategic, hit-and-run missions, aircrew and hostage rescue, sabotage, counter-terrorism, VIP protection and the abduction of high-value personnel, such as war criminals and high ranking military officers.

In future conflicts, the role of special forces is likely to be increasingly focused on intelligence gathering and target designation; operators on the ground are always the most reliable methods for being appraised of the current situation. This has been proven time and again during operations in Bosnia, Kosovo, Afghanistan and Iraq. In all these conflicts, special forces carried out close target recces (CTRs) on both high-value targets and enemy fielded forces, which greatly increased the operational effectiveness of both airborne and ground-based assets. A further benefit of such activities is that they minimise both collateral damage and Blue-on-Blue contacts – key issues of modern warfare.

Regardless of the change in mission focus, special forces will still train and equip themselves for all eventualities – skill slip is hard to put right once it has gone. Other dramatic changes will include the increased use of unmanned robotic systems such as mini-UAVs, which can both target and destroy enemy assets. In addition, the use of armed robotic vehicles capable of infiltrating heavily defended urban areas could be a possibility. While it may sound far-fetched, it is already happening in Iraq as part of a massive programme aimed at detaching friendly personnel from risk of death or injury during high intensity, high risk military operations.

Not only will these developments come on-line in the next decade, there will be others that will totally transform the appearance of the future generation special forces operator. In the US, this programme is known as Land Warrior, soon to be superseded by Objective Force Warrior. In the UK, the programme is known as Future Integrated Soldier Technology (FIST). There is also new weaponry coming on-line that will practically guarantee a first round hit.

As for future transportation needs, there are many innovative concepts currently under development for the special forces operator of the future. The following pages give a glimpse of just a few examples of the transportation systems our special forces are likely to have around the year 2025.

Land Warrior

Face of the Future Operator

Of all the future combat soldier programmes under development at present, there are few that compare to those planned for the US Army.

US special forces soldiers are among the best trained and equipped in the world, but from 2005 onwards they will be unmatched in terms of fighting ability by a system called Land Warrior.

Land Warrior integrates current small arms with high-tech equipment in a way that would have been unimaginable for an SF soldier of the Vietnam era. The idea of such a concept first came about in 1991, following a study by the US Army who recommended the development of an integrated weapon system based around the common soldier, essentially making him a weapons platform.

Land Warrior has been developed with three priorities. These are:
• Lethality
• Survivability
• Command and control
Its sub-systems are as follows:
• Weapon
• Integrated helmet
• Protective clothing and individual equipment
• Computer/radio and software

The weapon system is built around the M-16/M-4 modular carbine and features a laser range finder/digital compass, a daylight video camera, a laser aiming light and a thermal sight.

This system allows the soldier to fight effectively day and night, and in all weather. It even provides the ability to shoot around corners without risk of exposure to enemy fire.

The integrated helmet is lighter than a current Kevlar helmet and features a mounted monocular day display, a night sensor with flat panel display, a laser detection module complete with ballistic/laser eye protection, a microphone and a headset.

The protective clothing and individual equipment subsystem incorporates modular body armour and upgrade plates that can stop small-arms rounds fired at point-blank range and includes an integrated load-bearing frame, chemical/biological protective garments and a modular rucksack.

In operation, the combat soldier attaches the computer/radio subsystem to his load-bearing frame, which also contains a GPS locator. Over this goes the rucksack for the soldier's personal gear, which has a handgrip attached to the soldier's chest as a controlling mouse for changing computer screens, radio frequencies and sending digital information.

The subsystem comes in two variations: a leader version with two radios and a flat panel display/keyboard, and a soldier version with just a single radio. With this equipment, both soldier and leader can exchange information and even images. For example, if a soldier stops a vehicle and he is suspicious of its occupants, he can send back a video image of them to his tactical commanders and a decision can be taken as to what action is needed.

The software subsystem element of Land Warrior includes tactical and mission support modules, as well as maps and tactical overlays that can be updated by means of a power management module.

In total, the Land Warrior programme will cost around $2 billion. However, the system is set to revolutionise the way in which an SF soldier operates and fights.

Objective Force Warrior

The Objective Force Warrior (OFW) will be a formidable warrior in an invincible team, able to see first, understand first, act first – and finish decisively.

OFW is a US Army Science and Technology programme that will provide the basis for a major block upgrade to the current Land Warrior System by enhancing its lethality and survivability with ideas taken from the Future Warrior concept programme.

OFW is designed to support a 'soldier-centric' force, as part of the Objective Force

The many faces of the next generation operators. At the time of writing, some are on trial in Iraq.

strategy, both integrating with and complementing the capabilities of the Future Combat System (FCS).

Its notional concepts seek to create a lightweight, overwhelmingly lethal, fully integrated individual combat system, including weapon, head-to-toe individual protection, netted communications, soldier-worn power sources and enhanced human performance.

- Lethality Vision: an OFW family of lightweight weapons with advanced fire control systems optimised for urban combat, and able to synchronise with direct and indirect fire from the FCS
- Survivability Vision: ultra-lightweight, low bulk, multi-functional and full spectrum protective
- Sensors and Communications (C_4ISR) Vision: netted OFW small unit/teams equipped with robust communications, state-of-the-art sensors, organic tactical intelligence collection assets allowing enhanced

situational understanding, embedded training, on-the-move planning and linkage to other force assets
- Power Vision: 72-hour continuous autonomous team operations, using high density, low weight/volume, self-generating/regenerating, reliable, power source system
- Mobility, Sustainability and Human Performance Vision: unconstrained vertical and lateral movement at full combat/assault capability during mission execution; optimised cognitive and physical fightability, on-board physiological/medical sensor suite with enhanced prompt casualty care

OFW will have 'full-spectrum capabilities', meaning troops can use it for any possible mission from peacekeeping to high-intensity conflicts. It will be able to network with other assets such as manned and unmanned ground and aerial vehicles to form an enhanced battlefield picture. The OFW programme's long-term equipment weight goal is 18kg (40lb) per soldier, which will be achieved by

The OICW in action during field trials – it's going to be one awesome weapon!

Objective Individual Combat Weapon (OICW)
Key programme capabilities

- 500 per cent increase in probability of incapacitation
- New soldier capability to defeat targets in defilade
- Effective range to 1,000m (3,000ft)
- Day/night fire control; wireless weapon interface
- Substantial weight reduction
- Ergonomic design

System features

- Lethality capability: 20mm HE [high explosive] (air bursting) projectiles and 5.56 mm kinetic energy projectiles
- Weapon length: 84cm (33in)
- Weapon weight: 5kg (12lb)
- Rates of fire: 20mm – 10rpm, 5.56mm, equal to M16A2
- Range: 20mm – 1,000m, 5.56mm equal to or better than M16A2
- Combination 5.56mm and 20mm HE
- Single trigger controls for both barrels
- Ambidextrous weapon and switches
- Simple red dot day/night sighting system
- Laser adjustment for targets in buildings and in defilade
- Unique recoil mitigation and tactical operational awareness

Technology advancements

- Weapon recoil mitigation
- Fusing miniaturisation and accuracy
- Warhead performance and packaging
- Target acquisition and man in the loop
- Laser ranging accuracy at extended ranges
- Extensive composite use

using integrated, lightweight systems as well as off-loading some weight to a robotic mule. OFW is due to enter service in 2010.

Objective Individual Combat Weapon (OICW)

From 2005 onwards, the US Army will field a revolutionary new assault rifle. The OICW is a lightweight, highly accurate weapon capable of firing both kinetic energy projectiles and air-bursting fragmentation munitions.

It will allow soldiers to engage targets at much greater distances than today's generation of assault rifles. The OICW will increase the lethality and survivability of the next generation of combat infantryman and is the sole lethality component of the OFW programme. It will effectively replace the M16/M203 grenade launcher combination on a one for one basis, but in terms of sheer lethality there is no comparison in performance.

For example, if a soldier comes under enemy fire from a well-protected trench system, he points his OICW and its built-in FCS in the general direction of the target. He then selects the laser rangefinder switch and aims it at the nearest fixed object to the trench, such as a tree. This pinpoints the precise target range at which the HE round needs to explode; within a microsecond this information is relayed to the 20mm ammunition fusing system and the round is fired. As the round nears the trench it explodes, sending lethal fragments downwards, capable of penetrating light armour.

Planned Programmes

CV-22 Osprey

One of the most interesting programmes under development at present is the CV-22 Osprey. The CV-22 Osprey is a hybrid aircraft, combining the best capabilities of an aeroplane and a helicopter. It is capable of vertical/short take-off and landing (VSTOL) operations and offers twice the performance of the current USAF MH-53J. CV-22 is a multi-mission aircraft that is designed to give future special forces the ability to rapidly self deploy without the aid of transport aircraft.

The CV-22 is being acquired to meet one of the most demanding and stringent mission requirements ever set by US Special Operations Command. It is required to travel 800km (500 miles) at or below 150m (500ft) above ground level, locate a small landing zone, infiltrate and extract a team of 18 special operations forces, and return to base. This must be done covertly, at night and in adverse weather. CV-22 is one of the variants of the V-22 Osprey family and differs from the others planned for the US Navy,

Army and USMC. These differences relate to its equipment and capabilities, which are optimised for the highly demanding Special Forces Mission requirement.

Although the CV-22 maintains maximum commonality where possible with the baseline MV-22 (Marines variant) design, it does have several key differences. These relate to enhanced survivability by virtue of the electronic warfare suite specific to the SOF mission, as well as enhanced armament for self-protection. In addition to this, the CV-22 will have a Suite of Integrated Radio Frequency Countermeasures (SIRFC), which includes an active jammer that can geo-locate threats by using its missile warning receivers, as well as incorporate real-time intelligence from a multi-mission advanced tactical terminal (MATT).

Other differences include a terrain following and terrain avoidance radar (TF/TA), extra fuel capacity amounting to some 4,000 litres (900 gallons), plus rope ladders, survivor

The future of long-range SF missions is in the hands of the Osprey, an impressive aircraft that has had a troubled life so far, despite its unique qualities and capabilities.

locator system, upgraded computers and additional radios.

The primary tactic of CV-22 aircrew during operations will be to avoid detection if possible, and if detected to avoid engagement. This is because no current attack helicopter is able to provide an escort as they simply cannot keep up with it or indeed match its operational range. Instead, the primary method of threat avoidance is through detailed preflight mission planning and perceived threat assessment. This is carried out by means of real-time intelligence and datalinking from both ground- and air-based assets.

Special forces aircrew virtually always operate under cover of darkness and where possible use 'nap-of-the-earth' flying to mask their ingress or egress from a target area. This is made easier by the use of both terrain following radar and forward-looking infrared sensors (FLIR).

Should the CV-22 be fired upon by MANPADS, it has the ability to defend itself by means of active countermeasures, such as infrared, radar jamming and decoy flares.

The USAF currently aims to procure around 50 CV-22s by 2009, but this timeline may not be met due to numerous delays to the

programme, which have been caused by a mixture of accidents and budget concerns. The USAF, however, is anxious to see CV-22 enter service as soon as possible as it will add a new and much needed long-range capability to extract SOF personnel and American citizens from deep behind enemy lines. CV-22 can also be used for CSAR, amphibious assault, CASEVAC, land assault, medium cargo lift and even a gunship version.

CV-22 is manned by a pilot, co-pilot and support aircrew relevant to the mission, and can carry 20 fully armed soldiers or 4,500kg (10,000lb) of external cargo. The CV-22 will be capable of flying over 2,000 nautical miles with just one air-refuelling. In the world of special operations that is a quantum leap in operational capability, which will no doubt lead to an innovative new series of special forces tactics, techniques and procedures relevant solely to this type of aircraft.

Avpro Exint Pod

Currently undergoing evaluation by both British and American armed forces, the Avpro Aerospace Exint (Extraction-Insertion) Pod is a one-man pod 4m (12ft) in length and was first conceived after Operation Desert Storm

The Avpro Exint Extraction/Insertion Pod is designed for use on the Apache attack helicopter as a means of covert SF infiltration. It is deployable by parachute, should the need arise.

The Avpro Manta wing-in-ground effect concept.

for the speedy insertion or extraction of special forces and the recovery of downed aircrew.

Although Exint was originally developed for use by the British SAS for carriage on the Harrier Jump-Jet, it quickly became apparent that Exint could also be carried on any attack helicopter with a weapons pylon. Such types include the WH-64 Apache, AH-1 Cobra, Black Hawk and the Mangusta. In effect, Exint converts attack helicopters into a CSAR platform and a long-range SF insertion/extraction system.

Should a mission become compromised, an attack helicopter can fight back. Because it is small, it has a greater chance of evading AAA and SAMs. When not being used in the personnel carrying role, Exint can be used for the carriage of high-value equipment or pilots' personal kit. This capability effectively allows attack helicopters to self-deploy without the need for support helicopters.

Within each pod there is a radio, GPS, air conditioning system and a state-of-the-art parachute system which allows the Exint Pod to be released from either an aircraft or a helicopter during special operations. For extra safety, as the pod nears the ground or water, proximity sensors fire airbags to absorb the landing impact; these then deflate to form an effective flotation device.

A standard helicopter would fit two Exint Pods, however, in the case of the WH-64 Apache, it can carry as many as four. This means that an Apache can fly up to four SF soldiers and their kit on a single mission. With the Apaches' long range, that is an impressive capability as no enemy will be expecting attack helicopters to perform in this way.

Avpro Manta

Manta was conceived by Avpro Aerospace, as part of the UK's Defence Evaluation Research Agency (DERA) 2015 study into future amphibious warfare capabilities.

It is a wing-in-ground effect vehicle concept with a variety of applications, both civil and military. Currently, its principal intended use is as a large landing craft capable of performing a similar mission to the

Landing Craft Air Cushion (LCAC) of the US Marine Corps and the Japanese Navy.

The craft would fly over the sea at an altitude of 4.5m (15ft). At this altitude, the vehicle operates in ground effect, essentially floating on a cushion of air. The vehicle configuration proposed is designed to carry a 60 tonne payload over a range of 350 nautical miles at 565km/h (350mph) in sea states up to level 5.

These impressive specifications make the vehicle suitable for roles other than as a landing craft. For example, the craft's large payload bay and ability to operate in rough seas allows it to be used for search and rescue/medivac duties. Its cruise speed is significantly higher than that of helicopters and therefore it could reach the scene of a maritime accident more quickly. It could also be used as a high-speed transporter.

A further Royal Navy requirement for the Manta is that it should be capable of operating

from an internal bay of a base ship such as a marine assault ship. The vehicle has been laid out with folding wings, canards and tails so that it can fit in an internal bay whose dimensions are 15.25m wide × 14.46m high × 45.72m deep (50ft × 46ft × 150ft).

Manta is equipped with an air cushion, like that of a hovercraft, which allows it to be driven over beaches, minefields or underwater obstructions. One configuration proposed has four propfan engines, as these are better suited than turbofans to the cruise-speed and low-speed manoeuvring requirements of the Manta. However, at this time there is no Western propfan of the required 3,400kg (7,500lb) shp rating, so either a new engine would have to be developed or an existing one modified to make it viable.

The Manta would include a digital fly-by-wire (FBW) or fly-by-light (FBL) flight control system to provide a safe and controllable vehicle while maximising the benefits of the wing-in-ground (WIG) effect. The fuselage is of rectangular cross-section to provide maximum usable payload volume with entry being via the front or rear doors of the payload bay. The rear door is a ramp type, hinged at the bottom, while the front doors are hinged at the sides and open outwards.

Although ground effect will occur when the craft is at low altitude over any surface, its main operating environment would be over water. However, the craft could operate over ice flows, snow and beaches if required. The Manta has to compete with conventional landing craft, heavy-lift helicopters and transport aircraft, so why should it be developed?

Firstly, it combines some of the best

elements of all these vehicles in a single platform. It is large enough to carry payloads similar to those carried by heavy-lift aircraft. For example, the maximum payload of the C-17A Globemaster III is 77 tonnes and that of the Manta is 60 tonnes.

But the most significant reason is this: in a comparison study made between the Manta and the LCAC by the highly respected Cranfield University, they set an identical task for both platforms to carry out. In the case of the LCAC, it took 120 minutes to perform the task, while the Manta only took seven minutes. A remarkable feat.

In summary, the Manta offers the versatility of a hovercraft, the speed of a jet aircraft and the manoeuvrability of a helicopter, making it a tactical commander's dream.

Marauder

One of the most innovative special forces craft under development at present is the Avpro Aerospace Marauder. The twin-engined Marauder is a hybrid of a flying boat and a hydrofoil and operates just above the surface of water by means of a phenomenon known as ground effect.

In essence, air is trapped between the wing and the surface over which the Marauder is flying. This effectively creates a cushion of air on which it can ride, and since there is no friction it requires little or no power to maintain movement. The fundamental advantage of such a concept is that it can approach an enemy coastline in complete silence as it simply cuts its engines and glides in to the drop zone.

Should the Marauder have to make a quick getaway, it simply reverts back to being a flying boat and takes off in a conventional manner. In this mode it has little to fear from enemy aircraft as it is highly stealthy, having a Radar Cross Section (RCS) of that of a small bird. The Marauder has a crew of two and can carry up to 12 fully equipped soldiers in a bay within its composite hull. Many roles are envisaged for the Marauder, including search and rescue, anti-shipping, anti-narcotics, Airborne Early Warning (AEW) and, of course, covert insertion and extraction of special forces.

Avpro Aerospace Titan X-Wing concept

The Avpro Aerospace Titan X-Wing has been designed to be capable of meeting the US requirement for a heavy new-lift VTOL vehicle. As such the design proposed has a maximum payload of 60 tonnes and can accommodate two LAV-25 vehicles in its payload bay. It could carry a significant defensive/offensive armament, comprising forward and rearward cannon turrets and air-to-air missiles (AIM-9L and AIM-120). To improve the combat effectiveness of the vehicle its operational range can be extended by air refuelling (AR) while the aircraft is operating in conventional mode with the X-Wing stationary.

The main roles envisioned for Titan are heavy lift tasks and special forces operations, where its vtol capabilities could be exploited at both ends of the route. Its cruise speed will be significantly higher than conventional heavy-lift helicopters such as the Chinook and Super Stallion. This benefits the field commander by not only providing quicker placements of troops and equipment, but also allowing a greater number of sorties to be performed in a given time frame.

The principal design feature is a relatively conventional fuselage to house the payload, crew, systems and some of the fuel. Its fuselage is more streamlined than existing heavy-lift helicopters, since the vehicle is designed to be capable of a cruise speed in excess of 480km/h (300mph) in aeroplane mode.

An innovative gas-driven X-wing rotor would provide VTOL lift in the same way as a conventional helicopter rotor, but would be driven by high pressure air bled from the twin turbofan engines. The air would exit the

The Avpro Titan X-Wing concept is a vertical take-off/landing vehicle with the flexibility of a helicopter and the range of a long-range transport aircraft – an ideal replacement for the Chinook and C-130 Hercules.

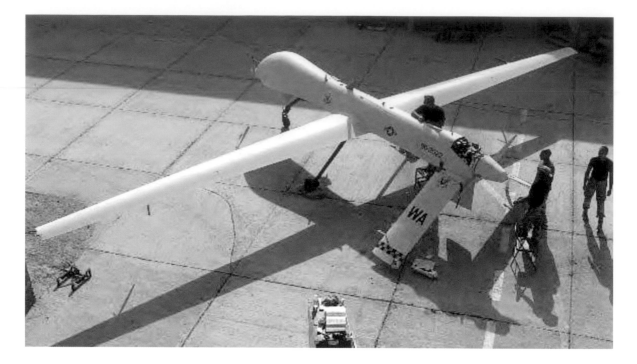

UAVs such as the Predator are increasingly used for covert SF operations, as they can carry weaponry and sensors to almost any place in the world.

blades through nozzles located at the blades' tips, causing them to rotate. The rotor could be brought to rest to allow the vehicle to fly like a conventional aircraft, with the stationary rotor blades performing the same function as the wing on a fixed-wing aircraft. With the blades stationary, no bleed air would be taken from the engines, hence all the air entering the engine would be used to provide forward thrust for flight.

To provide large payload capability (especially when operating in VTOL mode) in high-speed cruise, it is essential to keep Titan's empty weight to a minimum. For this reason, advanced composite materials, mainly carbon/epoxy, would be used for the primary structure wherever possible. Production and maintenance procedures for composites have matured rapidly and their use as the primary structural material for a new aircraft does not present a significant technological risk. Conversely, their advantages over metals, such as low weight, high strength, improved fatigue resistance, damage tolerance and negligible corrosion, make them ideal for the proposed vehicle and its likely operating environment.

The leading edges of the rotors contain multi-element phased array radars with electronic beam steering. This provides the crew with 360° radar coverage while the

X-wing is rotating. With the X-wing stationary, 360° coverage is still maintained because each blade can cover a 90° scan zone. The data obtained from the radar could be data-linked from the vehicle to AWACS or JSTARS aircraft or direct to other friendly forces.

While the X-wing has many advantages over the pure helicopter, especially in the heavy-lift transport role, another advanced hybrid is being developed as a potential replacement for the USMC AH-1W Super Cobra attack helicopter.

The Canard Rotor Wing (CRW) is being developed at Boeing's Phantom Works in St Louis, in response to a US Defense Advanced Projects Agency (DARPA) programme.

Final Words

In modern warfare, you must take the fight to the enemy day or night – and never give him or her a chance to rest or recover. The only forces that are able to prosecute such a war are our special forces.

For them, it does not matter whether the fight is in the mountains of Afghanistan or the deserts of Iraq – they will do their duty regardless, come what may.

Looking mean and sinister, an operator from 4 RAR poses for a photo before the invasion of Iraq in 2003. Note his heavily customised weapon and combat gear.

'Special forces are not supermen, nor indeed are they gods. They are common soldiers, who soldier uncommonly well. And we are blessed to have such people protecting us.'

Abbreviations

AAA	Anti-Aircraft Artillery		LZ	Landing Zone
ABG	Armoured Battle Group		MANPADS	Man Portable Air Defence System
AFV	Armoured Fighting Vehicle		MBT	Main Battle Tank
APC	Armoured Personnel Carrier		MLRS	Multiple Launch Rocket System
AWACS	Airborne Warning and Control System		MO	Modus operandi
C2	Command and Control		MoD	(UK) Ministry of Defence
C4I	Command, Control, Communications, Computers and Intelligence		MSR	Main Supply Route
			NATO	North Atlantic Treaty Organisation
CALCM	Conventionally Armed Air Launched Cruise Missiles		NVG	Night-Vision Goggles
			ORBAT	Order of Battle
CAP	Combat Air Patrol		QRF	Quick Reaction Force
CAS	Close Air Support		RV	Rendezvous
CIA	Central Intelligence Agency		SAM	Surface-to Air-Missile
CQB	Close Quarters Battle		SAR	Synthetic Aperture Radar
CSAR	Combat Search and Rescue		SAS	Special Air Service
DoD	(US) Department of Defense		SAW	Squad Assault Weapon
EOD	Explosives Ordnance Disposal		SBS	Special Boat Service
ERV	Emergency Rendezvous Point		SEAD	Suppression Enemy Air Defences
FCS	Future Combat System		SES	Surface Effect Ship
FRV	Forward Rendezvous Point		SF	Special Forces
GPMG	General Purpose Machine Gun		SMG	Sub-machine Gun
HAHO	High Altitude High Opening		SOAR	Special Operations Aviation Regiment
HALO	High Altitude Low Opening		SOCOM	Special Operations Command
HARM	High-Speed Anti-radiation Missile		SOG	Special Operations Group
IR	Infrared		STOVL	Short Take-Off and Vertical Landing
JSTARS	Joint Surveillance and Target Attack Radar		SWAT	Special Weapons and Tactics
LCAC	Landing Craft Air Cushion		UAV	Unmanned Air Vehicle
LMG	Light Machine Gun		UCAV	Unmanned Combat Air Vehicle
LPH	Landing Platform Helicopter		VCP	Vehicle Checkpoint
LRRP	Long-Range Reconnaissance Patrol		WIG	Wing-in-Ground
LSW	Light Support Weapon		WMD	Weapons of Mass Destruction

Author's appeal

As the global fight against terrorism continues, many of our brave countrymen are being lost in the fight for our freedom and way of life.

In light of this, a percentage of the royalties from this book is being donated to the Special Forces Welfare Foundation, an organisation that supports the families of those who have lost a loved one.

If you would like to help the foundation in its work, or make a donation, please write to:

Special Forces Welfare Foundation
Avpro Aerospace, PO Box 9128
Bollo Lane, London W3 6GE
UK

Your kindness and generosity is greatly appreciated by all concerned.

Mike Ryan

Index